P9-EDK-112

Great Golf Humour

Great Golf Humour

Humour

A Collection of
Stories & Articles
Edited by
Mervyn J. Huston

Hurtig Publishers
Edmonton

Copyright © 1977 by Mervyn J. Huston

No part of this book may be reproduced or
transmitted in any form by any means,
electrical or mechanical, including photocopying
and recording, or by any information
storage or retrieval system, without written
permission from the publisher, except
for brief passages quoted by a reviewer in a
newspaper or magazine.

Hurtig Publishers
10560 105 Street
Edmonton, Alberta

Design: David Shaw & Associates Ltd.

ISBN 0-88830-141-3

Printed and bound in Canada
by T.H. Best Printing Company Limited

This book is dedicated to
The Cunningham Foursome
and
The Mayfair Squires

AUGUSTANA UNIVERSITY COLLEGE
LIBRARY

Contents

Acknowledgements

The Editor wishes to thank the following for permission to include in this anthology previously copyrighted material:

Blond Briggs Publishers for Patrick Campbell's "The Way It Ought To Be Done" from *How To Become a Scratch Golfer*. The Hamlyn Publishing Group Limited for Bernard Darwin's "On Diegeling" from *Second Shots*. Harold Ober Associates, Incorporated, for Paul Gallico's "The Witch of Woonsapucket" (copyright 1939 by the Curtis Publishing Company; renewed 1966 by Paul Gallico). B.T. Batsford Limited for Ronald Heager's "Golf is a Funny Game" from *Golfers Bedside Book*. The Hamlyn Publishing Group Limited for George Houghton's "The Colonel and the Hunt" from *The Secret Diary of A Golf Addict's Caddie*. The Providence Journal-Bulletin for John L. Hulteng's "Watching My Wife." The Journal of Irreproducible Results, Incorporated, for M.J. Huston's "Golf and the POO Muscle." Little, Brown, and Company in association with Sports Illustrated Books for Dan Jenkin's excerpt from "Wide Open" from *The Dogged Victims of Inexorable Fate* (copyright 1970 by Dan Jenkins). David Higham Associates Limited for David Langdon's excerpts from *How to Talk Golf (A to Z of Golfing Terms)*. Hawthorn Books, Incorporated, for Rex Lardner's "Four-Balls, Two-Balls, and Mixed Foursomes" from *Downhill Lies and Other Falsehoods Or How to Play Dirty Golf* (copyright 1973; all rights reserved). Charles Scribner's Sons for Ring Lardner's "A Caddy's Diary" from *How To Write Short Stories* (copyright 1922 by Curtis Publishing Company). Doubleday and Company, Incorporated, for Don Marquis's "The Rivercliff Golf Killings" from *Sun Dial Time* (copyright 1927 by Don Marquis). Doubleday and Company, Incorporated, for Morie Morrison's "Goat Getting" from *Here's How To Play Money Golf* (copyright 1953 by Erwin G. Morrison). Prentice-Hall, Incorporated, for Robinson Murray's "Crying Towel" from

Are Golfers Human? (copyright 1951 by Prentice-Hall, Incorporated). Harper and Row for George Plimpton's excerpt, Chapter 40, from *The Bogey Man* (copyright 1968 by George Plimpton). William Heinemann Limited for Stephen Potter's "U.S. *versus* U.K." from *The Complete Golf Gamesmanship*. Hutchinson Publishing Group Limited for Patrick Smart's "The Captain and the Secretary" from *If You Must Play Golf*. Doubleday and Company, Incorporated, for Charles E. Van Loan's "The Ooley-Cow" from *Fore!* (copyright 1917 by Curtis Publishing Company). Mitchell Press Limited for Roland Wild's excerpt from *Golf The Loneliest Game*. The Estate of P.G. Wodehouse and A.P. Watt and Son for P.G. Wodehouse's "The Awakening of Rollo Podmarsh" from *The Golf Omnibus*. The author's agent, Lurton Blassingame, for Glynn Harvey's "Who Wants to Marry Money?" (copyright 1955 by Crowell-Collier, Incorporated). Hutchinson Publishing Group Limited for Michael Green's "Perils of the First Tee" from *The Art of Coarse Golf*. Hutchinson Publishing Group Limited for Michael Green's "A Child's Guide to Golf" from *The Art of Coarse Golf*. A.S. Barnes and Company, Incorporated, for Joe James's "Are You Making Enough Fun?" from *How To Give Up Golf*. Golf Digest Magazine, U.S.A., for J. Cronley's "Muny Golf Takes Cuts — Right, Mac?" (copyright 1973 by Golf Digest, Incorporated). Curtis Brown Limited for A.A. Milne's "The Charm of Golf" from *Not That It Matters*. E.P. Dutton, Publishers, for Barrie Payne's "One in a Trillion" from Chick Evans and Barrie Payne's *Ida Brooke: The Humor and Philosophy of Golf* (copyright 1929 by E.P. Dutton; renewed © 1956 by Chick Evans and Barrie Payne). Macmillan, London, and Basingstoke for H. Leach's extract from *The Happy Golfer*.

The Editor has made very effort to trace owners of copyright material used in this book. If he has inadvertently trespassed on any rights, his apologies are hereby tendered.

The Editor would like to thank Bryan M. Huston and Miss Frances Mielke for assistance with the bibliography and Elvin A. Christenson and Kenneth L. Crockett for the use of their libraries.

Introduction

Golf is a pain in the rear. Golf is also a joy. That's the paradox of the game which gives it its fascination. The occasional flashes of joy in the general gloom of despondency are sufficient to bring the millions of golfers of the world back to the links week after week and year after year. But some days you wonder, don't you? Like my friend Ralph who gives up the game finally and irrevocably every time he goes over a hundred. Until next day.

Golf is what you make it — a joy or a pain. Your approach to the game reflects your approach to life, for golf is the mirror of life. Golf embraces elation and despair, success and failure, pleasure and suffering. When you look down the fairway at the distant pin, you face the Greek masks of tragedy and comedy hovering over the hole. Will the trip be a scaling of Mount Olympus with all the gods smiling, or, as is more likely, a descent once again into the steaming bunker of Hades, with demons (and your opponents) chortling in unholy glee? That is the question and the challenge. But away with tragedy for the nonce. This book will be devoted to the fun of the game.

When I undertook to compile an anthology of golf writings, I faced a mountain of material. There is more fine writing about golf than any other sport — with the possible exception of girl-chasing. The quality of golf writing is, for the most part, very high. There are excellent historical books dealing with such matters as: the beginning of the game, the expansion of golf in various countries, the story of individual courses, the development of specific tournaments, and the evolution of equipment. There is an excellent literature devoted to biographies of great golfers and accounts of their famous, and infamous, matches. There are short stories, novels, plays, poetry, and whodunits based on golf and serious books dealing with the psychology, sociology, and philosophy of the game. Since the next best thing to playing golf is reading about it, this literature provides a fascinating outlet for the enthusiasm of the golfing aficionado.

A plethora of books exists on how to win by improving your game. These are written by pros, each of whom rediscovers the wheel and puts a fancy new hub-cap on it. You know the sort of thing: improve your swing by tucking a hanky in your right armpit, or by tying your shoe laces to your belt buckle, or dangling a chestnut on a string from the peak of your cap. These books are a complete waste of time — I know because I've tried them all. Another type of "how to" book is devoted to explaining ways to win *without* improving your game. These are much more useful to the average golfer since the techniques do not require great strength or athletic ability. All that is required is a torpid conscience, which is easily come by.

There is also a rich treasury of golfing humour, which is not surprising when you consider that golf is a microcosm of the human comedy. I find these writings so delightful that I decided to confine my selections for this anthology to such pieces in the happy belief that others would find as much enjoyment in them as I do. There is such a wealth of material to choose from that decisions for inclusion or rejection have frequently been difficult. The criterion for inclusion is a simple one based only on what I have found most amusing. I have endeavoured, however, to provide as much variety as possible in styles, genres, authors, and sources. The common denominator of all of them is simply that they are great good fun. Enjoy!

This book is designed for all golfers with the probable exception of the pros. It is my observation that pros don't have a sense of humour — about golf at any rate. You don't expect a lawyer to be amused at a lost appeal, or an engineer at a tumbled down bridge, or a dentist at an impacted molar, so it is not surprising that a golf pro is not amused by a shank, even if someone else's (it might be contagious). But most golfers are aware of their own foibles, and certainly those of their colleagues, and find some amusement in even their own tantrums — in retrospect — even if the horrors of the moment are apt to overwhelm the best adjusted psyches. The golfers who will get the most fun out of this book are those who get the most enjoyment from their own games.

The low handicapper expects to have a good round and is devastated when he doesn't; the high handicapper expects to have a lousy round and is delighted when he doesn't. Who has the most fun? My own theory is that enjoyment of golf peaks at a handicap of sixteen and tapers off above and below that figure. The high handicapper can be an embarrassment to himself and a trial to his friends. Below sixteen, the golfer starts taking the game increasingly seriously with a corresponding decrease in fun. Nobody with any sense really wants to be a scratch golfer although everyone tries. If you ask any golfer what handicap would give him the optimum enjoyment, he will think for a moment and then give you a figure four below his present handicap. At both handicap extremes there is a decreasing number of people who will want to play with you. Low handicappers are the biggest snobs on earth. I've had good golfers say in the bar "we must have a game sometime" and then hide in the bushes when I turn up. Theoretically, the handicap system allows a pleasant battle between a high and a low handicapper. But it doesn't work that way. If the expert beats the tyro, no credit accrues; if the rabbit beats the tiger, he is accused of having a phoney handicap. In general, golfers wisely tend to play with those of comparable handicaps.

My credentials to undertake this project of gathering a collection of writings about golf are sound. I love the game and it hates me — the love-hate syndrome. Typical. Furthermore, I relate to the vast majority of golfers because I have retained my duffer status despite heroic efforts to do otherwise. Those golfers who become proficient go on to new frustrations but tend to lose sympathy for those who go into rigour when facing a ball in a sandtrap, who are thrilled by a par hole, whose score fluctuates by fifteen strokes, or who can run into disaster in the middle of the fairway. I find that most golf writers and editors who lay modest claim to duffer status manage to drop a casual comment about the time they played with Palmer or Nicklaus (with whom they are on a first name basis) in the Pro-Am at Carnoustie, or some such. I don't have to play with Nicklaus to realize I'm a rabbit. Hell, Elvin Christenson can clobber me soundly and Pepper Moon can make me look like a nurd — and whoever heard of them at St. Andrews? No sir, as a duffer, I'm the real McCoy.

I therefore have the characteristics of the average golfer. I believe that Mulligan did more for golf than Vardon, and I don't really think that women have any place on a golf course at all but only say so when in the nethermost regions of the men's locker-room. I am convinced that every bit of bad luck that has ever befallen anyone has happened to me, and then some. My ball has disappeared down a gopher hole; I've had my ball nestle into a pile of moose manure, and if you don't think that presents a challenge you don't know much about moose (don't expect sympathy from your friends); I've been chased off a course by a mother bear; and I've stomped in a complete fury through some of the most beautiful scenery in the world and seen none of it. One the other hand, I've had a ball take six skips across a water hazard to land in the middle of the fairway; I've had a ball bounce off a ball-washer into the hole; and one time a raven picked up my ball and dropped it on the green — but not in the hole, dammit. Like all golfers, I accept the good fortune as my just desserts and yet feel that the bad luck is completely unwarranted and can't possibly happen again. Therefore, tomorrow I will put everything together and play a brilliant game.

Also, like all happy golfers, I feel that my golfing cronies are the greatest in the world. If you don't think so about yours then there's probably nothing wrong with your associates but there may be something wrong with you. I play most of my golf with a group of scoundrels known as the "Squires." They wouldn't give their grandmother an extra stroke in a thunderstorm, and they accept your nassau losses with sadistic glee. But they're wonderful companions, which is what golf is all about. We were sitting on the 19th hole one time when Murray drew our attention to a lone figure trudging up the 18th fairway in solitary acerbity. "Here comes George," said Murray, "surrounded by his friends." George plays a much better game of golf than I do, but I wouldn't change places with him for all the lost balls in the ocean at Pebble Beach.

On Saturdays I play with a more mystical group named the "Cunningham Foursome" after our senior member of that ilk. This foursome is unusual in a number of respects. For one thing, it comprises a president (non-playing), a first, second, third, and fourth vice-president, and two deputy vice-presidents. (Yes, seven in all.) We wear trews of Cunningham tartan although the ethnic backgrounds are Scottish, Norwegian, Irish, Italian, Welsh, Icelandic, and Liverpudlian. Minutes are kept of all gatherings and read, although never approved, at the next meeting. Last summer, one of our members got married on a Saturday. The ceremony was held in the late afternoon so as not to interfere with our accustomed round. We completed the match barely in time to shower and get the groom to the church. So you can see our group has its priorities set right.

Another feature of the Foursome is that it has a constitution which all new members must sign in a ceremony of induction complete with drawn claymores. This document is our effort to delineate the mystique of golf and may elicit a responsive chord in your heart.

The Cunningham Foursome Constitution

WE, the members of the Cunningham Foursome, join together for purposes of good fellowship and the playing of golf.

We believe that golf is a delightful pastime but not an end in itself. Golf provides an opportunity for companionship and for the demonstration of noble qualities. We shall strive at all times to play the best golf we are capable of, as is appropriate in any competitive sport, but we shall do so with sportsmanship and good manners. We shall always conduct ourselves in the best traditions of the ancient and honourable sport, and play with due regard to rules, customs, protocol, ethics, courtesy, and gentlemanly behaviour. We accept that other foursomes may have better scores, but we pledge ourselves that none shall excel us in the other more important aspects of the game.

Golf is diabolically designed to engender frustration, exasperation, and despair and thus bring out the best or worst in a man. We recognize and accept this challenge. The perversity of a small ball shall not embitter our lives nor distort our personalities. We accept, however, that colleagues may occasionally be tried beyond human endurance and we shall seek for charity in our hearts in their times of tribulation. We shall each endeavour to minimize this drain upon the charity of the others. Profanity will be used sparingly and only when provocation is unendurable. The solace of the 19th hole will be employed with restraint.

We shall not berate a partner even if, or particularly if, he has it coming to him. We will not take undue delight in the disasters of our opponents, nor the good fortune of our own team. We recognize, however, that human nature being what it is, one is less upset by the difficulties of opponents than by the bad luck of oneself, but we shall endeavour to bring sympathy and kindliness to the former and restraint and good humour to the latter.

We will not hold forth unduly on our own problems or accomplishments, and we will listen a reasonable length of time while others are sounding off.

Banter is a characteristic of good fellowship. We will do our kidding in good taste and with due regard to the sensitivities and momentary frustrations of the recipient. On the other hand, we will accept chaffing with good humour and grace even when we feel like wrapping a nine iron around someone's neck.

Betting is an appropriate part of competitive golf. Bets, however, will be at a level sufficient to add piquancy to the game without undue strain on the losers or unseemly joy to the winners.

We support the tradition that the companionship of a match shall continue in the camaraderie of the 19th hole over selected flagons of usquebaugh. Winners shall be determined and debts paid off forthwith; we accept that this ritual will be enjoyed more by some than by others; tolerance will be maintained during expressions of satisfaction or of chagrin.

The objective of golf is good fellowship.

I shall now give you some comments on the various pieces in the book and the reasons for their inclusion, although, truth to tell, this was largely dictated simply by what tickled my funny-bone. Harry Leon Wilson in "All Golf is Divided into Three Parts" has emphasized the importance of what he calls "subgolfers" in the golfing scheme of things and has wittily described their problems in trying to improve. A.A. Milne, in "The Charm of Golf" maintains that golf is popular simply because it is the best game in the world at which to be bad. Rex Beach, in "Excerpt from A New Way to Better Golf" says golf is a game only to the dub. Stephen Potter has applied his theory of gamesmanship to golf very effectively as demonstrated in "U.S. *verses* U.K." which deals with international sculduggery. Rex Lardner in "Four-Balls, Two-Balls and Mixed Foursomes" has dealt with the topic at a more mundane level and has pointed out the role which women can play in this time-honoured chicanery. Morie Morrison in "Goat Getting" has explained how to choose your ploys according to the emotional make-up of your opponent.

Many of the pieces deal in a light-hearted way with the various vicissitudes met by the average golfer. For example: the ordeal of driving from the first tee in front of an audience ("Perils of the First Tee" by Michael Green); the real meaning of golf terminology ("Excerpts from How to Talk Golf" by David Langdon); home practice ("The 7th Hole" by Fred Beck and O.K. Barnes); reaction to a bad round ("Crying Towel" by Robinson Murray); the pressure of putting ("Excerpt from the Happy Golfer" by Henry Leach); copying the pros ("On Diegeling" by Bernard Darwin); mastering a particular club ("The Pitching Wedge" by Hollis Alpert, Ira Mothner, and Harold Schonberg); getting good advice ("Other People's Golf" by Bernard Darwin); facing the tumult of a municipal course ("Muny Golf Takes Guts — Right, Mac?" by Jay Cronley); dealing with rip-off artists ("The Ooley-Cow" by Charles E. Van Loan); exasperation with an opponent ("The Rivercliff Golf Killings" by Don Marquis); and freak shots ("Excerpt from the Bogey Man" by George Plimpton).

Although professional golf, for the most part, is a deadly serious affair, Ronald Heager in "Golf Is a Funny Game" has recorded some delightful happenings in tournament play. Then there is the hilarious account by Patrick Campbell in "The Way It Ought To Be Done" of an exhibition match played by Sam Snead in Israel. Dan Jenkins in "Excerpt from Wide Open" lets his imagination soar like a sky shot from the rough in an account of a fictitious National Open. Alpert, Mothner, and Schonberg give a delightful account of the television coverage of the first double bogey golf tournament in "The Wide, Wide World of Double Bogey Golf."

"A Caddy's Diary" by the great Ring Lardner is a superb piece of humorous writing which carries with it a moral which all golfers could heed. Michael Green in "A Child's Guide to Golf" presents a daughter's account of her father playing golf — out of the mouths of babes comes dismaying truth. Stephen Leacock, the great Canadian humorist, describes the single-mindedness of a golf nut in "The Golfomaniac." "The Captain and the Secretary" by Patrick Smart is a wild account of the in-fighting that goes on in a private club. Three pieces, by Roland Wild, John L. Hulteng, and Barry Payne, deal with different aspects of women and golf. And I have included an article of my own out of sheer vanity.

P.G. Wodehouse, who is considered by many to be the dean of humorous golf fiction, is represented by "The Awakening of Rollo Podmarsh." Another story based on the premise that romance and golf are not necessarily incompatible is Glynn Harvey's "Who Wants to Marry Money?" I have included "Cowboy on the Green" by Max Evans because I was intrigued by the absurdity of a cowboy in stetson hat and high heels playing tournament golf. I chose "The Witch of Woonsapucket" from the many fine stories written by Paul Gallico because most golfers, good or bad, subscribe to some form of superstition about their game. George Houghton is a prolific writer of good golf humour from which I selected "The Colonel and the Hunt" for its zany theme.

Stories and articles, fun and nonsense, wit and wisdom, all combining to make a rich treasury of *Great Golf Humour*.

Mervyn J. Huston
Edmonton, Alberta, Canada
June, 1977

The Awakening of Rollo Podmarsh
P.G. Wodehouse

Down on the new bowling green behind the clubhouse some sort of competition was in progress. The seats about the smooth strip of turf were crowded, and the weak-minded yapping of the patients made itself plainly audible to the Oldest Member as he sat in his favorite chair in the smoking room. He shifted restlessly, and a frown marred the placidity of his venerable brow. To the Oldest Member a golf club was a golf club, and he resented the introduction of any alien element. He had opposed the institution of tennis courts; and the suggestion of a bowling green had stirred him to his depths.

A young man in spectacles came into the smoking room. His high forehead was aglow, and he lapped up a ginger ale with the air of one who considers that he has earned it.

"Capital exercise!" he said, beaming upon the Oldest Member.

The Oldest Member laid down his *Vardon on Casual Water,* and peered suspiciously at his companion.

"What did you go round in?" he asked.

"Oh, I wasn't playing golf," said the young man. "Bowls."

"A nauseating pursuit!" said the Oldest Member coldly, and resumed his reading.

The young man seemed nettled.

"I don't know why you should say that," he retorted. "It's a splendid game."

"I rank it," said the Oldest Member, "with the juvenile pastime of marbles."

The young man pondered for some moments.

"Well, anyway," he said at length, "it was good enough for Drake."

"As I have not the pleasure of the acquaintance of your friend Drake, I am unable to estimate the value of his endorsement."

"*The* Drake. The Spanish Armada Drake. He was playing bowls on Plymouth Hoe when they told him that the Armada was in sight. 'There is time to finish the game,' he replied. That's what Drake thought of bowls."

"If he had been a golfer he would have ignored the Armada altogether."

"It's easy enough to say that," said the young man, with spirit, "but can the history of golf show a parallel case?"

"A million, I should imagine."

"But you've forgotten them, eh?" said the young man satirically.

"On the contrary," said the Oldest Member. "As a typical instance, neither more nor less remarkable than a hundred others, I will select the story of Rollo Podmarsh." He settled himself comfortably in his chair, and placed the tips of his fingers together. "This Rollo Podmarsh —"

"No, I say!" protested the young man, looking at his watch.

"This Rollo Podmarsh —"

"Yes, but —"

This Rollo Podmarsh (said the Oldest Member) was the only son of his mother, and she was a widow; and like other young men in that position he had rather allowed a mother's tender care to take the edge off what you might call his rugged manliness. Not to put too fine a point on it, he had permitted his parent to coddle him ever since he had been in the nursery; and now, in his twenty-eighth year, he invariably wore flannel next to his skin, changed his shoes the moment they got wet, and — from September to May, inclusive — never went to bed without partaking of a bowl of hot arrowroot. Not you would say, the stuff of which heroes are made. But you would be wrong. Rollo Podmarsh was a golfer, and consequently pure gold at heart; and in his hour of crisis all the good in him came to the surface.

In giving you this character sketch of Rollo, I have been at pains to make it crisp, for I observe that you are wriggling in a restless manner and you persist in pulling out that watch of yours and gazing at it. Let me tell you that, if a mere skeleton outline of the man has this effect upon you, I am glad for your sake that you never met his mother. Mrs. Podmarsh could talk with enjoyment for hours on end about her son's character and habits. And, on the September evening on which I introduce her to you, though she had, as a fact, been speaking only for some ten minutes, it had seemed like hours to the girl, Mary Kent, who was the party of the second part to the conversation.

Mary Kent was the daughter of an old school friend of Mrs. Podmarsh, and she had come to spend the autumn and winter with her while her parents were abroad. The scheme had never looked particularly good to Mary, and after ten minutes of her hostess on the subject of Rollo she was beginning to weave dreams of knotted sheets and a swift getaway through the bedroom window in the dark of the night.

"He is a strict teetotaller," said Mrs. Podmarsh.

"Really?"

"And has never smoked in his life."

"Fancy that!"

"But here is the dear boy now," said Mrs. Podmarsh fondly.

Down the road toward them was coming a tall, well-knit figure in a Norfolk coat and gray flannel trousers. Over his broad shoulders was suspended a bag of golf clubs.

"Is *that* Mr. Podmarsh?" exclaimed Mary.

She was surprised. After all she had been listening to about the arrowroot and the flannel next the skin and the rest of it, she had pictured the son of the house as a far weedier specimen. She had been expecting to meet a small, slender young man with an eyebrow mustache, and pince-nez; and this person approaching might have stepped straight out of Jack Dempsey's training camp.

"Does he play golf?" asked Mary, herself an enthusiast.

"Oh, yes," said Mrs. Podmarsh. "He makes a point of going out on the links once a day. He says the fresh air gives him such an appetite."

Mary, who had taken a violent dislike to Rollo on the evidence of his mother's description of his habits, had softened toward him on discovering that he was a golfer. She now reverted to her previous opinion. A man who could play the noble game from such ignoble motives was beyond the pale.

"Rollo is exceedingly good at golf," proceeded Mrs. Podmarsh. "He scores more than a hundred and twenty every time, while Mr. Burns, who is supposed to be one of the best players in the club, seldom manages to reach eighty. But Rollo is very modest — modesty is one of his best qualities — and you would never guess he was so skillful unless you were told.

"Well, Rollo darling, did you have a nice game? You didn't get your feet wet, I hope? This is Mary Kent, dear."

Rollo Podmarsh shook hands with Mary. And at her touch the strange dizzy feeling which had come over him at the sight of her suddenly became increased a thousandfold. As I see that you are consulting your watch once more, I will not describe his emotions as exhaustively as I might. I will merely say that he had never felt anything resembling this sensation of dazed ecstasy since the occasion when a twenty-foot putt of his, which had been going well off the line, as his putts generally did, had hit a worm cast sou'sou'east of the hole and popped in, giving him a snappy six. Rollo Podmarsh, as you will have devined, was in love at first sight. Which makes it all the sadder to think Mary at the moment was regarding him as an outcast and a blister.

Mrs. Podmarsh, having enfolded her son in a vehement embrace, drew back with a startled exclamation, sniffing.

"Rollo!" she cried. "You smell of tobacco smoke."

Rollo looked embarrassed.

"Well, the fact is, mother —"

A hard protuberance in his coat pocket attracted Mrs.

Podmarsh's notice. She swooped and drew out a big-bowled pipe.

"Rollo!" she exclaimed, aghast.

"Well, the fact is, mother —"

"Don't you know," cried Mrs. Podmarsh, "That smoking is poisonous, and injurious to the health?"

"Yes. But the fact is, mother —"

"It causes nervous dyspepsia, sleeplessness, gnawing of the stomach, headache, weak eyes, red spots on the skin, throat irritation, asthma, bronchitis, heart failure, lung trouble, catarrh, melancholy, neurasthenia, loss of memory, impaired will power, rheumatism, lumbago, sciatica, neuritis, heartburn, torpid liver, loss of appetite, enervation, lassitide, lack of ambition, and falling out of hair."

"Yes, I know, mother. But the fact is, Ted Ray smokes all the time he's playing, and I thought it might improve my game."

And it was at these splendid words that Mary Kent felt for the first time that something might be made of Rollo Podmarsh. That she experienced one-millionth of the fervor which was gnawing at his vitals I will not say. A woman does not fall in love in a flash like a man. But at least she no longer regarded him with loathing. On the contrary, she found herself liking him. There was, she considered, the right stuff in Rollo. And if, as seemed probable from his mother's conversation, it would take a bit of digging to bring it up, well — she liked rescue work and had plenty of time.

Mr. Arnold Bennett, in a recent essay, advises young bachelors to proceed with a certain caution in matters of the heart. They should, he asserts, first decide whether or not they are ready for love; then, whether it is better to marry earlier or later; thirdly, whether their ambitions are such that a wife will prove a hindrance to their career. These romantic preliminaries concluded, they may grab a girl and go to it. Rollo Podmarsh would have made a tough audience for these precepts. Since the days of Antony and Cleopatra probably no one had ever got more swiftly off the mark. One may say that he was in love before he had come within two yards of the girl. And each day that passed found him more nearly up to his eyebrows in the tender emotion.

He thought of Mary when he was changing his wet shoes; he dreamed of her while putting flannel next his skin; he yearned for her over the evening arrowroot. Why, the man was such a slave to his devotion that he actually went to the length of purloining small articles belonging to her. Two days after Mary's arrival Rollo Podmarsh was driving off the first tee with one of her handkerchiefs, a powder puff, and a dozen hairpins secreted in his left breast pocket. When dressing for dinner he used to take them out and look at them, and at night he slept with them under his pillow. Heavens, how he loved that girl!

One evening when they had gone out into the garden together to look at the new moon — Rollo, by his mother's advice, wearing a woollen scarf to protect his throat — he endeavored to bring the conversation round to the important subject. Mary's last remark had been about earwigs. Considered as a cue, it lacked a subtle something; but Rollo was not the man to be discouraged by that.

"Talking of earwigs, Miss Kent," he said, in a low musical voice, "have you ever been in love?"

Mary was silent for a moment before replying.

"Yes, once. When I was eleven. With a conjurer who came to perform at my birthday party. He took a rabbit and two eggs out of my hair, and life seemed one grand sweet song."

"Never since then?"

"Never."

"Suppose — just for the sake of argument — suppose you ever did love anyone — er — what sort of a man would it be?"

"A hero," said Mary promptly.

"A hero?" said Rollo, somewhat taken aback. "What sort of hero?"

"Any sort. I could only love a really brave man — a man who had done some wonderful heroic action."

"Shall we go in?" said Rollo hoarsely. "The air is a little chilly."

We have now, therefore, arrived at a period in Rollo Podmarsh's career which might have inspired those lines of Henley's about "The night that covers me, black as the pit from pole to pole." What with one thing and another, he was in an almost Job-like condition of despondency. I say "one thing and another," for it was not only hopeless love that weighed him down. In addition to being hopelessly in love, he was greatly depressed about his golf.

On Rollo in his capacity of golfer I have so far not dwelt. You have probably allowed yourself, in spite of the significant episode of the pipe, to dismiss him as one of those placid, contented — shall I say dilettante? — golfers who are so frequent in these degenerate days. Such was not the case. Outwardly placid, Rollo was consumed inwardly by an ever-burning fever of ambition. His aims were not extravagent. He did not want to become amateur champion, nor even to win a monthly medal; but he did, with his whole soul, desire one of these days to go round the course in under a hundred. This feat accomplished, it was his intention to set the seal on his golfing career by playing a real money match; and already he had selected his opponent, a certain Colonel Bodger, a tottery performer of advanced years who for the last decade had been a martyr to lumbago.

But it began to look as if even the modest goal he had marked out for himself was beyond his powers. Day after day he would step on to the first tee, glowing with zeal and hope, only to crawl home in the quiet evenfall with another hundred and twenty on his card. Little wonder, then, that he began to lose his appetite and would moan feebly at the sight of a poached egg.

With Mrs. Podmarsh sedulously watching over her son's health, you might have supposed that this inability on his part to teach the foodstuffs to take a joke would have caused consternation in the home. But it so happened that Rollo's mother had recently been reading a medical treatise in which an eminent physician stated that we all eat too much nowadays, and that the secret of a happy life is to lay off the carbohydrates to some extent. She was, therefore, delighted to observe the young man's moderation in the matter of food, and frequently held him up as an example to be noted and followed by little Lettice Willoughby, her granddaughter, who was a good and consistent trencherwoman, particularly rough on the puddings. Little Lettice, I should mention, was the daughter of Rollo's sister Enid, who lived in the neighborhood. Mrs. Willoughby had been compelled to go away on a visit a few days before and had left her child with Mrs. Podmarsh during her absence.

You can fool some of the people all the time, but Lettice Willoughby was not of the type that is easily deceived. A nice, old-fashioned child would no doubt have accepted without questioning her grandmother's dictum that roly-poly pudding could not fail to hand a devastating wallop to the blood pressure, and that to take two helpings of it was practically equivalent to walking right into the family vault. A child with less decided opinions of her own would have been impressed by the spectacle of her uncle refusing sustenance, and would have received without demur the statement that he did it because he felt that abstinence was good for his health. Lettice was a modern child and knew better. She had had experience of this loss of appetite and its significance. The first symptom which had preceded the demise of poor old Ponto, who had recently handed in his portfolio after holding office for ten years as the Willoughby family dog, had been this same disinclination to absorb nourishment. Besides, she was an observant child, and had not failed to note the haggard misery in her uncle's eyes. She tackled him squarely on the subject one morning after breakfast. Rollo had retired into the more distant parts of the garden, and was leaning forward, when she found him, with his head buried in his hands.

"Hallo, uncle," said Lettice.

Rollo looked up wanly.

"Ah, child!" he said. He was fond of his niece.

"Aren't you feeling well, uncle?"

"Far, far from well."

"It's old age, I expect," said Lettice.

"I feel old," admitted Rollo. "Old and battered. Ah, Lettice, laugh and be gay while you can."

"All right, uncle."

"Make the most of your happy, careless, smiling, halcyon childhood."

"Right-o, uncle."

"When you get to my age, dear, you will realize that it is a sad, hopeless world. A world where, if you keep your head down, you forget to let the clubhead lead; where even if you do happen by a miracle to keep 'em straight with your brassie, you blow up on the green and foozle a six-inch putt."

Lettice could not quite understand what Uncle Rollo was talking about, but she gathered broadly that she had been correct in supposing him to be in a bad state, and her warm, childish heart was filled with pity for him. She walked thoughtfully away, and Rollo resumed his reverie.

Into each life, as the poet says, some rain must fall. So much had recently been falling into Rollo's that, when Fortune at last sent along a belated sunbeam, it exercised a cheering effect out of all proportion to its size. By this I mean that when, some four days after his conversation with Lettice, Mary Kent asked him to play golf with her, he read into the invitation a significance which only a lover could have seen in it. I will not go so far as to say that Rollo Podmarsh looked on Mary Kent's suggestion that they should have a round together as actually tantamount to a revelation of undying love; but he certainly regarded it as a most encouraging sign. It seemed to him that things were beginning to move, that Rollo Preferred were on a rising market. Gone was the gloom of the past days. He forgot those sad, solitary wanderings of his in the bushes at the bottom of the garden; he forgot that his mother had bought him a new set of winter woollies which felt like horsehair; he forgot that for the last few evenings his arrowroot had tasted strange. His whole mind was occupied with the astounding fact that she had voluntarily offered to play golf with him, and he walked out on to the first tee filled with a yeasty exhilaration which nearly caused him to burst into song.

"How shall we play?" asked Mary. "I am a twelve. What is your handicap?"

Rollo was under the disadvantage of not actually possessing a handicap. He had a sort of private system of bookkeeping of his own by which he took strokes over if they did not seem to him to be up to sample, and allowed himself five-foot putts at discretion. So he had never actually handed in the three cards necessary for handicapping purposes.

"I don't exactly know," he said. "It's my ambition to get round in under a hundred, but I've never managed it yet."

"Never?"

"Never! It's strange, but something always seems to go wrong."

"Perhaps you'll manage it today," said Mary encouragingly, so encouragingly that it was all that Rollo could do to refrain from flinging himself at her feet and barking like a dog. "Well, I'll start you two holes up, and we'll see how we get on. Shall I take the honor?"

She drove off one of those fair-to-medium balls which go with a twelve handicap. Not a great length, but nice and straight.

"Splendid!" cried Rollo devoutly.

"Oh, I don't know," said Mary. "I wouldn't call it anything special."

Titanic emotions were surging in Rollo's bosom as he addressed his ball. He had never felt like this before, especially on the first tee — where as a rule he found himself overcome with a nervous humility.

"Oh, Mary! Mary!" he breathed to himself as he swung.

You who squander your golden youth fooling about on a bowling green will not understand the magic of those three words. But if you were a golfer, you would realize that in selecting just that invocation to breathe to himself Rollo Podmarsh had hit, by sheer accident, on the ideal method of achieving a fine drive. Let me explain. The first two words, tensely breathed, are just sufficient to take a man with the proper slowness to the top of his swing; the first syllable of the second "Mary" exactly coincides with the striking of the ball; and the final "ry!" takes care of the follow-through. The consequence was that Rollo's ball, instead of hopping down the hill like an embarrassed duck, as was its usual practice, sang off the tee with a scream like a shell, nodded in passing Mary's ball, where it lay some hundred and fifty yards down the course, and carrying on from there, came to rest within easy distance of the green. For the first time in his golfing life Rollo Podmarsh had hit a nifty.

Mary followed the ball's flight with astonished eyes.

"But this will never do!" she exclaimed. "I can't possibly start you two up if you're going to do this sort of thing."

Rollo blushed.

"I shouldn't think it would happen again," he said. "I've never done a drive like that before."

"But it must happen again," said Mary firmly. "This is evidently your day. If you don't get round in under a hundred today, I shall never forgive you."

Rollo shut his eyes, and his lips moved feverishly. He was registering a vow that, come what might, he would not fail her. A minute later he was holing out in three, one under bogey.

The second hole is the short lake hole. Bogey is three, and Rollo generally did it in four; for it was his custom not to count any balls he might sink in the water, but to start afresh with one which happened to get over, and then take three putts. But today something seemed to tell him that he would not require the aid of this ingenious system. As he took his mashie from the bag, he *knew* that his first shot would soar successfully onto the green.

"Ah, Mary!" he breathed as he swung.

These subtleties are wasted on a worm, if you will pardon the expression, like yourself, who, possibly owing to a defective education, is content to spend life's springtime rolling wooden balls across a lawn; but I will explain that in altering and shortening his soliloquy at this juncture Rollo had done the very thing any good pro would have recommended. If he had murmured, "Oh, Mary! Mary!" as before he would have overswung. "Ah, Mary!" was exactly right for a half swing with the mashie. His ball shot up in a beautiful arc, and trickled to within six inches of the hole.

Mary was delighted. There was something about this big, diffident man which had appealed from the first to everything in her that was motherly.

"Marvelous!" she said. "You'll get a two. Five for the first two holes! Why, you simply must get round in under a hundred now." She swung, but too lightly; and her ball fell in the water. "I'll give you this," she said, without the slightest chagrin, for this girl had a beautiful nature. "Let's get on to the third. Four up! Why, you're wonderful!"

And not to weary you with too much detail, I will simply remark that, stimulated by her gentle encouragement, Rollo Podmarsh actually came off the ninth green with a medal score of forty-six for the half round. A ten on the seventh had spoiled his card to some extent, and a nine on the eighth had not helped, but nevertheless here he was in forty-six, with the easier half of the course before him. He tingled all over — partly because he was wearing the new winter woollies to which I have alluded previously, but principally owing to triumph, elation, and love. He gazed at Mary as Dante might have gazed at Beatrice on one of his particularly sentimental mornings.

Mary uttered an exclamation.

"Oh, I've just remembered," she exclaimed. "I promised to write last night to Jane Simpson and give her that new formula for knitting jumpers. I think I'll phone her now from the clubhouse and then it'll be off my mind. You go on to the tenth, and I'll join you there."

Rollo proceeded over the brow of the hill to the tenth tee, and was filling in the time with practice swings when he heard his name spoken.

"Good gracious, Rollo! I couldn't believe it was you at first."

He turned to see his sister, Mrs. Willoughby, the mother of the child Lettice.

"Hallo!" he said. "When did you get back?"

"Late last night. Why, it's extraordinary!"

"Hope you had a good time. What's extraordinary? Listen, Enid. Do you know what I've done? Forty-six for the first nine! Forty-six! And holing out every putt."

"Oh, then that accounts for it."

"Accounts for what?"

"Why, your looking so pleased with life. I got an idea from Letty, when she wrote to me, that you were at death's door. Your gloom seems to have made a deep impression on the child. Her letter was full of it."

Rollo was moved.

"Dear little Letty! She is wonderfully sympathetic."

"Well, I must be off now," said Enid Willoughby. "I'm late. Oh, talking of Letty. Don't children say the funniest things! She wrote in her letter that you were very old and wretched and that she was going to put you out of your misery."

"Ha, ha, ha!" laughed Rollo.

"We had to poison poor old Ponto the other day, you know, and poor little Letty was inconsolable till we explained to her that it was really the kindest thing to do, because he was so old and ill. But just imagine her thinking of wanting to end *your* sufferings!"

"Ha ha!" laughed Rollo. "Ha ha h—!"

His voice trailed off into a broken gurgle. Quite suddenly a sinister thought had come to him.

The arrowroot had tasted strange!

"Why, what on earth is the matter?" asked Mrs. Willoughby, regarding his ashen face.

Rollo could find no words. He yammered speechlessly. Yes, for several nights the arrowroot had tasted very rummy. Rummy! There was no other adjective. Even as he plied the spoon he had said to himself: "This arrowroot tastes rummy!" And — he uttered a sharp yelp as he remembered — it had been little Lettice who had brought it to him. He recollected being touched at the time by the kindly act.

"What *is* the matter, Rollo?" demanded Mrs. Willoughby sharply. "Don't stand there looking like a dying duck."

"I am a dying duck," responded Rollo hoarsely. "A dying man, I mean. Enid, that infernal child has poisoned me!"

"Don't be ridiculous! And kindly don't speak of her like that!"

"I'm sorry. I shouldn't blame her, I suppose. No doubt her motives were good. But the fact remains."

"Rollo, you're too absurd."

"But the arrowroot tasted rummy."

"I never knew you could be such an idiot," said his exasperated sister with sisterly outspokenness. "I thought you would think it quaint. I thought you would roar with laughter."

"I did — till I remembered about the rumminess of the arrowroot."

Mrs. Willoughby uttered an impatient exclamation and walked away.

Rollo Podmarsh stood on the tenth tee, a volcano of mixed emotions. Mechanically he pulled out his pipe and lit it. But he found that he could not smoke. In this supreme crisis of his life tobacco seemed to have lost its magic. He put the pipe back in his pocket and gave himself up to his thoughts. Now terror gripped him; anon a sort of gentle melancholy. It was so hard that he should be compelled to leave the world just as he had begun to hit 'em right.

And then in the welter of his thoughts there came one of practical value. To wit, that by hurrying to the doctor's without delay he might yet be saved. There might be antidotes.

He turned to go and there was Mary Kent standing beside him with her bright, encouraging smile.

"I'm sorry I kept you so long," she said. "It's your honor. Fire away, and remember that you've got to do this nine in fifty-three at the outside."

Rollo's thoughts flitted wistfully to the snug surgery where Dr. Brown was probably sitting at this moment surrounded by the finest antidotes.

"Do you know, I think I ought to —"

"Of course you ought to," said Mary. "If you did the first

nine in forty-six, you can't possibly take fifty-three coming in."

For one long moment Rollo continued to hesitate — a moment during which the instinct of self-preservation seemed as if it must win the day. All his life he had been brought up to be nervous about his health, and panic gripped him. But there is a deeper, nobler instinct than that of self-preservation — the instinctive desire of a golfer who is at the top of his form to go on and beat his medal-score record. And little by little this grand impulse began to dominate Rollo. If, he felt, he went off now to take antidotes, the doctor might possibly save his life; but reason told him that never again would he be likely to do the first nine in forty-six. He would have to start all over afresh.

Rollo Podmarsh hesitated no longer. With a pale, set face he teed up his ball and drove.

If I were telling this story to a golfer instead of to an excrescence — I use the word in the kindliest spirit — who spends his time messing about on a bowling green, nothing would please me better than to describe shot by shot Rollo's progress over the remaining nine holes. Epics have been written with less material. But these details would, I am aware, be wasted on you. Let it suffice that by the time his last approach trickled onto the eighteenth green he had taken exactly fifty shots.

"Three for it!" said Mary Kent. "Steady now! Take it quite easy and be sure to lay your second dead."

It was prudent counsel, but Rollo was now thoroughly above himself. He had got his feet wet in a puddle on the sixteenth, but he did not care. His winter woollies seemed to be lined with ants, but he ignored them. All he knew was that he was on the last green in ninety-six, and he meant to finish in style. No tame three putts for him! His ball was five yards away, but he aimed for the back of the hole and brought his putter down with a whack. Straight and true the ball sped, hit the tin, jumped high in the air, and fell into the hole with a rattle.

"Oo!" cried Mary.

Rollo Podmarsh wiped his forehead and leaned dizzily on his putter. For a moment so intense is the fervor induced by the game of games, all he could think of was that he had gone round in ninety-seven. Then, as one waking from a trance, he began to appreciate his position. The fever passed, and a clammy dismay took possession of him. He had achieved his life's ambition; but what now? Already he was conscious of a curious discomfort within him. He felt as he supposed Italians of the Middle Ages must have felt after dropping in to take pot luck with the Borgias. It was hard. He had gone round in ninety-seven, but he could never take the next step in the career which he had mapped out in his dreams — the money match with the lumbago-stricken Colonel Bodger.

Mary Kent was fluttering round him, bubbling congratulations, but Rollo sighed.

"Thanks," he said. "Thanks very much. But the trouble is, I'm afraid I'm going to die almost immediately. I've been poisoned!"

"Poisoned!"

"Yes. Nobody is to blame. Everything was done with the best intentions. But there it is."

"But I don't understand."

Rollo explained. Mary listened pallidly.

"Are you sure?" she gasped.

"Quite sure," said Rollo gravely. "The arrowroot tasted rummy."

"But arrowroot always does."

Rollo shook his head.

"No," he said. "It tastes like warm blotting paper, but not rummy."

Mary was sniffing.

"Don't cry," urged Rollo tenderly. "Don't cry."

"But I must. And I've come out without a handkerchief."

"Permit me," said Rollo, producing one of her best from his left breast pocket.

"I wish I had a powder puff," said Mary.

"Allow me," said Rollo. "And your hair has become a little

disordered. If I may —" And from the same reservoir he drew a handful of hairpins.

Mary gazed at these exhibits with astonishment.

"But these are mine," she said.

"Yes. I sneaked them from time to time."

"But why?"

"Because I loved you," said Rollo. And in a few moving sentences which I will not trouble you with he went on to elaborate this theme.

Mary listened with her heart full of surging emotions, which I cannot possibly go into if you persist in looking at that damned watch of yours. The scales had fallen from her eyes. She had thought slightingly of this man because he had been a little overcareful of his health, and all the time he had had within him the potentiality of heroism. Something seemed to snap inside her.

"Rollo!" she cried, and flung herself into his arms.

"Mary!" muttered Rollo, gathering her up.

"I told you it was all nonsense," said Mrs. Willoughby, coming up at this tense moment and going on with the conversation where she had left off. "I've just seen Letty, and she said she meant to put you out of your misery but the chemist wouldn't sell her any poison, so she let it go."

Rollo disentangled himself from Mary.

"What?" he cried.

Mrs. Willoughby repeated her remarks.

"You're sure?" he said.

"Of course I'm sure."

"Then why did the arrowroot taste rummy?"

"I made inquiries about that. It seems that mother was worried about your taking to smoking, and she found an advertisement in one of the magazines about the Tobacco Habit Cured in Three Days by a secret method without the victim's knowledge. It was a gentle, safe, agreeable method of eliminating the nicotine poison from the system, strengthening the weakened membranes, and overcoming the craving; so she put some in your arrowroot every night."

There was a long silence. To Rollo Podmarsh it seemed as

though the sun had suddenly begun to shine, the birds to sing, and the grasshoppers to toot. All Nature was one vast substantial smile. Down in the valley by the second hole he caught sight of Wallace Chesney's plus fours gleaming as their owner stooped to play his shot, and it seemed to him that he had never in his life seen anything so lovely.

"Mary," he said, in a low, vibrant voice, "will you wait here for me? I want to go into the clubhouse for a moment."

"To change your wet shoes?"

"No!" thundered Rollo. "I'm never going to change my wet shoes again in my life." He felt in his pocket, and hurled a box of patent pills far into the undergrowth. "But I *am* going to change my winter woollies. And when I've put those dashed barbed-wire entanglements into the clubhouse furnace, I'm going to phone to old Colonel Bodger. I hear his lumbago's worse than ever. I'm going to fix up a match with him for a shilling a hole. And if I don't lick the boots off him you can break the engagement!"

He kissed her, and with long, resolute steps strode to the clubhouse.

The Pitching Wedge
Hollis Alpert, Ira Mothner,
and Harold Schonberg

The pitching wedge is regarded with suspicion even by good golfers. Some will do anything to avoid it. They will play a nine iron flat, hoping for the best. They will play a seven-iron pitch-and-run, preferring in effect to kick the ball on the green rather than lift it. Suddenly even these good players are Double Bogey Golfers, sharing the same paralysis when faced with an itsy-bitsy, 30-yard pitch to the green.

Yet the pitching wedge is such an easy club to use.

All that is needed, really, is a left arm with the kind of control that Isaac Stern has in his wrist and fingers, a right with the bowing action of Jascha Heifetz, and the muscular coordination of Olga Korbut.

Observe the instrument. It is about the shortest club in the bag. It has a pronounced bend in the blade. One might even consider it wedge-shaped.

There is a reason for that. Mankind, struggling through the millennia, eventually figured out that the greater the angle applied by a striking force to a spherical object, the greater the loft that is achieved. This discovery was a breakthrough as important as the invention of peanut brittle.

Therefore, the pitching wedge has been designed to send a golf ball into or nearly into orbit when struck with appropriate force. Is there anything more thrilling in golf — except, of course, a good drive, or a good fairway wood shot, or a good middle iron, or a successful blast from the trap — than to hit a high, soaring wedge, watch it float into the stratosphere and flirt with falcons before descending gracefully eight inches from the pin?

In addition, the good players manage to put backspin on the wedge and other iron shots. Forget that. For the Double Bogey Golfer, there is no such thing as backspin.

The trouble is that most golfers want to help natural law. They cannot bring themselves to believe that the angle of intersection equals the angle of loft. They are doubters, skeptics, unbelievers. And so they try to *push* the ball upstairs, or *lift* it upstairs, unwilling to let the laws of nature operate in a normal manner.

The end result is catastrophic.

Watch the Double Bogey Golfer on this 30-yard pitch shot. He grimly advances to the ball, nervous because a good pitch will put him on the green in three, and if he two-putts he will have a splendid bogey instead of his usual two- or three-over.

He stands over his pitch shot. Then he steps away.

"Are we playing winter rules?" he wants to know.

The question is received with the scorn it deserves.

The Double Bogey Golfer sighs and looks at the ball. He looks at the flag. He looks at the ball again and looks at the flag again.

"Goshsake!" somebody says. "There's a foursome behind us."

Finally he lines up, grasping his club in a death vise, the rubber bulging from between his fingers. He brings his wedge back as far as possible and swings down, teeth clenched, elbows flying, muscles bulging. At the very last instant, he comes up on the ball — head up, shoulder up, wrists up. He is trying to *lift* the damn thing.

One of three things invariably happens: the ball shanks far to the right, in darkest rough; it dribbles 10 feet down the fairway; or it is sculled, running like a scared squirrel over the green, coming to rest in a far-side sand trap.

The Double Bogey Golfer starts screaming.

"Goodness gracious me!" he yells.

Gone are his visions of the bogey. He will be lucky to hole out in seven.

It is, as the great philosophers have observed, man's lot to make easy things hard. By rights the pitching wedge should be one of the Double Bogey Golfer's most potent weapons. All it needs is the kind of practice that the aforesaid Messrs. Stern and Heifetz have brought to their performances of the Beethoven Violin Concerto. They do not *fight* the instrument; and indeed, the violin, like the pitching wedge, requires no great strength to use. All that is needed is a little finesse, and a little confidence in a basic law of nature (angle = loft). A little practice, no more than four or five hours a day, will then groove a swing that gives nice contact with the ball. The basic thing is to sweep through the ball rather than try to lift it or guide it.

The use of the wedge is contingent upon the fairway lie, as almost anyone can figure out. The Double Bogey Golfer should never use the wedge unless the ball is sitting pretty on grass. If it is in a hole, forget it. Use an eight iron. If the ball is on a bare spot, zing it down its predestined path with a seven iron. Recognize your limitations.

But if conditions are ideal, then grab the pitching wedge. Don't worry about stance, open position, closed position, 60 percent of your weight on the inside of your left foot, and the other arcane things through which the teaching pro drives a Mercedes Benz and drives the Double Bogey Golfer to near-insanity. There are only three things to remember for the chip shot. Don't bring the club too far back. Sweep through the ball in the direction of the flag (if you take a divot, fine; if you don't take a divot, fine); and follow through.

So now observe the same Double Bogey Golfer on the same kind of 30-yard pitch shot. He has read this chapter. He advances to the ball with infinite cockiness. This time he asks no silly questions about winter rules. He lines up. He brings his club head back, not too far back. He swings down, right elbow nicely tucked in. He follows through. Then he watches a sculled ball run like a scared squirrel over the green, coming to rest in the far-side sand trap.

The goddam stupid jerk is *still* trying to lift the ball.

The Witch of Woonsapucket
Paul Gallico

Do you believe in witches, keep away from black cats, worry if you bust a mirror and stay home in bed on Friday the thirteenth? I am only asking, because personally, I am not superstitious myself, though I must confess that I am more than a little partial to a small ivory lucky elephant about the size of a walnut that Freddy McRae brought back for me from a golfing tour he made through India one winter, and that I carry in my left pants pocket just in case. And, boy, if I hadn't had it along with me that time the P.G.A. Championship got itself h'anted, I hate to think what would have happened to poor Elmer Brown, who was just a big dumb kid, but sweet and decent, and that swell Mary Summers he was so stuck on.

I mean, when it comes to that stuff about witches riding on broomsticks and Old Ned moving into a guy's golf bag and telling him what stick to use and where to place the ball to turn a tough par-five hole into a drive, a pitch, and a putt, your Uncle William Fowler, Esq., just gives it the broad "haw." But there's something cute about that little elephant and it doesn't take up much space anyway; and to think I almost forgot it when I changed suits before I went up to Woonsapucket for the P.G.A. Championship last year because I was so sore at old A.R. spoiling the party for me.

Being the assistant advertising manager of Mallow & Co., in charge of promotion, means that I do all the dirty work. And that was just what I was called upon to do when, the day before I was to leave for Massachusetts, I went in to see A.R. in response to his buzzer. Any time I am yanked in to A.R.'s office and he is sitting there with his glasses on the end of his nose and a paper in his hand, I know that there is going to be some trouble for William.

"Ha! Ahmmm! Hrrrmph! Fowler. I have here a memo compiled for me by Mr. Gudgins of the business department. It is a list of the professionals under contract to us and their — ah — accomplishments. Topheavy! Carrying some deadwood. Uncertain times, Fowler. Business unsteady. Everyone nervous. Good time to retrench. Must cut down, eh? This fellow Brown — hrrrmph! — Elmer Brown from — ah — Osceola, Iowa. What has he done to earn his pay?"

Well, he had me there, because Elmer hadn't exactly set any fairways on fire since I had signed him up three years before when it had looked as though he might be going to win the Open. But he was such a decent, earnest guy that I thought I'd at least have one crack at saving him, so I said:

"Gee whiz, A.R., he's just a kid. He placed seventh in the Open in '36, and had it won if he hadn't folded on the last five holes, and —"

"Ha! Exactly, Fowler. There is no room on the Mallow & Co. payroll for professionals who fold. This young man has done nothing since then, according to my memo, but place ninth in the Los Angeles Open, and twelfth at the Masters Tournament in Augusta. His contract has expired. I do not wish it renewed. He has brought no credit to A.R. Mallow products. Ha! Hum!" With the last "Ha! Hum!" he pushed his glasses back up on the bridge of his nose, which was always the signal that A.R. meant what he said and there was no use arguing.

Of course they would hold the P.G.A. in a place by the

name of Woonsapucket, Mass., five miles from Salem, but to the boys who cover for the papers, a thousand miles from anywhere. As far as our business is concerned, the lines are all pretty well laid out in that tournament, which is just for the pros, and there's no scrambling or chiseling or gambling to be done as there is around an Open, beyond a little polite needling. We always like it when one of our pros wins, and advertise it, but it doesn't count with the public like the Open. So for me it's just an annual week's vacation where I can relax, follow the boys around, and have myself some laughs. But it's a bad way to start a good time to have to give a nice kid the heave-oh. I guess maybe I'm just too tender-hearted.

There wasn't even a hotel at Woonsapucket and there was no room to stay at the Woonsapucket Golf Club, which was eight miles outside of Salem, so they had the boys quartered around in private houses, the citizens chipping in with room and board as a matter of civic pride. I found I was sharing a room in a swell old house with our Freddy McRae, who had as good a chance as anyone to win the tournament. I told him that I was going to have to give Elmer Brown the axe. He shrugged his shoulders and said: "That's a shame. He's a good kid, even though he is an awful hick. That's all that's the matter with him. He hasn't got that hay out of his hair yet. He's shy and scared. Every time he steps on a tee with someone who's got a name, he's licked."

I went out to the club Saturday morning, the day before the tournament started. It was a pretty course, long, and winding through woods every inch of the way. I had been wondering whether I would break the news to Elmer before or after the tournament. I suppose it would have been kinder to wait until it was all over, and keep that load off his mind, but I thought that maybe if I told him right away it would make him just mad enough to go out there and play some golf. And if he could make any kind of a showing in the tournament, maybe I could risk giving A.R. another argument.

I found him putting on the practice green. Not that he was

hard to find, because he had a build like Lou Nova's. He was grain-fed, big, husky, with corn-tassel hair and blue eyes and a broad mouth. He'd been brought up on a farm out in Iowa.

I didn't waste much time after the handshake and the usual about how his game was going. I came right out with it and said: "Look here, Elmer. I'm sorry to have to be the one to tell you this, but you're on the spot."

He straightened up from a putt he was going to make. Gloom was smeared as thick as butter all over his big, good-natured pan. And he looked scared too. He said: "Oh gee. Do you mean —?"

I started to give him a lot of stuff right out of A.R.'s book — retrenchment, unsettled conditions, nothing personal, economy wave, things ought to be better next year — when he cut in with:

"Aw, gee, Mr. Fowler. I know. You don't have to let me down easy. I know I ain't been winning enough to clean the rust off a mashie. If it hadn't been for you folks I'd a had to go back to the farm long ago. I guess I knew it was coming."

There was a sort of silence in which I felt rotten, and he leaned over and banged a nine-footer into the cup. Then he straightened up and said:

"Mr. Fowler, would it do any good if I won the P.G.A.?"

I looked at him. "It would help, kid. It would give me an argument with A.R. Even if the P.G.A. doesn't count a hell of a lot selling merchandise, A.R. is smart enough to know that the man who wins it is also capable of winning the Open, or one of those other big publicity tournaments like the Masters."

He said: "Gee, Mr. Fowler, I just gotta win, then. I just gotta." It was pipe-lined straight from his heart. And before I could speak the question I had written on my face, he said:

"I got a girl, Mr. Fowler. Gee, she's sweet."

I said "Oh-oh!" The last time one of our pros got himself a girl, it came so close to costing us the Open I didn't even want to think about it. But he hadn't heard me. That far-away look of men in love and fighters who have been popped on the chin came into his eyes, and he was off. "Gee, Mr. Fowler, she's the most wonderful person I ever met."

So I got the whole story from him. He had been assigned to the Wellbye cottage, kept by a spinster, Miss Sarah Wellbye, and the house had been in the family for more than two hundred and fifty years. Miss Wellbye's niece, Mary Summers, was staying there with her for her vacation. Mary was a college girl, a stenographer in Boston, and had black hair and blue eyes and wasn't any bigger than a milking stool, but gee, she was sweet and smart as a buggy whip, and he had fallen in love with her the first day he saw her, a week ago, when he arrived there to practice, and he couldn't understand why, but she liked him too, and they were going to be married when the tournament was over; the thousand dollars' prize money would get them started.

Well, the more he rattled on, the glummer I got. There he was, all full of young love and wanting to get married to a nice girl, and I had just fired him. And I knew just how tough it was for a young pro who wasn't winning anything to keep himself fed, let alone marry.

And as for winning the P.G.A.! I didn't have the heart to tell him. As McRae said, he was a shy, hero-worshipping type who got the meemies every time he played anybody with a name like MacDonough, or Crabby Wilson, or Craig, or Steubner. All they had to do was throw a ball on the tee and he was licked. And the P.G.A. was match play against the toughest, coldest, most hard-boiled, goat-getting crew in the racket. He didn't stand any more chance with them than I would of breaking 80 at Pinehurst with a croquet mallet and a butterfly net.

But I gave him a little pep talk and wished him luck and then beat it off to the locker room to have myself a little snort. It certainly was a swell introduction to a lousy time.

They really give a golfer a workout the way they play that P.G.A. It stretches out over a week. The first two days they play eighteen holes, each of qualifying medal play, starting Sunday. The low sixty-three qualify, along with last year's champion, who qualifies automatically, making sixty-four in all. On Tuesday they play two eighteen-hole matches, which knocks the field down to sixteen by nightfall, and from then on, it's thirty-six holes a day to the end.

Outside of Elmer's troubles there wasn't a thing to worry about. All of our boys, and we had four in the tournament, qualified nicely, and, for that matter, so did Elmer, but that didn't surprise me, because the guy wasn't so bad at medal play. He could cock a ball a mile when he really let out and wasn't under pressure. He was so big and powerful that he never used more than a three-quarter swing. But that didn't mean anything, because by Tuesday night Elmer would have departed for Osceola, Iowa. The poor sucker had managed to get himself into the tough side of the draw. And, brother, that upper bracket read just like the Social Register of golf. It was loaded for bear. At least a dozen of them were champions or former champions. Angus MacDonough, the Fairgreen pro who had won the Open that year, was in the lower half, and had a cinch. Also I met Elmer's girl, Mary Summers.

There's something sweet, right away, about the name Mary, and she lived up to all of it. She had that quiet sincerity that seems to go with dark hair and blue eyes. She wore her hair very smooth and glossy so that you wanted to touch it with your hand, but, for all her tiny figure — she came just about up to Elmer's shoulder — she had a good, strong, firm chin and a mouth that looked as if its owner might mean business sometimes. And was she stuck on big Elmer! She didn't seem to mind that he wasn't the brightest guy on earth. All she cared was that he was sweet and kind, and could break her in two, maybe, if he ever took a full backswing before he hugged her. Why do all those cute tricks go for guys like that when here is your Uncle Fowler around just dying for something soft and agreeable who will soothe his feverish head when he brings it home at night, hot and throbbing from the daily effort of thinking up ways to make more dubs buy more A.R. Mallow products?

We met on the clubhouse porch after the qualifying round. Elmer was drinking himself a glass of milk and kidding with the guys, because they all liked him, he was so modest and decent and unspoiled; and he called out: "Mr. Fowler, I want you to meet Mary Summers. Mary, this is Mr. Fowler of the A.R. Mallow Company. That's the company that — that — I have been working for. He thinks I have a chance to win."

Mary gave me one of those deep, kind, welcoming smiles as though, by thinking that, I belonged, and shook my hand and said: "This is the first golf match I ever saw, Mr. Fowler, but surely Elmer will win because he plays so beautifully. And of course you know why it is so important to us. Elmer told me that — that you know," and she suddenly gave Elmer's arm a little hug with such a natural, tender gesture that I thought I'd got one of our Tuff-Hide balls stuck in my throat because all the time I was looking right over her shoulder at what amounted to Elmer's walking papers. It was the draw-sheet on the club bulletin board, and Elmer was down to play old Archie Crobb in the first round. Uhuh. You got the name right away. It was just like taking a kid out of the amateur ranks for his first professional prize-fight and saying: "Come on in here, son, and meet your opponent. His name is Joe Louis."

Archie was a crochety old Scotchman, but he had been around for years and had the smoothest swing of the pack. And how he loved to take those youngsters apart in match play!

"Do come and take dinner with us at Wellbye Cottage, Mr. Fowler," Mary was saying.

"Gee, yes," Elmer added. "It's the most interesting house you ever saw. It's full of things, just like a museum, from before the Revolution even. . . ."

But I was hardly listening to them. All I could think of was that poor kid trying to tell his girl that he was out of the tournament, out of a job, and flat broke. I mumbled something about thanks and congratulations and, sure, that Elmer would come through, and got away. I even had half a notion of going to Archie and asking him not to pour it into the kid too badly, though a lot of difference it made whether he went out three and two or nine and eight. But Arch was too mean, anyway. He loved to rub their noses in it. So I just went into the locker room down to the crying corner where the guys who had failed to qualify were gathered. I felt at home there, it was so nice and gloomy.

Were you ever around a golf tournament on the day when they play those two eighteen-holes sudden-death matches? Brother, it's a shambles, and you know it. The corpses of the famous dead lie piled eight high in the locker room, the grill room is made hideous with the groans of the wounded and dying, and those that survive come off the course with a look of madness in their eyes. The word "Upset" falls with a monotonous and sickly thud upon the eardrums. I lost Whitey Brompton, one of our best men, to an unknown pro from Alabama who hit the ball as though he had a twitch, and Reggie Ring, another of our topnotchers, had the tough luck to meet Crabby Wilson, the Sweetwood pro, when Crabby was red-hot. That made two. And I just did pull Freddy McRae through in extra holes in the afternoon. Excitement? Plenty of it, with stars dumped right and left.

Oh yes, and Elmer was still in the tournament when the day was over. He beat Archie Crobb one up on the nineteenth hole, and in the afternoon took over Nelson Rohm, the crack Midwest pro, one up on the eighteenth. I didn't see it happen; nobody did, for that matter, but the scorer who went with them, because they had no gallery. But from what the scorers told me afterwards, Elmer just had all the luck that can happen to one guy at a time. Crobb had him dormy on the fifteenth. On the sixteenth they were both on in two, but off the pin. Elmer had to make a birdie to have a chance to stay in the show, so he jumped at the putt and rolled four feet past the hole. He sank the one coming back, but it was too late then, because Crobb shoved his putt to within eight inches of the hole for a sure half. The old guy waited for Elmer to knock the ball away and concede the victory. Elmer didn't say anything, so Crobb took his time studying the putt, while the kid stood off to one side with a funny expression on his face, staring at Archie. Crobb putted carefully and surely so that he couldn't miss, and then, by gum, the ball shot off in the funniest way and finished eight inches to one side of the hole. Archie glared as though he couldn't believe it and took a five to Elmer's four. Elmer squared the match on the eighteenth and won it on the nineteenth with a neat birdie.

In the afternoon round, against Nelson Rohm, he was cooked again. They were all square on the eighteenth tee. Elmer topped his drive, took an extra one in the rough, and lay four on the edge of the green. Nelson hit a daisy, his best drive of the day, and had the easiest kind of a niblick pitch to the pin for a sure four or a possible three. The scorer said Elmer must have been thinking of that train ride back to Iowa from the horrified way he stared at Nelson while the Midwest pro measured the distance, niblick in hand and got ready to give him the axe. And then, apparently for no reason at all, Rohm hit his niblick shot right up onto the clubhouse porch nearly killing an eightball who was carrying a tray of drinks. He had to play it off flagstone from behind a pillar and bounced it into some shrubbery and from there into a bunker. He took a nice juicy seven. Elmer won the hole and the match with a six. Funny, huh?

I went to look up Elmer to congratulate him and give him another pep talk. That girl, and luck, were sure working wonders for him. I found Mary, but she hadn't seen him since he had come off the course. She was a little troubled because, she said, he had walked right past without looking at her, but I smoothed that out by explaining that when a guy comes off the green after winning a tough match he sometimes doesn't know his own mother.

Do you know where I finally found Elmer, and it was late too, and the locker room practically deserted? In the washroom, staring at himself in the mirror with the wildest, scaredest, funniest expression I ever saw on any human face. Funny, too, that he didn't seem to see me come up behind him, because when I clouted him on the shoulder with a "Good work, kid!" he jumped as though he had seen the devil and let out a yell. He came down on his feet, but his knees were shaking.

He said: "Ow! I — uh — er — th-th-thanks, Mr. F-F-Fowler," and turned and ran right out of the washroom and out of the building too.

I put it down as a case of unstrung golf nerves after a couple of harrowing matches.

Which just goes to show you how wrong Mr. Fowler can be.

And one after another, my guys got themselves kicked out of the tournament. You remember who met in the finals, don't you? That's right, Elmer Brown and Angus MacDonough. Elmer had walked right through Alex Gliddy, Crabby Wilson, and Chubby Craig, three of the best and toughest golfers in the business. I didn't see the matches because I was busy trying to root our stars through, but they said those three played the worst golf in their lives. Gliddy got an attack of hooking and parked five tee shots in a row out of bounds. Crabby Wilson couldn't putt for sour apples. He three-putted seven greens. And Chubby Craig, the greatest iron player in the game, actually got to shanking. Elmer, on the other hand, apparently couldn't do anything wrong. He holed out from bunkers. His ball took all the right kicks. If he got into trouble with his tee shot, he'd blast the next one so close to the cup he could blow it in. It was the talk of the tournament.

Yes, and there was some other kind of talk going on too, and I couldn't run it down. It was more a feeling that was in the air that you couldn't get hold of. The pros were off Elmer. They were giving him funny looks, and not speaking to him or kidding with him any more. And they used to love him. But the strangest thing I heard late Friday, when the semi-finals were finished, was that when Elmer's match with Chubby was over — he beat Chubby 8 and 7 — Craig refused to shake hands with him. Instead, they said, he waved one fist in front of Elmer's face in a queer way and snarled some word at him, and then turned and walked off the green. I thought maybe I'd better find Elmer and see what this was all about. But I couldn't locate him anywhere around the clubhouse. It was beginning to bother me, so I went into the locker room and had a couple of snorts. All right, maybe I had four, then. Anyway, when I got into my car parked behind the clubhouse I thought perhaps I wouldn't drive it just yet, but would sit there awhile and try to figure things out. I guess I must have fallen asleep, because when I woke up it was dark. It was nine o'clock by my wristwatch. I was just going to drive myself home when I saw a figure sneaking out the back door of the clubhouse. By its size and a flash of light on yellow hair, I knew it was Elmer. At the same time another figure suddenly came up the path. I knew that one too, dark as it was. She said:

"Elmer, dear, I've been looking for you. What — what is wrong?"

The boy stood there in the dark for a moment. "N-nothing, M-Mary."

There was a long silence. Then Mary began to speak again, in a low, clear, steady voice.

"Elmer, this afternoon after the match was over, I was going through the woods to the car. Two of the golfers were walking just in front of me. I don't know their names, but they were two who played and had been put out. They were talking about you. They were saying that you had cheated."

There was another long silence in which I could hear my heart going "bonk — bonk — bonk. . . ."

"I went up to them, told them who I was. One of them said — 'Ma'm, we're sorry, because it's true. He admitted it. If you don't believe it, why don't you ask him?' and then they both walked away. Elmer — I am asking you now. Is it true?"

Did I listen for Elmer's answer? Yes, brother, you bet I did. It was a long time coming. At last he stammered: "M-M-Mary — gee, Mary — I — I — I can't say anything — I can't — I can't. . . ."

So there it was. It seemed like hours before Mary said in a sort of small, hurt voice: "I — I'm sorry, Elmer. I guess that's all, then. I just can't stand a cheat. If you win that tournament through cheating, why — why, don't ever speak to me again."

And then she turned and ran off down the path, and a moment later I heard a car starting and driving off. Elmer waited until the last sound had died away. Then he let out an awful groan, turned, and went back into the clubhouse. Me, I wasn't more than six steps behind him.

I found him sitting in a corner of the darkened locker room with his head in his hands. I slid alongside him, put my arm around his shoulder, and said: "What's the matter, kid? Why don't you tell me and get it off your chest?"

He gave a couple of shudders and finally said: "Mr. Fowler, I want to go home. I want to default tomorrow and get out of here. You can post my default for me. I want to get out tonight, now, right away."

I tried to jolly him. I said: "Oh, come on, Elmer, you can't do that. You're going great. You've got to stay in there and fight for old Alma Mallow. You're the only one we've got left. You can't leave now. If you do it'll cost you your job, and what's more, you'll never get another job because you'll be branded a quitter."

He shook his head and groaned: "I don't care. I don't want another job. I just want to get out of here." Suddenly he stopped, hesitated, and then blurted out all in a heap: "Mr. Fowler, I've done something awful. I — I'm a witch."

I thought it was still those snorts I'd had earlier. "You're a *what*?"

"A — a witch, Mr. Fowler. I — I cheated. I put a hex on Mr. Crobb, and Mr. Rohm, and Mr. Gliddy too, though I didn't mean to, honestly, Mr. Fowler, and I guess it got Mr. Craig too, though I didn't put it on him, but it won't stop. I gotta get out of here, Mr. Fowler, I just gotta. Can't you see?"

He wasn't kidding. He was on the level. He was so much on the level that there were tears in his eyes.

I said: "Listen, kid, why don't you tell me what the hell this is all about? I don't believe you're a cheat, and I don't believe in witches, and —"

"I didn't mean to do it, Mr. Fowler. I didn't believe in it either, but I was desperate. I had to win. Mr. Crobb had a *'gimme'* to win the match, and I was out of the tournament and my job, and I couldn't marry Mary. Otherwise I wouldn't have said the words. Honest I wouldn't, Mr. Fowler."

I saw I had kind of to nurse him along to get anything out of him, so I said: "What words?"

"The words in the book."

"Uhuh. What book?"

"The book I found in Mary's house. I just looked into it. It's old-like. They have a lot of things there from before the Revolution — pictures, and arrowheads and guns, and books, printed in the old kind of English, and there was this one book I just looked into, one night."

"What was the book?"

It was tough getting the story out of him because he was really unstrung, but it finally developed that he had found a copy of something called *Of Ye Plague of Wytches in Ye Collonies*, by the Reverend Hallelujah Snite, printed in Boston in 1699, and had read the thing out of curiosity and found some sort of words in it which, according to the Reverend Dr. Snite, the witches of old Salem used to summon Old Nick for a party. It was getting tough to keep from laughing, because I wanted to badly.

"Just what were the words?"

"Do I have to say them?"

"Go ahead. I'm a Psi Kappa Psi myself. . . ."

He gobbled a little and finally came out with some balderdash that sounded like "Abrogath Ahrimanes Abaddon," and then looked around him frightened, as though he expected to see Old Harry snap to attention out of a cloud of sulphur with an "At your service, sir!"

"So what happened?"

"Well, I was in this jam and was practically out of the tournament, and then I suddenly remembered those words. I didn't really believe in it, but I had to do something, Mr. Fowler. Mr. Crobb couldn't miss an eight-inch putt. So I said them."

"Out loud?"

"Oh, gee, no. Just to myself."

"Could old Archie see you?"

"No, sir. I was standing behind him out of his line so he couldn't see me at all. . . ."

"And Archie blew the putt! Wow!" I just couldn't hold it any longer and had to let go with a dozen guffaws that shook the locker room. "Kid, it's the discovery of the age. You write 'em down for me. Will I give it to that louse J. Sears Hammett of the Fairgreen Company the next time I play him a five-buck Nassau."

But the kid wasn't laughing. He said: "But you don't understand, Mr. Fowler. It's no joke. I didn't believe it at first, so when Mr. Rohm had me on the hook, I said them again and Mr. Rohm put his niblick shot into the clubhouse and took a seven. And when I played Mr. Gliddy I guess I must have said them once more without knowing it, and the Devil made him hook five tee shots in a row, and by then I was so scared I swore I'd never use them again, but it's too late now, I've sold myself to Satan. I didn't say anything when I played Mr. Wilson, but there he was just the same, keeping Mr. Wilson's putts out of the cup, and when I'd pull a six iron out of my bag I'd hear him say: 'Wrong club, sucker, it's a seven; play it high and fade it from right to left. Can't you see that wind in the top of the trees?' I've raised him, Mr. Fowler, and I can't get rid of him. If I'd only done it once, maybe he wouldn't have charged just for a demonstration. But he must want me awful bad, because he's working overtime. I can't make a bad shot. And I've lost my girl on account of him."

I said: "Listen, you big dope, those guys would have blown those shots anyway. Didn't you ever jab at a six-inch putt and see it stay out? Or get an attack of sausage fingers and see your game slip away? All that stuff is a lot of hooey anyway, but if it'll do you good and make you think you can beat those guys, what the hell! And anyway, they don't know about it, so —"

"That's one of the worst troubles, Mr. Fowler; they do!"

"What? How could they find out —?"

"I — I told them, Mr. Fowler — yesterday before I played Mr. Craig."

"You what? Why, you sap —"

It seems that the kid was scared and worried and uncertain whether he really had made a spell, or whatever it was, because he knew from his farm upbringing that Beelzebub doesn't do that kind of work for nothing, so he had asked old Crobb whether he had felt anything when he made that putt, and of course the old guy had said: "Yes, why?" Huh! Show me a golfer who won't grab for an alibi. The poor dope had told him, and of course Crobb had snarled: "Ay, I feltit something pushit my elbow. I no hae missit a wee putt like that gang on thirrty years." And Rohm then chimed in and said when he mishit that niblick shot it was just as though somebody else was swinging the club, and Gliddy recalled that coming down the seventeenth fairway he had actually said: "This damn driver of mine must be bewitched." And Crabby Wilson had said: "Hah! No wonder I couldn't get a putt down all day." And they they had all turned on him and accused him of cheating, hexing them, casting the evil eye, and conduct unbecoming a member of the P.G.A. The match when Chubby Craig shanked all day had finished it.

"They're in the grill room right now, holding a meeting over it, Mr. Fowler," concluded Elmer. "They're going to have me barred anyway. Let me go back to Osceola, Mr. Fowler. I can't go on. Satan's moved into my golf bag. I just gotta hang it up."

I said: "Listen, kid. You stay here until I get back. I'm going to that meeting. Those sharks aren't going to push one of my guys out of a tournament that way. You do as I say, understand?"

And I went busting into the grill room. I was just in time too. There was a big crowd of the pros there, and Archie Crobb was saying: "All those favoring to expel Elmer Brown and bar him frae the final say —" when I walked through the door and finished it for him:

"Say what? Are you guys nuts? What's the matter with Brown? Can't you birds take a licking without crying?"

Crabby Wilson said: "We can when it's on the level," and Nelson Rohm shouted: "What are you doing in here, Fowler? This is a closed meeting. You don't belong here."

I said: "Maybe I don't, but I'm not going to let you railroad one of my guys out of this tournament for nothing."

"For nothing!" shouted Crabby Wilson. "He put the whammie on me! Every time I'd go to putt, my eyes would water so I couldn't see the ball."

"He admittit himself he called on the De'il," said Crobb. "The mon's a witch. I haven't misstit a wee putt like thot in thirrr —"

I said: "You're a fool, Crobb. There aren't any male witches."

"Aweel, then, callit him a wizard, it's a' the same."

"I'll say he's a wizard, the way he plastered you five straight holes after you lost your nerve and blew a kick-in."

"What about his telling me he put a spell on me before I hit that shot to the eighteenth? The ball went up into the clubhouse, didn't it?" said Nelson Rohm.

"Yeah," I said. "He told you afterwards. I suppose you never missed a green in your life before. Sure, the kid's a little screwy like all you birds, but —"

Angus MacDonough chimed in here: "A mon has no richt to do wi bogles in a gowf match. I'll no have to do wi him. The De'il's in his bag."

I said: "O.K., boys. You do what you want, but I'm going out and dig up a couple of golf writers and give them the story of how a lot of grown men who got licked by a green kid had to work up an alibi for themselves."

I thought that would do it. It did, too. There were a lot of sensible guys there and they talked it over and finally agreed to do nothing and go ahead with the tournament.

"But you tell that young mon I'll no be bewitched," warned Angus. "The fairst spell I feel, I'll magic him wi a niblick."

I went back into the locker room and got Elmer and said: "Son, you'd better get all that nonsense out of your head. They were holding a meeting to consider the course for next year's tournament. You come on home with me and get a night's sleep and tomorrow you'll pin Angus's ears back for good old Mallow."

He shook his head. "Aw, what's the use, Mr. Fowler? I

don't want the job any more. I've lost Mary. She thinks I'm a cheat like the rest of them do."

So I piled into him about quitting and gave him a ten-minute speech that any football coach would have paid me for, winding up with: "You can't let this thing lick you this way. Go on out there and prove that you can whip —"

He interrupted me suddenly. A change seemed to have come over him. He jumped up and said: "I will, Mr. Fowler. By crickey, I will. I can make good. I will. *I know how.*"

I took him home with me. Boy, I was tickled to death. Mallow was going to collect another championship. I wouldn't have been so pleased if I'd known what he really meant. . . .

So the next morning we went out to play the final match against Angus MacDonough, with me carrying Elmer's bag. That's right. I had to caddie for him. Elmer's regular boy, a big African from Mobile by the name of Four Toes, met me down by the caddie pen, and he was on his way out, headed south. He said: "You gotta *ex*cuse me, Mistuh Fowler. Ah ain' gonna carry dat bag no mo'. De Debbil's done got in it. Ebbrybody say so. Ebbry time Ah give a club to Mistuh Brown de Debbil he say to him to take another. Ah heerd de voice an' seen de smoke commin' outen de bag. No *suh*! Ah ain't touchin' it no mo'." All the other caddies had disappeared. I picked up Elmer's clubs and went to the first tee. Elmer didn't even notice that I was carrying for him. He was like a guy all wrapped up in something. Angus turned his back on him and so did Angus's caddie, who was none other than Dutch Steubner, another Fairgreen pro. That witchcraft story had got all the caddies so scared they wouldn't go anywhere near Elmer. It was a good thing there weren't any of the top-flight golf writers around that tournament or they would have been asking plenty of questions. As it was, some of those smart guys from Boston were nosing around trying to track down some of the rumours they'd heard, and I had to tell plenty of lies. There was nothing unusual in Angus MacDonough refusing to look at an opponent, or speak to him, because he had the reputation of being a mean, goat-getting grouch in match play, but I wondered whether the reporters would catch on to the surreptitious signs he and Dutch and all the other golfers who were in the gallery made every time that Elmer would look at them — you know, fist doubled up with thumb and little finger sticking out, and X's and circles in the air.

I was glad when we got started. I wanted to get it over with. There were about a thousand or so in the gallery, and they must have felt there was something in the air, because they were sort of hushed when they moved off after us, following two nice drives that split the fairway, Elmer's some forty yards past Angus's. Angus knocked a four iron onto the green, about fourteen feet from the pin. Elmer pulled a number seven out of the bag. I said: "It's a six, kid. There's an upslope in front of the green. If you don't reach, it'll stop the ball dead."

Do you know what that fool kid did? He put his hands over his ears. Then he said: "Stand behind me, caddie." I got it, all right. He meant: "Get thee behind me, Satan." Then he hit a perfect seven iron. Only, as I said, it was a six-iron shot. The ball hit in front of the green, hesitated, and then rolled back down the slope. And his chip hit the bank and stopped outside of Angus's ball. Elmer had to putt first and rolled to within a foot of the cup for a fairly sure five. It was Angus's turn to putt. He took a long time over it and then hit one that certainly was a dilly. I never saw a worse shot on a green. He must have lunged at it. It wound up seven feet past the hole to one side. Angus stared at it as though he couldn't believe it. Then he turned angrily on Elmer, but before he could say anything, Elmer went over to Angus's ball, knocked it away with a "That's good," and walked off the green. There was a murmur of astonishment from the crowd.

I said: "What the devil did you do that for, you sap? He was a sure thing to miss that putt coming back and you'd have halved the hole. Now you're one down."

"No, I ain't," said Elmer softly, "no, I ain't. I'm one up. On that feller you just mentioned. And I'm going to whip him all the way."

So that's how it was going to be. Yes, and that's how it

was, too. When I brought him in to the clubhouse at the end of the first eighteen holes, he was exactly fourteen down. He underclubbed, he overclubbed, he conceded putts, he took penalties. The people in the gallery were sore as pups, grumbling and threatening to demand their money back or complain to the officials, but Angus was tickled to death, and so were the other pros. They acted just as though they had it coming to them. The newspaper boys kept barging up to me, asking: "What's he doing, throwing the match? What's the idea?" and I'd yell: "Oh leave us alone. Didn't you ever see a guy in a slump before? He'll be all right after lunch." But of course that last was hooey. It was all over. I could have killed Elmer, except that for the first time since it all started he seemed halfway happy and some of the fear was gone from his face. I left him alone in a corner of the grill drinking milk and went out by myself. I was too sick to eat. I passed a group of officials conferring in front of the clubhouse and heard they were going to call a meeting before the tee-off again after lunch. They had to, because everybody was squawking. I went into the woods bordering the sixth fairway to cool off. I didn't even want a drink. I had my hands stuffed down into my pockets and was kicking at things.

So that was how I came to haul that lucky elephant out of my pocket, because after a while I got to feeling it there, sort of hard and funny-shaped. I said: "You're a fine damn mascot, you are! You're supposed to be lucky, eh? You're nothing but a Jonah, and here you go," and with that I took a Bob Feller windup and heaved it as hard and as far as I could into a clump of bushes.

There was a gasp, and somebody said: "Ow!" I ran around to the other side of them to apologize to whoever I had beaned. You guessed it. It was Mary Summers. She was sitting on a log. There were tear-stains on her face where she had been crying. The elephant was lying at her feet.

I said: "Gee, Mary, I'm sorry. Where have you been? I've wanted to see you. Elmer —"

She began to cry again. "Oh Bill, I'm so miserable. I accused Elmer of cheating, and left him without giving him a real chance to explain. I don't care what he's done, I love him.

He isn't a cheat. And I saw what he was doing this morning. And instead of helping him, I — Oh, Bill —"

So then I told her the whole story, right from the beginning. And sometimes she laughed, but with tears and tenderness behind it, and sometimes she cried and made little gestures with her arms as though she were taking the absent Elmer into them. I wound up: "The poor kid is off his nut. He thinks he sinned saying those words, and has to atone for it by throwing the match to that old sour-puss Angus and beat the Devil that way, even though it costs him his job and the chance to marry you; and Angus, the old goat, behaves as though he had it coming to him, with the other pros egging him on, because by blaming it all on Elmer it gives them an alibi for their lousy golf. The reporters are hot on the trail of the story, though they haven't got it yet, but if it gets out, the kid'll be ruined. The officials are going to call a meeting in the clubhouse private office before the afternoon. Maybe they'll disqualify him right there. I don't know. It's an awful mess."

The girl took a deep breath and straightened up. Gee, she was a sweet sight with her blue eyes shining. She said: "Bill — Bill — we've got to do something. Right away."

"I know, but what? Maybe it's too late."

She was staring down at my elephant suddenly. She said: "Bill, what is that?"

I said: "That's my elephant. I carry it around in my pocket."

"What for?"

"For luck. But the luck was all bad, so I heaved it."

She picked it up, gazed at it for a moment, and then handed it to me. There was a strange look on her face.

"Put it back in your pocket, Bill. Maybe it will turn out to be the best friend you or I ever had." She glanced at her watch and gave a little gasp. "Oh! There isn't much time. Hurry, Bill! Go to that meeting. Don't let them leave. Do anything to hold them. I'll be there at two o'clock," and she was streaking off through the woods like a young deer.

I went back to the clubhouse, but quick. The afternoon tee-off time was two fifteen. At ten minutes to two the meeting was called by the officials. It was attended by Elmer and myself and Angus and Dutch, and all the pros that Elmer had beaten, and half a dozen others. Old Bill Wattley, the chief referee, didn't waste any time. He was boiling mad. He lit into poor Elmer and said that what he had done that morning was a disgrace to professional golfing, that people had paid good money to see a fair match. He lit into old Angus too, and the other pros, and said that he had heard a lot of silly stories, and there and now meant to get at the truth of the matter before he decided what action he would take.

Nobody wanted to say anything at first because, now that it was going to be dragged out in open meeting, they were a little ashamed, I guess; but finally old Archie Crobb spoke up and said: "Meester Wattley, 'tis ony richt he should gi' back to us what he tookit by foul means. He's admittit he has to do wi' bogles and Beelzebub and the sperrits o' the pit. I no hae missit a wee putt like that in thirrrty —"

Elmer suddenly got up, big, lanky, and miserable, and interrupted. "Aw, gee, Mr. Wattley, let me default and get out of here. I don't care what they say about me. Mr. Crobb is right. I didn't deserve to win. I —"

"Oh yes you did, Elmer," said Mary Summers. She had opened the door and come in very quietly. It was just two o'clock. She had a book under her arm, and she threw it down on the table. It was old and yellow, and from where I sat I could see it was the treatise by the Reverend Hallelujah Snite. Everybody stared at it as though it were a snake, including Elmer.

"Oh yes, you deserve to win, Elmer," Mary repeated, and then looked the whole crowd over coolly and a little as though they were insects. "I know the whole silly story. All you gentlemen who are so righteous, did you ever hear this: 'Let him who is without sin cast the first stone'?"

A fly buzzing on the windowpane sounded just like a dive-bomber, it was that quiet.

"Mr. Crobb," said Mary Summers, "turn out your pockets!"

Nobody moved. "Wha — what did ye say, lass?" said Old Crobb.

59

AUGUSTANA UNIVERSITY COLLEGE
LIBRARY

"I said turn out your pockets, Mr. Crobb. Put whatever you have here on the table. At once."

By jeepers, old Crobb did. He was hypnotized. His hands came up from his pockets full of junk which he laid on the table — some bills, coins, a little roll of tape, pocket-knife, half a dozen tees, and a little rabbit's-foot set in silver.

"Now you, Mr. Wilson," her voice rising, "and you . . . and you . . . and you . . . all of you. Out with them."

By jeepers, they were *all* hypnotized. Even I turned mine out before I knew it. And then Mary was at the table, picking out objects from each pile and sweeping them toward the center, the rabbit's-foot, punched coins, cat's-eyes, a piece of heather in a locket, framed four-leaf clovers, miniature horseshoes, little worsted Aucassins and Nicolettes, a curiously shaped stone or two, chunks of carved wood, a little silver devil on a ring, pairs of dice, medals, carved elephants, a piece of jade, and a silver pig.

She pointed to the pile. "What do you call these?" she said.

They all grinned sheepishly, and Archie Crobb said: "Eh, lass, what's wrang wi' a mascot?"

"Wrong? Do you know where the word 'mascot' comes from?" asked Mary Summers. "In old French the word 'masco' meant a sorceress or witch. You're all in it, every one of you. There isn't one of you who doesn't carry a talisman that you think gives you something on the other fellow, an edge, a spell, a lucky charm, something supernatural. And you dare to pick on Elmer? You ought to be ashamed of yourselves, all of you. That book there, that you're all so afraid of —" she flipped it open — "do you know what it is? It was written by a half-crazy, superstitious ninny about a pack of harmless, innocent old women who were drowned and stoned and hanged not more than five miles from here in Salem, to the everlasting shame of that city and a monument to ignorance and stupidity. Do you know what that spell is that terrified all you big brave men so that you couldn't hit a little golf ball? There it is. It was used by a lot of poor, ignorant, self-deluded wretches to curdle milk. And it never curdled anything but your dispositions. There, read it and see if it is any worse than that collection of ridiculous junk you carry around with you this year of 1942 to ward off bogies. Grown men, all of you. Very well. You're all even now. Put your nasty things back into your pockets and try to act like men and not a lot of frightened old women. Elmer Brown, you go right out and play that man golf, out in the woods there where everything is fresh and sweet and clean. And — and —" she hesitated suddenly and her lower lip began to tremble — "and — I don't care whether you win or lose, I'll marry you because I love you, and I don't care if we s-s-s-starve. . . . Oh, Elll-lllmer —"

And she was in his arms, crying, and all the pros were around her, patting her on the shoulder and apologizing and trying to make up to Elmer, and Mary kissed Elmer as though nobody was there, and Elmer suddenly raised up his arms with his fists clenched and shouted: "I've won! I've won! I've licked it. And now I'll lick you too, Angus MacDonough. Come on out on the course and take it. . . ."

Whew! I'm glad I don't have to describe that last eighteen holes for you. You read about it. The greatest comeback in the history of golf, they called it. And that Angus was playing too. You don't catch him giving anything away. But nobody ever saw golf like that kid played. He'd never really hit a ball before as hard as he could because of his size and strength, which might rob him of control. But now he had the control too. When they set par for that course it wasn't for the kind of golf Elmer shot. He simply made threes out of the fours, and fours out of the fives.

There weren't more than fifty people on the tee when we started, but by the time we reached the ninth, there were two thousand galloping on our heels, and Elmer, who had turned in 30, was only seven down. Even the cooks and waiters came out of the kitchen to see the miracle. As I toted Elmer's bag past the clubhouse from the ninth green to the tenth tee, a

Western Union boy handed me a telegram. It was from A.R. Mallow, who must have been listening in to the match on the radio. It said:

TRUST YOU HAVE NOT MADE MISTAKE OF LETTING BROWN GET AWAY FROM US STOP IF HE WINS RAISE SALARY TWELVE HUNDRED A YEAR STOP A.R.

Me make the mistake! Wasn't that just like A.R.?

You read how Elmer squared the match on the seventeenth to the greatest frenzy of cheering I ever heard, and then slipped up on the eighteenth to let Angus halve him. Then Angus got into trouble on the nineteenth and was only on the edge of the green in three, while Elmer was on in two, but with a nasty, curling, downhill ten-foot putt. Angus chipped into the cup from off the edge for his four, and the crowd gave him a great hand. A careful, certain four would keep the match open for Elmer another hole. A three would win it. But the putt was downhill, and if it missed the can, the ball would roll on and cost him the match and the championship if he missed coming back.

Elmer knelt down and studied the line. He studied it from every angle, inspected each blade of grass in the path to the hole. Everybody knew that he was going to go for the cup and the match.

He bent over his putt and waited to steady his nerves. And then I saw old Angus MacDonough do a funny thing. He fished into his pocket and hauled forth a little scrap of paper, studied it, glared at Elmer's back, and his lips moved; then he looked back at the paper again. Somehow, out of the corner of his eye, Elmer must have seen him too, for he straightened up all of a sudden, grinning.

Then he said: "The words, Mr. MacDonough, are: 'Abrogath Ahrimanes Abaddon,' but they don't mean a damn thing if you haven't got the golf to go with them. Watch this."

He leaned over and stroked the ball and I shut my eyes. Then I heard a gentle "Bonk!" as it fell into the cup, and everybody was yelling and screaming and dancing, and Mary

Summers was in the center of it all, with her arms around big stupid Elmer's neck. . . .

Boy, did I kiss that little old good-luck elephant of mine. Wouldn't it have been hell if I'd left it at home?

The Golfomaniac
Stephen Leacock

We ride in and out pretty often together, he and I, on a suburban train. That's how I came to talk to him. "Fine morning," I said as I sat down beside him yesterday and opened a newspaper.

"Great!" he answered. "The grass is drying out fast now and the greens will soon be all right to play."

"Yes," I said, "the sun is getting higher and the days are decidedly lengthening."

"For the matter of that," said my friend, "a man could begin to play at six in the morning easily. In fact, I've often wondered that there's so little golf played before breakfast. We happened to be talking about golf, a few of us last night — I don't know how it came up — and we were saying that it seems a pity that some of the best part of the day, say, from five o'clock to seven thirty, is never used."

"That's true," I answered, and then, to shift the subject, I said, looking out of the window:

"It's a pretty bit of country just here, isn't it?"

"It is," he replied, "but it seems a shame they make no use of it — just a few market gardens and things like that. Why, I noticed along here acres and acres of just glass — some kind of houses for plants or something — and whole fields of lettuce and things like that. It's a pity they don't make something of it. I was remarking only the other day as I came along in the train with a friend of mine, that you could easily lay out an eighteen-hole course anywhere here."

"Could you?" I said.

"Oh, yes. This ground, you know, is an excellent light soil to shovel up into bunkers. You could drive some big ditches through it and make one or two deep holes — the kind they have on some of the French links. In fact, improve it to any extent."

I glanced at my morning paper. "I see," I said, "that it is again rumored that Lloyd George is at last definitely to retire."

"Funny thing about Lloyd George," answered my friend. "He never played, you know; most extraordinary thing — don't you think? — for a man in his position. Balfour, of course, was very different: I remember when I was over in Scotland last summer I had the honor of going around the course at Dumfries just after Lord Balfour. Pretty interesting experience, don't you think?"

"Were you over on business?" I asked.

"No, not exactly. I went to get a golf ball, a particular golf ball. Of course, I didn't go merely for that. I wanted to get a mashie as well. The only way, you know, to get just what you want is to go to Scotland for it."

"Did you see much of Scotland?"

"I saw it all. I was on the links at St. Andrews and I visited the Loch Lomond course and the course at Inverness. In fact, I saw everything."

"It's an interesting country, isn't it, historically?"

"It certainly is. Do you know they have played there for over five hundred years! Think of it! They showed me at Loch Lomond the place where they said Robert the Bruce played the Red Douglas (I think that was the other party — at any rate, Bruce was one of them), and I saw where Bonnie Prince Charlie disguised himself as a caddie when the Duke of Cumberland's soldiers were looking for him. Oh, it's a wonderful country historically."

After that I let a silence intervene so as to get a new start. Then I looked up again from my newspaper.

"Look at this," I said, pointing to a headline, *United States Navy Ordered to Nicaragua*. "Looks like more trouble, doesn't it?"

"Did you see in the paper a while back," said my companion, "that the United States Navy Department is now making golf compulsory at the training school at Annapolis? That's progressive, isn't it? I suppose it will have to mean shorter cruises at sea; in fact, probably lessen the use of the Navy for sea purposes. But it will raise the standard."

"I suppose so," I answered. "Did you read about this extraordinary murder case on Long Island?"

"No," he said. "I never read murder cases. They don't interest me. In fact, I think this whole continent is getting over-preoccupied with them —"

"Yes, but this case had such odd features —"

"Oh, they all have," he replied, with an air of weariness. "Each one is just boomed by the papers to make a sensation —"

"I know, but in this case it seems that the man was killed with a blow from a golf club."

"What's that? Eh, what's that? Killed him with a blow from a golf club!"

"Yes, some kind of club —"

"I wonder if it was an iron — let me see the paper — though, for the matter of that, I imagine that a blow with even a wooden driver, let alone one of the steel-handled drivers — where does it say it? — pshaw, it only just says 'a blow with golf club.' It's a pity the papers don't write these things up with more detail, isn't it? But perhaps it will be better in the afternoon paper —"

"Have you played golf much?" I inquired. I saw it was no use to talk of anything else.

"No," answered my companion, "I am sorry to say I haven't. You see, I began late. I've only played twenty years, twenty-one if you count the year that's beginning in May. I don't know what I was doing. I wasted about half my life. In fact, it wasn't till I was well over thirty that I caught on to the game. I suppose a lot of us look back over our lives that way and realize what we have lost.

"And even as it is," he continued, "I don't get much chance to play. At the best I can only manage about four afternoons a week, though of course I get most of Saturday and all Sunday. I get my holiday in the summer, but it's only a month, and that's nothing. In the winter I manage to take a run south for a game once or twice and perhaps a little swack at it around Easter, but only a week at a time. I'm too busy — that's the plain truth of it." He sighed. "It's hard to leave the office before two," he said. "Something always turns up."

And after that he went on to tell me something of the technique of the game, illustrate it with a golf ball on the seat of the car, and the peculiar mental poise needed for driving, and the neat, quick action of the wrist (he showed me how it worked) that is needed to undercut a ball so that it flies straight up in the air. He explained to me how you can do practically anything with a golf ball, provided that you keep your mind absolutely poised and your eye in shape, and your body a trained machine. It appears that even Bobby Jones of Atlanta and people like that fall short very often from the high standard set up by my golfing friend in the suburban car.

So, later in the day, meeting someone in my club who was a person of authority on such things, I made inquiry about my friend. "I rode into town with Llewellyn Smith," I said. "I think he belongs to your golf club. He's a great player, isn't he?"

"A great player!" laughed the expert. "Llewellyn Smith? Why, he can hardly hit a ball! And anyway, he's only played about twenty years!"

A Child's Guide to Golf
Michael Green

"When the voices of children are heard on the green
And laughing is heard on the hill. . . ."

Blake

Askew's seven-year-old daughter was recently asked to write an essay in school on the subject of sport. This was the result.

66

I am going to write about golf. My Daddy plays golf with Uncle Mike. Uncle Mike is very old, as old as Daddy. Uncle Mike has to play golf with my Daddy because he has no children of his own to keep him amused. I do not like Uncle Mike. He is not as nice as my other uncle who comes to sleep when Daddy is away on business.

Uncle Mike used to give me presents sometimes, but he has stopped since I was sick in the back of his car. When Daddy and Uncle Mike go to play golf they come back smelling all funny. Daddy says it is Flowers.

One day Daddy took me to watch him play golf with Uncle Mike. Mummy made him do it as she had to have her hair done. Uncle Mike was not pleased and asked Daddy why he couldn't have left the brat at home, preferably in the kitchen with all the gas taps turned on.

When they got to the golf course they went into a little room in a big house and changed their clothes and then they came out and waited with a lot of other men while some others hit the ball. They were all old men too.

When a man hit a ball he said "Shave off" and ran to one side to watch it hit the trees and all the others said "Ardluck, Charlie," but secretly I think they were pleased.

When Uncle Mike came to hit the ball he spent a long time waving his big club, and then he lifted it ever so high in the air and dug up a piece of earth with it and he was not pleased because he had been naughty and all the men looked at each other and said, "Oh dear, what a naughty man."

And I said, "Are you digging for worms, Uncle Mike?" and they all laughed and one of them patted my head and said I was a clever girl, but I do not think Uncle Mike was pleased.

After Daddy had had his go he went into a little wood and Uncle Mike went into another little wood to look for their balls. Daddy found his ball under a bush. I got it out for him and he built a little mound of earth and put it on it and then he hit it out of the wood and went to help Uncle Mike who was looking into a drain.

I said to Uncle Mike, "Daddy just found his ball under a bush and I got it out for him," and Daddy tried to put his hand over my mouth but Uncle Mike said I was a good girl and gave me a sweetie.

Just then some naughty men came up and told Uncle Mike that if he had lost his ball he should let them have their little go, but Uncle Mike was rude.

Then Uncle Mike found his ball and he hit it into the drain again and we had to wait while a lot of other men had their go.

Daddy did not go into the wood again but he took ever such a little club and he went to play in a sandpit like we have in the school playground only much bigger. Daddy played a lovely game throwing sand all over everywhere so I went into another sandpit next door and built a beautiful sand castle with a real moat.

When I showed it to Daddy he went very red and said, "Good God, look what the child's done," and he and Uncle Mike went down on their hands and knees and flattened out my castle. While they were doing it a man came along on a sort of mowing machine and he said they ought to be ashamed of themselves and he would report them to the secretary, and Uncle Mike said that word again.

After that Daddy and Uncle Mike went to play on a little piece of flat ground with a lot of sandpits round it and a big stick in the middle and Daddy let me hold the stick. It was in a nasty little hole full of water. So when Uncle Mike hit his ball I stopped it from rolling into the nasty hole and Uncle Mike threw his club at Daddy and it hit him on the knee. Daddy said, "You can't blame me for what the child does," and Uncle Mike said the only consolation was that I was as happy as if I was in my right senses.

Then we saw two lady golfers, and they were very old, as old as Mummy, and Uncle Mike said something to Daddy and they went away and whispered and came back laughing.

Then we came to a huge river and Daddy and Uncle Mike tried to see who could get the most balls into it and my Daddy won because he hit the river more times, but he did not look pleased. Uncle Mike said would I like to go and look in the river for the balls, preferably in the deepest part, but I did not go.

Then they went to play on a bit with a stick in the middle again. Daddy took out his teeny-weeny club, the one he uses to practise with in the living-room. He stood on the grass near the long stick, and he looked hard at the ball and hard at the long stick and then he stood on one leg and then he started to breathe very heavily and then he asked Uncle Mike to stop blinking as he noise of his eyelids upset him.

Well, while Daddy was standing still and breathing hard I saw a squirrel and I whispered it to Uncle Mike, and he said, "Go and tell Daddy now." As Daddy was swinging his teeny-weeny club I ran up and I shouted, "Daddy, Daddy, Daddy, I've just seen a squirrel," and he jumped and he hit the ball ever so hard, much harder than he hits it even with that big club with the lump on the end, and the ball went away into a sandpit.

Then Daddy went all sort of pale and trembly, like Diana Bradshaw when she was sick in the playground, and he kept twitching and muttering, and then he said, "May God forgive me, but I want to kill my own daughter."

Uncle Mike said would I pull his little truck for him as that might keep me quiet, and he let me pull the truck and I found it ever so easy and I ran round and round and round one of the long sticks just like a race-track. But two nasty men came along and shouted at me and Uncle Mike took his little truck away from me and said if I had any more brains I would be half-witted.

Then we got back to where they started and we went into the big house and Daddy gave me a lemonade and Uncle Mike gave me sixpence and I put it into a big machine with coloured lights all over it, and I pressed a handle and a lot of sixpences came out of the bottom. Uncle Mike made a noise as if he was going to be ill and said it was the irony of life and now he had tasted the very dregs.

I shall not play golf when I grow up as it is a stupid, silly game. I told Mummy so when she was bathing me and she said I was quite right but men played it because they were silly, stupid people and Uncle Mike was the silliest and stupidest of them all.

Angela Askew (Form IV)

(There is a note on the end of the manuscript in the teacher's handwriting stating, "There is no need to try and spell out the exact words used by your Daddy and his friend.")

The Ooley-Cow
Charles E. Van Loan

After the explanation, and before Uncle Billy Poindexter and Old Man Sprott had been able to decide just what had hit them, Little Doc Ellis had the nerve to tell me that he had seen the fuse burning for months and months. Little Doc is my friend and I like him, but he resembles many other members of his profession in that he is usually wisest after the post mortem, when it is a wee bit late for the high contracting party.

And at all times Little Doc is full of vintage bromides and figures of speech.

"You have heard the old saw," said he. "A worm will turn if you keep picking on him, and so will a straight road if you ride it long enough. A camel is a wonderful burden bearer, but even a double-humped ship of the desert will sink on your hands if you pile the load on him a bale of hay at a time."

"A worm, a straight road, a camel and a sinking ship," said I. "Whither are we drifting?"

Little Doc did not pay any attention to me. It is a way he has.

"Think," said he, "how much longer a camel will stand up under punishment if he gets his load straw by straw, as it were. The Ooley-cow was a good thing, but Uncle Billy and Old Man Sprott did not use any judgment. They piled it on him too thick."

"Meaning," I asked, "to compare the Ooley-cow with a camel?"

"Merely a figure of speech," said Little Doc; "but yes, such was my intention."

"Well," said I, "your figures of speech need careful auditing. A camel can go eight days without a drink —"

Little Doc made impatient motions at me with both hands. He has no sense of humor, and his mind is a one-way track, totally devoid of spurs and derailing switches. Once started, he must go straight through to his destination.

"What I am trying to make plain to your limited mentality," said he, "is that Uncle Billy and Old Man Sprott needed a lesson in conservation, and they got it. The Ooley-cow was the easiest, softest picking that ever strayed from the home pasture. With care and decent treatment he would have lasted a long time and yielded an enormous quantity of nourishment, but Uncle Billy and Old Man Sprott were too greedy. They tried to corner the milk market, and now they will have to sign tags for their drinks and their golf balls the same as the rest of us. They have killed the goose that laid the golden eggs."

"A minute ago," said I, "the Ooley-cow was a camel. Now he is a goose — a dead goose, to be exact. Are you all done figuring with your speech?"

"Practically so, yes."

"Then," said I, "I will plaster up the cracks in your argument with the cement of information. I can use figures of speech myself. You are barking up the wrong tree. You are away off your base. It wasn't the loss of a few dollars that made Mr. Perkins run wild in our midst. It was the manner in which he lost them. Let us now dismiss the worm, the camel, the goose and all the rest of the menagerie, retaining only the Ooley-cow. What do you know about cows, if anything?"

"A little," answered my medical friend.

"A mighty little. You know that a cow has hoofs, horns and a tail. The same description would apply to many creatures, including Satan himself. Your knowledge of cows is largely academic. Now me, I was raised on a farm, and there were cows in my curriculum. I took a seven-year course in the gentle art of acquiring the lacteal fluid. Cow is my specialty, my long suit, my best hold. Believe it or not, when we christened old Perkins the Ooley-cow we builded better than we knew."

"I follow you at a great distance," said Little Doc. "Proceed with the rat killing. Why did we build better than we knew when we did not know anything?"

"Because," I explained, "Perkins not only looks like a cow and walks like a cow and plays golf like a cow, but he has the predominant characteristic of a cow. He has the one distinguishing trait which all country cows have in common. If you had studied that noble domestic animal as closely as I have, you would not need to be told what moved Mr. Perkins to strew the entire golf course with the mangled remains of the two old pirates before mentioned. Uncle Billy and Old Man Sprott were milking him, yes, and it is quite likely that the Ooley-cow knew that he was being milked, but that knowledge was not the prime cause of the late unpleasantness."

"I still follow you," said Little Doc plaintively, "but I am losing ground every minute."

"Listen carefully," said I. "Pin back your ears and give me your undivided attention. There are many ways of milking a cow without exciting the animal to violence. I speak now of the old-fashioned cow — the country cow — from Iowa, let us say."

"The Ooley-cow is from Iowa," murmured Little Doc.

"Exactly. A city cow may be milked by machinery, and in a dozen different ways, but the country cow does not know anything about new-fangled methods. There is one thing — and one thing only — which will make the gentlest old mooley in Iowa kick over the bucket, upset the milker, jump a four-barred fence and join the wild bunch on the range. Do you know what that one thing is?"

"I haven't even a suspicion," confessed Little Doc.

Then I told him. I told him in words of one syllable, and after a time he was able to grasp the significance of my remarks. If I could make Little Doc see the point, I can make you see it too. We go from here.

Wesley J. Perkins hailed from Dubuque, but he did not hail from there until he had gathered up all the loose change in Northeastern Iowa. When he arrived in sunny Southern California he was fifty-five years of age, and at least fifty of those years had been spent in putting aside something for a rainy day. Judging by the diameter of his bankroll, he must have feared the sort of a deluge which caused the early settlers to lay the ground plans for the Tower of Babel.

Now it seldom rains in Southern California — that is to say, it seldom rains hard enough to produce a flood — and as soon as Mr. Perkins became acquainted with climatic conditions he began to jettison his ark. He joined an exclusive downtown club, took up quarters there and spent his afternoons playing dominoes with some other members of the I've-got-mine Association. Aside from his habit of swelling up whenever he mentioned his home town, and insisting on referring to it as "the Heidelberg of America," there was nothing about Mr. Perkins to provoke comment, unfavorable or otherwise. He was just one more Iowan in a country where Iowans are no novelty.

In person he was the mildest-mannered man that ever foreclosed a short-term mortgage and put a family out in the street. His eyes were large and bovine, his mouth dropped perpetually and so did his jowls, and he moved with the slow, uncertain gait of a venerable milch cow. He had a habit of lowering his head and staring vacantly into space, and all these things earned for him the unhandsome nickname by which he is now known.

"But why the Ooley-cow?" someone asked one day. "It doesn't mean anything at all!"

"Well," was the reply, "neither does Perkins."

But this was an error, as we shall see later.

It was an increasing waistline that caused the Ooley-cow to look about him for some form of gentle exercise. His physician suggested golf, and that very week the board of directors of the Country Club was asked to consider his

73

application for membership. There were no ringing cheers, but he passed the censors.

I will say for Perkins that when he decided to commit golf he went about it in a very thorough manner. He had himself surveyed for three knickerbocker suits, he laid in a stock of soft shirts, imported stockings and spiked shoes, and he gave our professional *carte blanche* in the matter of field equipment. It is not a safe thing to give a Scotchman permission to dip his hand in your change pocket, and MacPherson certainly availed himself of the opportunity to finger some of the Dubuque money. He took one look at the novice and unloaded on him something less than a hundredweight of dead stock. He also gave him a lesson or two, and sent him forth armed to the teeth with wood, iron and aluminum.

Almost immediately Perkins found himself in the hands of Poindexter and Sprott, two extremely hard-boiled old gentlemen who have never been known to take any interest in a financial proposition assaying less than seven per cent, and that fully guaranteed. Both are retired capitalists, but when they climbed out of the trenches and retreated into the realm of sport they took all their business instincts with them.

Uncle Billy can play to a twelve handicap when it suits him to do so, and his partner in crime is only a couple of strokes behind him; but they seldom uncover their true form, preferring to pose as doddering and infirm invalids, childish old men, who only think they can play the game of golf, easy marks for the rising generation. New members are their victims; beginners are just the same as manna from heaven to them. They instruct the novice humbly and apologetically, but always with a small side bet, and no matter how fast the novice improves he makes the astounding discovery that his two feeble old tutors are able to keep pace with him. Uncle Billy and Old Man Sprott are experts at nursing a betting proposition along, and they seldom win any sort of a match by a margin of more than two up and one to go. Taking into account the natural limitations of age they play golf very well, but they play a cinch even better — and harder. It is common scandal that Uncle Billy has not bought a golf ball in ten years. Old Man Sprott bought one in 1915, but it was under the mellowing influence of the third toddy and, therefore, should not count against him.

The Ooley-cow was a cinch. When he turned up, innocent and guileless and eager to learn the game, Uncle Billy and his running mate were quick to realize that Fate had sent them a downy bird for plucking, and in no time at all the air was full of feathers.

They played the Ooley-cow for golf balls, they played him for caddie hire, they played him for drinks and cigars, they played him for luncheons and they played him for a sucker — played him for everything, in fact, but the locker rent and the club dues. How they came to overlook these items is more than I know. The Ooley-cow would have stood for it; he stood for everything. He signed all the tags with a loose and vapid grin, and if he suffered from writer's cramp he never mentioned the fact. His monthly bill must have been a thing to shudder at, but possibly he regarded this extra outlay as part of his tuition.

Once in a while he was allowed to win, for Poindexter and Sprott followed the system practiced by other confidence men; but they never forgot to take his winnings away from him the next day, charging him interest at the rate of fifty per cent for twenty-four hours. The Ooley-cow was so very easy that they took liberties with him, so good-natured about his losses that they presumed upon that good nature and ridiculed him openly; but the old saw sometimes loses a tooth, the worm turns, the straight road bends at last, so does the camel's back, and the prize cow kicks the milker into the middle of next week. And, as I remarked before, the cow usually has a reason.

One morning I dropped into the downtown club which Perkins calls his home. I found him sitting in the reception room, juggling a newspaper and watching the door. He seemed somewhat disturbed.

"Good morning," said I.

"It is not a good morning," said he. "It's a bad morning. Look at this."

He handed me the paper, with his thumb at the head of the Lost-and-Found column, and I read as follows:

LOST — *A black leather wallet, containing private papers and a sum of money. A suitable reward will be paid for the return of same, and no questions asked. Apply to W.J.P., Argonaut Club, City.*

"Tough luck," said I. "Did you lose much?"

"Quite a sum," replied the Ooley-cow. "Enough to make it an object. In large bills mostly."

"Too bad. The wallet had your cards in it?"

"And some papers of a private nature."

"Have you an idea where you might have dropped it? Or do you think it was stolen?"

"I don't know what to think. I had it last night at the Country Club just before I left. I know I had it then, because I took it out in the lounging room to pay a small bet to Mr. Poindexter — a matter of two dollars. Then I put the wallet back in my inside pocket and came straight here — alone in a closed car. I missed it just before going to bed. I telephoned to the Country Club. No sign of it there. I went to the garage myself. It was not in the car. Of course it may have been there earlier in the evening, but I think my driver is honest, and —"

At this point we were interrupted by a clean-cut looking youngster of perhaps seventeen years.

"Your initials are W.J.P., sir?" he asked politely.

"They are."

"This is your ad in the paper?"

"It is."

The boy reached in his pocket and brought out a black leather wallet. "I have returned your property," said he, and waited while the Ooley-cow thumbed a roll of yellow-backed bills.

"All here," said Perkins with a sigh of relief. Then he looked up at the boy, and his large bovine eyes turned hard as moss agates. "Where did you get this?" he demanded abruptly. "How did you come by it?"

The boy smiled and shook his head, but his eyes never left Perkins' face. "No questions were to be asked, sir," he said.

"Right!" grunted the Ooley-cow. "Quite right. A bargain's a bargain. I — I beg your pardon, young man — Still, I'd like to know — Just curiosity, eh? — No? — Very well then. That being the case" — he stripped a fifty-dollar note from the roll and passed it over — "would you consider this a suitable reward?"

"Yes, sir, and thank you, sir."

"Good day," said Perkins, and put the wallet into his pocket. He stared at the boy until he disappeared through the street door.

"Something mighty queer about this," mused the Ooley-cow thoughtfully. "Mighty queer. That boy — he looked honest. He had good eyes and he wasn't afraid of me. I couldn't scare him worth a cent. Couldn't bluff him — Yet if he found it somewhere, there wasn't any reason why he shouldn't have told me. He didn't steal it — I'll bet on that. Maybe he got it from someone who did. Oh, well, the main thing is that he brought it back — Going out to the Country Club this afternoon?"

I said that I expected to play golf that day.

"Come out with me then," said the Ooley-cow. "Poindexter and Sprott will be there too. Yesterday afternoon I played Poindexter for the lunches today. Holed a long putt on the seventeenth green, and stuck him. Come along, and we'll make Poindexter give a party — for once."

"It can't be done," said I. "Uncle Billy doesn't give parties."

"We'll make him give one," chuckled the Ooley-cow. "We'll insist on it."

"Insist if you want to," said I, "but you'll never get away with it."

"Meet me here at noon," said the Ooley-cow. "If Poindexter doesn't give the party, I will."

I wasn't exactly keen for the Ooley-cow's society, but I

accepted his invitation to ride out to the club in his car. He regaled me with a dreary monologue, descriptive of the Heidelberg of America, and solemnly assured me that the pretty girls one sees in Chicago are all from Dubuque.

It was twelve-thirty when we arrived at the Country Club, and Uncle Billy and Old Man Sprott were there ahead of us.

"Poindexter," said Perkins, "you are giving a party today, and I have invited our friend here to join us."

Uncle Billy looked at Old Man Sprott, and both laughed uproariously. Right there was where I should have detected the unmistakable odor of a rodent. It was surprise number one.

"Dee-lighted!" cackled Uncle Billy. "Glad to have another guest, ain't we, Sprott?"

Sprott grinned and rubbed his hands. "You bet! Tell you what let's do, Billy. Let's invite everybody in the place — make it a regular party while you're at it!"

"Great idea!" exclaimed Uncle Billy. "The more the merrier!" This was surprise number two. The first man invited was Henry Bauer, who has known Uncle Billy for many years. He sat down quite overcome.

"You shouldn't do a thing like that, Billy," said he querulously. "I have a weak heart, and any sudden shock —"

"Nonsense! You'll join us?"

"Novelty always appealed to me," said Bauer. "I'm forever trying things that nobody has ever tried before. Yes, I'll break bread with you, but — why the celebration? What's it all about?"

That was what everybody wanted to know and what nobody found out, but the luncheon was a brilliant success in spite of the dazed and mystified condition of the guests, and the only limit was the limit of individual capacity. Eighteen of us sat down at the big round table, and sandwich-and-milk orders were sternly countermanded by Uncle Billy, who proved an amazing host, recommending this and that and actually ordering Rhine wine cup for all hands. I could not have been more surprised if the bronze statue in the corner of the grill had hopped down from its pedestal to fill our glasses. Uncle Billy collected a great pile of tags beside his plate, but the presence of so much bad news waiting at his elbow did not seem to affect his appetite in the least. When the party was over he called the head waiter. "Mark these tags paid," said Uncle Billy, capping the collection with a yellow-backed bill, "and hand the change to Mr. Perkins."

"Yes sir," said the head waiter, and disappeared.

I looked at the Ooley-cow, and was just in time to see the light of intelligence dawn in his big soft eyes. He was staring at Uncle Billy, and his lower lip was flopping convulsively. Everybody began asking questions at once.

"One moment, gentlemen," mooed the Ooley-cow, pounding on the table. "One moment!"

"Now don't get excited, Perkins," said Old Man Sprott. "You got your wallet back, didn't you. Cost you fifty, but you got it back. Next time you won't be so careless."

"Yes," chimed in Uncle Billy, "you oughtn't to go dropping your money round loose that way. It'll teach you a lesson."

"It will indeed." The Ooley-cow lowered his head and glared first at one old pirate and then at the other. His soft eyes hardened and the moss-agate look came into them. He seemed about to bellow, paw up the dirt and charge.

"The laugh is on you," cackled Poindexter, "and I'll leave it to the boys here. Last night our genial host dropped his wallet on the floor out in the lounging room. I kicked it across under the table to Sprott and Sprott put his foot on it. We intended to give it back to him today, but this morning there was an ad in the paper — reward and no questions asked — so we sent a nice bright boy over to the Argonaut Club with the wallet. Perkins gave the boy a fifty-dollar note — very liberal, I call it — and the boy gave it to me. Perfectly legitimate transaction. Our friend here has had a lesson, we've had a delightful luncheon party, and the joke is on him."

"And a pretty good joke, too!" laughed Old Man Sprott.

"Yes," said the Ooley-cow at last, "a pretty good joke. Ha, ha! A mighty good joke." And place it to his credit that he managed a very fair imitation of a fat man laughing, even to the shaking of the stomach and the wrinkles round the eyes. He looked down at the tray in front of him and fingered the few bills and some loose silver.

"A mighty good joke," he repeated thoughtfully, "but what I can't understand is this — why didn't you two jokers keep the change? It would have been just that much funnier."

The Ooley-cow's party was generally discussed during the next ten days, the consensus of club opinion being that someone ought to teach Poindexter and Sprott the difference between humor and petty larceny. Most of the playing members were disgusted with the two old skinflints, and one effect of this sentiment manifested itself in the number of invitations that Perkins received to play golf with real people. He declined them all, much to our surprise, and continued to wallop his way round the course with Uncle Billy and Old Man Sprott, apparently on as cordial terms as ever.

"What are you going to do with such a besotted old fool as that?" asked Henry Bauer. "Here I've invited him into three foursomes this week — all white men, too — and he's turned me down cold. It's not that we want to play with him, for as a golfer he's a terrible thing. It's not that we're crazy about him personally, for socially he's my notion of zero minus; but he took his stinging like a dead-game sport and he's entitled to better treatment than he's getting. But if he hasn't any better sense than to pass his plate for more, what are you going to do about it?"

" 'Ephraim is joined to idols,' " quoted Little Doc Ellis. "Let him alone!"

"No, it's the other way round," argued Bauer. "His idols are joined to him — fastened on like leeches. The question naturally arises, how did such a man ever accumulate a fortune? Who forced it on him, and when, and where, and why?"

That very afternoon the Ooley-cow turned up with his guest, a large, loud person, also from the Heidelberg of America, who addressed Perkins as "Wesley" and lost no time in informing us that Southern California would have starved

to death but for Iowa's capital. His name was Cottle —
Calvin D. Cottle — and he gave each one of us his card as
he was introduced. There was no need. Nobody could have
forgotten him. Some people make an impression at first sight
— Calvin D. Cottle made a deep dent. His age was perhaps
forty-five, but he spoke as one crowned with Methuselah's
years and Solomon's wisdom, and after each windy
statement he turned to the Ooley-cow for confirmation.

"Ain't that so, Wesley? Old Wes knows, you bet your life!
He's from my home town!"

It was as good as a circus to watch Uncle Billy and Old
Man Sprott sizing up this fresh victim. It reminded me of two
wary old dogs circling for position, manoeuvering for a safe
hold. They wanted to know something about his golf
game — what was his handicap, for instance?"

"Handicap?" repeated Cottle. "Is that a California idea?
Something new, ain't it?"

Uncle Billy explained the handicapping theory.

"Oh!" said Cottle. "You mean what do I go round in —
how many strokes. Well, sometimes I cut under a hundred;
sometimes I don't. It just depends. Some days I can hit 'em,
some days I can't. That's all there is to it."

"My case exactly," purred Old Man Sprott. "Suppose we
dispense with the handicap?"

"That's the stuff!" agreed Cottle heartily. "I don't want to
have to give anybody anything; I don't want anybody to give
me anything. I like an even fight, and what I say is, may the
best man win! Am I right, gentlemen?"

"Absolutely!" chirped Uncle Billy. "May the best man win!"

"You bet I'm right!" boomed Cottle. "Ask Old Wes here
about me. Raised right in the same town with him, from a kid
knee-high to a grasshopper! I never took any the best of it in
my life, did I, Wes? No, you bet not! Remember that time I got
skinned out of ten thousand bucks on the land deal? A lot of
fellows would have squealed, wouldn't they? A lot of fellows
would have hollered for the police; but I just laughed and
gave 'em credit for being smarter than I was. I'm the same
way in sport as I am in business. I believe in giving everybody

credit. I win if I can, but if I can't — well, there's never any hard feelings. That's me all over. You may be able to *lick* me at this golf thing — likely you will; but you'll never *scare* me, that's a cinch. Probably you gentlemen play a better game than I do — been at it longer; but then I'm a lot younger than you are. Got more strength. Hit a longer ball when I do manage to land on one right. So it all evens up in the long run."

Mr. Cottle was still modestly cheering his many admirable qualities when the Perkins party went in to luncheon, and the only pause he made was on the first tee. With his usual caution Uncle Billy had arranged it so that Dubuque was opposed to Southern California, and he had also carefully neglected to name any sort of a bet until after he had seen the stranger drive.

Cottle teed his ball and stood over it, gripping his driver until his knuckles showed white under the tan. "Get ready to ride!" said he. "You're about to leave this place!"

The clubhead whistled through the air, and I can truthfully say that I never saw a man of his size swing any harder at a golf ball — or come nearer cutting one completely in two.

"Topped it, by gum," ejaculated Mr. Cottle, watching the maimed ball until it disappeared in a bunker. "Topped it! Well, better luck next time! By the way, what are we playing for? Balls, or money, or what?"

"Whatever you like," said Uncle Billy promptly. "You name it."

"Good! That's the way I like to hear a man talk. Old Wes here is my partner, so I can't bet with him, but I'll have a side match with each of you gentlemen — say, ten great, big, smiling Iowa dollars. Always like to bet what I've got the most of. Satisfactory?"

Uncle Billy glanced at Old Man Sprott, and for an instant the old rascals hesitated. The situation was made to order for them, but they would have preferred a smaller wager to start with, being petty larcenists at heart.

"Better cut that down to five," said Perkins to Cottle in a low tone. "They play a strong game."

"Humph!" grunted his guest. "Did you ever know me to pike in my life? I ain't going to begin now. Ten dollars or nothing!"

"I've got you," said Old Man Sprott.

"This once," said Uncle Billy. "It's against my principles to play for money; but yes, this once."

And then those two old sharks insisted on a foursome bet as well.

"Ball, ball, ball," said the Ooley-cow briefly, and proceeded to follow his partner into the bunker. Poindexter and Sprott popped conservatively down the middle of the course and the battle was on.

Battle, did I say? It was a massacre of the innocents, a slaughter of babes and sucklings. Our foursome trailed along behind, and took note of Mr. Cottle, of Dubuque, in his fruitless efforts to tear the cover off the ball. He swung hard enough to knock down a lamppost, but he seldom made proper connections, and when he did the ball landed so far off the course that it took him a dozen shots to get back again. He was hopelessly bad, so bad that there was no chance to make the side matches close ones. On the tenth tee Cottle demanded another bet — to give him a chance to get even, he said. Poindexter and Sprott each bet him another ten dollar note on the last nine, and this time Uncle Billy did not say anything about his principles.

After it was all over Cottle poured a few mint toddies into his system and floated an alibi to the surface.

"It was those confounded sand greens that did it," said he. "I'm used to grass, and I can't putt on anything else. Bet I could take you to Dubuque and flail the everlasting daylights out of you!"

"Shouldn't be surprised," said Uncle Billy. "You did a lot better on the last nine — sort of got into your stride. Any time you think you want revenge —"

"You can have it," finished Old Man Sprott as he folded a

crisp twenty-dollar note. "We believe in giving a man a chance — eh, Billy?"

"That's the spirit!" cried Cottle enthusiastically. "Give a man a chance; it's what I say, and if he does anything, give him credit. You beat me today, but I never saw this course before. Tell you what we'll do: Let's make a day of it tomorrow. Morning and afternoon both. Satisfactory? Good! You've got forty dollars of my dough and I want it back. Nobody ever made me quit betting yet, if I figure to have a chance. What's money? Shucks! My country is full of it! Now then, Wesley, if you'll come out on the practice green and give me some pointers on this sand thing, I'll be obliged to you. Ball won't run on sand like it will on grass — have to get used to it. Have to hit 'em a little harder. Soon as I get the hang of the thing we'll give these Native Sons a battle yet! Native Sons? Native Grandfathers! Come on!" Uncle Billy looked at Old Man Sprott and Old Man Sprott looked at Uncle Billy, but they did not begin to laugh until the Ooley-cow and his guest were out of earshot. Then they clucked and cackled and choked like a couple of hysterical old hens.

"His putting!" gurgled Uncle Billy. "Did he have a putt to win a hole all the way round?"

"Not unless he missed count of his shots. Say, Billy!"

"Well?"

"We made a mistake locating so far west. We should have stopped in Iowa. By now we'd have owned the entire state!"

I dropped Mr. Calvin D. Cottle entirely out of my thoughts; but when I entered the locker room shortly after noon the next day something reminded me of him. Possibly it was the sound of his voice.

"Boy! Can't we have 'nother toddy here? What's the matter with some service? How 'bout you, Wes? Oh, I forgot — you never take anything til after five o'clock. Think of all the fun you're missing. When I get to be an old fossil like you maybe I'll do the same. Good rule — You gentlemen having anything? No? Kind of careful, ain't you? Safety first, hey? — Just one toddy, boy, and if that mint ain't fresh, I'll — Yep, you're cagey birds, you are, but I give you credit just the same. And some cash. Don't forget that. Rather have cash than credit any time, hey? I bet you would! But I don't mind a little thing like that. I'm a good sport. You ask Wes here if I ain't. If I ain't a good sport I ain't anything — Still, I'll be darned if I see how you fellows do it! You're both old enough to have sons in the Soldiers' Home over yonder, but you take me out and lick me again — lick me and make me like it! A couple of dried-up mummies with one foot in the grave, and I'm right in the prime of life! Only a kid yet! It's humiliating, that's what it is, humiliating! Forty dollars apiece you're into me — and a flock of golf balls on the side! Boy! Where's the mint toddy? Let's have a little service here!"

I peeped through the door leading to the lounging room. The Dubuque-California foursome was grouped at a table in a corner. The Ooley-cow looked calm and placid as usual, but his guest was sweating profusely, and as he talked he mopped his brow with the sleeve of his shirt. Uncle Billy and Old Man Sprott were listening politely, but the speculative light in their eyes told me that they were wondering how far they dared go with this outlander from the Middle West.

"Why," boomed Cottle, "I can hit a ball twice as far as either one of you! 'Course I don't always know where it's going, but the main thing is I got the *strength*. I can throw a golf ball farther than you old fossils can hit one with a wooden club, yet you lick me easy as breaking sticks. Can't understand it at all — Twice as strong as you are — Why, say, I bet I can take one hand and outdrive you! *One Hand!*"

"Easy, Calvin," said the Ooley-cow reprovingly. "Don't make wild statements."

"Well, I'll bet I can do it," repeated Cottle stubbornly. "If a man's willing to bet his money to back up a wild statement, that shows he's got the right kind of a heart anyway. I ought to be able to stick my left hand in my pocket and go out there and trim two men of your age. I ought to, and I'll be damned if I don't think I can!"

"Tut, tut!" warned the Ooley-cow. "That's foolishness."

"Think so?" Cottle dipped his hand into his pocket and brought out a thick roll of bills. "Well, this stuff here says I can do it — at least I can *try* — and I ain't afraid to back my judgment."

"Put your money away," said Perkins. "Don't be a fool!"

Cottle laughed uproariously and slapped the Ooley-cow on the back.

"Good old Wes!" he cried. "Ain't changed a bit. Conservative! Always conservative! Got rich at it, but me I got rich taking chances. What's a little wad of bills to me, hey? Nothing but chicken-feed! I'll bet any part of this roll — I'll bet *all* of it — and I'll play these sundried old sports with one hand. Now's the time to show whether they've got any sporting blood or not. What do you say, gentlemen?"

Uncle Billy looked at the money and moistened his lips with the tip of his tongue.

"Couldn't think of it," he croaked at length.

"Pshaw!" sneered Cottle. "I showed you too much — I scared you!"

"He ain't scared," put in Old Man Sprott. "It would be too much like stealing it."

"I'm the one to worry about that," announced Cottle. "It's my money, ain't it? I made it, didn't I? And I can do what I damn please with it — spend it, bet it, burn it up, throw it away. When you've worried about everything else in the world, it'll be time for you to begin worrying about young Mr. Cottle's money! This slim little roll — bah! Chicken-feed! Come get it if you want it!" He tossed the money on the table with a gesture which was an insult in itself. "There it is — cover it! Put up or shut up!"

"Oh, forget it!" said the Ooley-cow wearily. "Come in and have a bite to eat and forget it!"

"Don't want anything to eat!" was the stubborn response. "Seldom eat in the middle of the day. But I'll have 'nother mint toddy — Wait a second, Wes. Don't be in such a rush. Lemme understand this thing. These — these gentlemen here, these two friends of yours, these dead-game old Native Sons have got eighty dollars of my money — not that it makes any difference to me, understand, but they've got it — eighty dollars that they won from me playing golf. Now I may have a drink or two in me and I may not, understand, but anyhow I know what I'm about. I make these — gentlemen a sporting proposition. I give 'em a chance to pick up a couple of hundred apiece, and they want to run out on me because it'll be like stealing it. What kind of a deal is that, hey? It it sportsmenship? Is it what they call giving a man a chance? Is it —"

"But they know you wouldn't have a chance," interrupted the Ooley-cow soothingly. "They don't want a sure thing."

"They've had one so far, haven't they?" howled Cottle. "What are they scared of now? 'Fraid I'll squeal if I lose? Tell 'em about me, Wes. Tell 'em I never squealed in my life. I win if I can, but if I can't — 's all right. No kick coming. There never was a piker in the Cottle family, was there, Wes? No, you bet not! We're sports, every one of us. Takes more than one slim little roll to send us up a tree! If there's anything that makes me sick, it's a cold-footed, penny-pinching, nickel-nursing, sure-thing player!"

"Your money does not frighten me," said Uncle Billy, who was slightly nettled by this time. "It is against my principles to play for a cash bet —"

"But you and your pussy-footed old side-partner got into me for eighty dollars just the same!" scoffed Cottle. "You and your principles be damned!"

Uncle Billy swallowed this without blinking, but he did not look at Cottle. He was looking at the roll of bills on the table.

"If you are really in earnest —" began Poindexter, and glanced at Old Man Sprott.

"Go ahead, Billy," croaked that aged reprobate. "Teach him a lesson. He needs it."

"Never mind the lesson," snapped Cottle. "I got out of school a long time ago. The bet is that I can leave my left arm in the clubhouse safe — stick it in my pocket — and trim you birds with one hand."

"We wouldn't insist on that," said Old Man Sprott. "Play with both hands if you want to."

"Think I'm a welsher?" demanded Cottle. "The original proposition goes. 'Course I wouldn't really cut the arm off and leave it in the safe, but what I mean is, if I use two arms in making a shot, right there is where I lose. Satisfactory?"

"Perkins," said Uncle Billy, solemnly wagging his head, "you are a witness that this thing has been forced on me. I have been bullied and browbeaten and insulted into making this bet —"

"And so have I," chimed in Old Man Sprott. "I'm almost ashamed —"

The Ooley-cow shrugged his shoulders.

"I am a witness," said he quietly. "Calvin, these gentlemen have stated the case correctly. You have forced them to accept your proposition —"

"And he can't blame anybody if he loses," finished Uncle Billy as he reached for the roll of bills.

"You bet!" ejaculated Old Man Sprott. "He was looking for trouble, and now he's found it. Count it Billy, and we'll each take half."

"That goes, does it?" asked Cottle.

"Sir?" cried Uncle Billy.

"Oh, I just wanted to put you on record," said Cottle, with a grin. "Wesley, you're my witness too. I mislaid a five-hundred-dollar note the other day, and it may have got into my change pocket. Might as well see if a big bet will put these safety-first players off their game! Anyhow, I'm betting whatever's there. I ain't sure how much it is."

"I am," said Uncle Billy in a changed voice. He had come to the five-hundred-dollar bill, sandwiched in between two twenties. He looked at Old Man Sprott, and for the first time I saw doubt in his eyes.

"Oh, it's there, is it?" asked Cottle carelessly. "Well, let it all ride. I never backed out on a gambling proposition in my life — never pinched a bet after the ball started to roll. Shoot the entire works — 's all right with me!"

Uncle Billy and Old Man Sprott exchanged significant glances, but after a short argument and some more abuse from Cottle they toddled over to the desk and filled out two blank checks — for five hundred and eighty dollars apiece.

"Make 'em payable to cash," suggested Cottle. "You'll

probably tear 'em up after the game. Now the next thing is a stakeholder —"

"It that — necessary?" asked Old Man Sprott.

"Sure!" said Cottle. "I might run out on you. Let's have everything according to Hoyle — stakeholder and all the other trimmings. Anybody'll be satisfactory to me; that young fellow getting an earful at the door, he'll do."

So I became the stakeholder — the custodian of eleven hundred and sixty dollars in coin and two checks representing a like amount. I thought I detected a slight nervousness in the signatures, and no wonder. It was the biggest bet those old petty larcenists had ever made in their lives. They went in to luncheon — at the invitation of the Ooley-cow, of course — but I noticed that they did not eat much. Cottle wandered out to the practice green, putter in hand, forgetting all about the mint toddy which, by the way, had never been ordered.

"You drive first, sir," said Uncle Billy to Cottle, pursuing his usual system. "We'll follow you."

"Think you'll feel easier if I should hit one over into the eucalyptus trees yonder?" asked the man from Dubuque. "Little nervous, eh? Does a big bet scare you? I was counting on that — Oh, very well, I'll take the honor."

"Just a second," said Old Man Sprott, who have been prowling about in the background and fidgeting with his driver. "Does the stakeholder understand the terms of the bet? Mr. Cottle is playing a match with each of us individually —"

"Separately and side by each," added Cottle.

"Using only one arm," said Old Man Sprott.

"If he uses both arms in making a shot," put in Uncle Billy, "he forfeits both matches. Is that correct, Mr. Cottle?"

"Correct as hell! Watch me closely, young man. I have no mustache to deceive you — nothing up my sleeve but my good right arm. Watch me closely!"

He teed his ball, dropped his left arm at his side, grasped the driver firmly in his right hand and swung the club a couple of times in tentative fashion. The head of the driver described a perfect arc, barely grazing the top of the tee. His two-armed swing had been a thing of violence — a baseball wallop, constricted, bound up, without follow-through or timing, a combination of brute strength and awkwardness. Uncle Billy's chin sagged as he watched the easy, natural sweep of that wooden club — the wrist-snap applied at the proper time, and the long graceful follow-through which gives distance as well as direction. Old Man Sprott also seemed to be struggling with an entirely new and not altogether pleasant idea.

"Watch me closely, stakeholder," repeated Cottle, addressing the ball. "Nothing up my sleeve but my good right arm. Would you gentlemen like to have me roll up my sleeve before I start?"

"Drive!" grunted Uncle Billy.

"I'll do that little thing," said Cottle, and this time he put the power into the swing. The ball, caught squarely in the middle of the clubface, went whistling toward the distant green, a perfect screamer of a drive without a suspicion of hook or slice. It cleared the cross-bunker by ten feet, carried at least a hundred and eighty yards before it touched grass, and then bounded ahead like a scared rabbit, coming to rest at least two hundred and twenty-five yards away. "You like that?" asked Cottle, moving off the tee. "I didn't step into it very hard or I might have had more distance. Satisfactory, Stakeholder?" And he winked at me openly and deliberately.

"What — what sort of a game is this?" gulped Old Man Sprott, finding his voice with an effort.

"Why," said Cottle, smiling cheerfully, "I wouldn't like to say offhand and so early in the game, but you might call it golf. Yes, call it golf, and let it go at that."

At this point I wish to go on record as denying the rumor that our two old reprobates showed the white feather. That first tee shot, and the manner in which it was made, was enough to inform them that they were up against a sickening surprise party; but, though startled and shaken, they did not weaken. They pulled themselves together and drove the best they knew how, and I realized that for once I was to see their true golfing form uncovered.

Cottle tucked his wooden club under his arm and started down the course, and from that time on he had very little to say. Uncle Billy and Old Man Sprott followed him, their heads together at a confidential angle, and I brought up the rear with the Ooley-cow, who had elected himself a gallery of one.

The first hole is a long par four. Poindexter and Sprott usually make it in five, seldom getting home with their seconds unless they have a wind behind them. Both used brassies and both were short of the green. Then they watched Cottle as he went forward to his ball.

"That drive might have been a freak shot," quavered Uncle Billy.

"Lucky fluke, that's all," said Old Man Sprott, but I knew and they knew that they only hoped they were telling the truth.

Cottle paused over his ball for an instant, examined the lie and drew a wooden spoon from his bag. Then he set himself, and the next instant the ball was on its way, a long, high, shot, dead on the pin.

"And maybe that was a fluke!" muttered the Ooley-cow under his breath. "Look! He's got the green with it!"

From the same distance I would have played a full mid-iron and trusted in Providence, but Cottle had used his wood, and I may say that never have I seen a ball better placed. It carried to the little rise of turf in front of the putting green, hopped once, and trickled close to the cup. I was not the only one who appreciated that spoon shot.

"Say," yapped Old Man Sprott, turning to Perkins, "what are we up against here? Miracles?"

"Yes, what have you framed up on us?" demanded Uncle Billy vindictively.

"Something easy, gentlemen," chuckled the Ooley-cow. "A soft thing from my home town. Probably he's only lucky."

The two members of the Sure-Thing Society went after their customary fives and got them, but Cottle laid his approach putt stone dead at the cup and holed out in four. He missed a three by the matter of half an inch. I could stand the suspense no longer. I took Perkins aside while the contestants were walking to the second tee.

"You might tell a friend," I suggested. "In strict confidence, what are they up against?"

"Something easy," repeated the Ooley-cow, regarding me with his soft, innocent eyes. "They wanted it and now they've got it."

"But yesterday, when he played with both arms —" I began.

"That was yesterday," said Perkins. "You'll notice that they didn't have the decency to offer him a handicap, even when they felt morally certain that he had made a fool bet. Not that he would have accepted it — but they didn't offer it. They're wolves, clear to the bone, but once in a while a wolf bites off more than he can chew." And he walked away from me. Right there I began reconstructing my opinion of the Ooley-cow.

In my official capacity as stakeholder I saw every shot that was played that afternoon. I still preserve the original score card of the amazing round of golf. There are times when I think I will have it framed and present it to the club, with red-ink crosses against the thirteenth and fourteenth holes. I might even set a red-ink star against the difficult sixth hole, where Cottle sent another tremendous spoon shot down the wind, and took a four where most of our Class-A men are content with a five. I might make a notation against the tricky ninth, where he played a marvellous shot out of a sand trap to halve a hole which I would have given up as lost. I might make a footnote calling attention to his deadly work with his short irons. I say I think of all these things, but perhaps I shall never frame that card. The two men most interested will never forget the figures. It is enough to say that Old Man Sprott, playing such golf as I had never seen him play before, succumbed at the thirteenth hole, six down and five to go. Uncle Billy gave up the ghost on the fourteenth green, five and four, and I handed the money and the checks to Mr. Calvin D. Cottle, of Dubuque. He pocketed the loot with a grin.

"Shall we play the bye-holes for something?" he asked. "A drink — or a ball, maybe?" And then the storm broke. I do not pretend to quote the exact language of the losers. I merely state that I was surprised, yes, shocked at Uncle Billy Poindexter. I had no idea that a member of the Episcopal church — but let that pass. He was not himself. He was the biter bitten, the milker milked. It makes a difference. Old Man Sprott also erupted in an astounding manner. It was the Ooley-cow who took the center of the stage.

"Just a minute, gentlemen," said he. "Do not say anything which you might afterward regret. Remember the stakeholder is still with us. My friend here is not, as you intimate, a crook. Neither is he a sure-thing player. We have some sure-thing players with us, but he is not one of them. He is merely the one-armed golf champion of Dubuque — and the Middle West."

Imagine an interlude here for fireworks, followed by pertinent questions.

"Yes, yes, I know," said Perkins soothingly. "He can't play a lick with two arms. He never could. Matter of fact, he never learned. He fell off a haystack in Iowa — how many years ago was it, Cal?"

"Twelve," said Mr. Cottle. "Twelve next July."

"And he broke his left arm rather badly," explained the Ooley-cow. "Didnt have the use of it for — how many years, Cal?"

"Oh, about six, I should say."

"Six years. A determined man can accomplish much in that length of time. Cottle learned to play golf with his right arm — fairly well, as you must admit. Finally he got the left arm fixed up — they took a piece of bone out of his shin and grafted it in — new-fangled idea. Decided there was no sense in spoiling a one-armed star to make a dub two-armed golfer. Country full of 'em already. That's the whole story. You picked him for an easy mark, a good thing. You thought he had a bad bet and you had a good one. Don't take the trouble to deny it. Gentlemen, allow me to present the champion one-armed golfer of Iowa and the Middle West!"

"Yes," said Cottle modestly, "when a man does anything, give him credit for it. Personally I'd rather have the cash!"

"How do you feel about it now?" asked the Ooley-cow.

Judging by their comments, they felt warm — very warm. Hot, in fact. The Ooley-cow made just one more statement, but to me that statement contained the gist of the whole matter.

"This," said he, "squares us on the wallet proposition. I didn't say anything about it at the time, but that struck me as a scaly trick. So I invited Cal to come out and pay me a visit — Shall we go back to the clubhouse?"

I made Little Doc Ellis see the point; perhaps I can make you see it now.

Returning to the original simile, the Ooley-cow was willing to be milked for golf balls and luncheons and caddie hire. That was legitimate milking, and he did not resent it. He would have continued to give down in great abundance, but when they took fifty dollars from him, in the form of a bogus reward, he kicked over the bucket, injured the milkers and jumped the fence.

Why? I'm almost ashamed to tell you, but did you ever hear of a country cow — an Iowa cow — that would stand for being milked from the wrong side?

I think this will be all, except that I anticipate a hard winter for the golfing beginners at our club.

One in a Trillion
Barrie Payne

Once upon a time there was a golfer who had a perfect wife.

When he told how his drive on the Sixth hit the pin, described in detail his birdie on the Tenth that should have been an eagle, and drew a diagram of the heelprint that ruined his shot on the Twelfth, she listened with rapt attention and begged him to tell the story all over again.

She applauded his many shots on the Nineteenth and said she just adored the odor of gin.

When, after being held up by a funeral procession threesome, he arrived home late for dinner, she kissed him and said, "I'm glad you took plenty of time for your game. Why didn't you stay and play nine more holes?"

In reply to his dutiful request to play with him on Sunday The Perfect Wife said, "I'm sorry, dear, but I've got a foursome arranged with three other ladies. I hope you don't mind."

One day he broke his pet mashie on a hidden rock and came home heart-broken. Instead of the usual, "Well, what of it? Can't you buy another?" his peerless mate wept sympathetically and offered to wear mourning for the dear departed.

The Wonder Woman was constantly urging him to play more golf, even at the risk of neglecting his business. "Golf means health," she said, "and health is more important than money."

If she happened to be present when he hit a long drive she always cried, "Attaboy! Two-eighty right down the middle!" instead of the customary "Where did it go? Into the rough? I didn't see it."

This Miracle of Femininity never tried to putt with a driver. She never attempted an explosion-shot with a brassie. She never lingered in the fairway on a crowded course to pick four-leaf clovers. She never chose a moment in the middle of his swing to remind him that his tie was twisted. She never laughed when he topped one into the creek.

When she dubbed a shot she invariably blamed herself. She always said, "I guess I didn't do what you told me" instead of "I did exactly as you said and look what happened! As a golf instructor you're the worst foul ball in the National League."

When her ball was lost she immediately said, "Let 'em go through" instead of "Let 'em wait. They shouldn't be so impatient."

When he came home tired after playing thirty-six holes she usually said, "I'll phone the Smiths we can't play bridge tonight. You ought to get some sleep."

Another of her favorite remarks: "I wrote mother not to

come this month. I knew you were busy with golf and wouldn't have time to entertain her."

When her husband happened to mention the name of Bobby Jones she didn't ask, "Who's Bobby Jones?"

On a certain occasion she sent him this telegram: "Our house burned down today, but don't worry. We managed to save your golf clubs."

As I remarked in the beginning, once upon a time there was a golfer who had a perfect wife.

All fairy tales begin with "Once upon a time —."

Excerpt From
The Happy Golfer
Henry Leach

The strange case of Sir Archibald Strand is one that caused much excited attention among the members of the golf community in general some months ago, and it is still discussed in the club-houses. Sir Archibald Strand, Bart., is a fair example of the thorough, enthusiastic, middle-aged player, who treats golf as something rather more than a game, which is as it should be. He is one of tolerably equable temperament, a good sportsman, and a man of strong character and physique, who did a long term of military service in India. Nowadays he spends an appreciable portion of his time in golfing, and a fair part of the remainder in contemplating the enduring mysteries and problems of the links. The game worries him exceedingly, occasionally it leads him to unhappiness, but, on the whole, he feels he likes it. He is a member of several London clubs, including Sunningdale, Walton Heath, Mid-Surrey, Coombe Hill, and Woking, and of his seaside clubs those he most frequents are the Royal St. George's at Sandwich, and Rye. His handicap is 5, and generally he is what we consider and call a good reliable 5.

He and his opponent, to whom, as a matter of discretion and confidence, we must refer as Mr. A., had just ended their match at Mid-Surrey one pleasant day, and Sir Archibald was trying his last putt over again as golfers often do. It was a putt of two feet. He had missed it before; but now, of course, he rolled the ball in every time. A question arose about circumstances altering cases, as they so commonly do in golf, and of responsibility weighing heavily on the mind that hesitates; and Sir Archibald declared that nobody in good health could be such a fool as to miss a two-feet putt like that, if he really examined the line thoroughly and took the proper pains. Just then the open champion of the period was passing by the green, and they called him up and asked his views upon the missing of two-feet putts. Taylor denied that a man was a fool for missing them. He mentioned the psychology of the business, and very forcibly argued that a two-feet putt was a very difficult thing, that the more important it was the more difficult it became, and that the longer one thought about it the more impossible did it seem to hole it. "Ah!" he murmured, "if I had never missed any putts of one foot, let alone the putts of two! I tell you, sir, the two-feet putt, when it has to be done — mind you when it has got to be done — is one of the most difficult things in the world to do, and never mind the fact that your babies can do it all the time! Take that from me, sir!" This was a touch of the real Taylor, the true philosopher, one who knows the game.

Mr. A., who is sometimes aggressive in manner, brought the matter in discussion to a pretty point at once. "Look here, Strand," said he, "I will tell you what I will do. I will place this ball here, so, exactly two feet from the hole, and I will give you a fortnight, but not less than a fortnight, to hole that putt. You are not to practise it here at this hole on this green in the meantime: but you may place the ball in position if you like, and look at it. And a fortnight to-day, at ten o'clock in the morning, you must make the putt, and I will bet you fourteen guineas, being a guinea a day for waiting, that you do not hole it. We will have the position of the hole properly marked, so that a fortnight hence it shall be in the same place."

The champion said he would tell Lees, the greenskeeper, and that should be done. Strand, with a laugh, accepted the wager, and the matter was settled.

The events that followed were curious. In the clubhouse, there was then little disposition to attend to the accounts of the proceedings that were furnished by both parties. The men who had finished their rounds were too much occupied with their own trouble or joys.

At his club in town that evening, Sir Archibald, over dinner, related the circumstances of the wager to a few friends, with an appearance of considerable satisfaction with himself, and seemed a little surprised that the other members of the party did not at once approve of his proceeding as sound and business-like.

"Of course, you know, Strand, my good man," said Mr. Ezekiel Martin, a successful stockbroker, "these putts are missed sometimes, and I don't suppose it makes it any easier for you by waiting a fortnight. It's like carrying over in the House till one is a very tired bull."

"Nonsense!" exclaimed Sir Archibald, "I could go out now and hole that putt nineteen times of twenty in the dark!"

"I believe you could," answered Martin, "but doing it in the dark, when you cannot see the hole and realise all the imaginary difficulties, is very different from doing it in broad daylight; and putting now, on the spur of the moment, as it were is very different from putting when you have a whole fortnight to think about what you are going to do."

"I don't see it," replied Sir Archibald, yet he began to feel a little uneasy. On returning home that night, instead of going to bed at once he went into his study, laid a tumbler on its side on the carpet, and putted from a measured two feet for about half an hour. He holed most of them, and tumbled into bed feeling that Martin had been "pulling his leg," as people say. In the morning he engaged a gardener to smooth down a peice of his lawn, planting in a little putting-green turf, and he had a hole made in it, and a circle with two feet radius drawn round the hole, so that he could putt from every point. When this work was done, he spent an hour in practising there, and succeeded well. He only missed about one in ten.

He tried seven different putters, with approximately equal results. In the afternoon he went down to Mid-Surrey, played a match, and lost it by missing a short putt at the home hole. After tea, he went out on to the eighteenth green, found the spot where the hole was the day before, examined it carefully, and saw that there were slight differences in the texture of the grass round about, and that there was a little depression to the left side. He had not noticed this before. However, he said to himself, it would be easy to make allowances for these things, but he began now to doubt whether thirteen days ahead he would use his wry-necked putting cleek or bolt the put with an aluminum putter. Where there are troubles of that kind it is often better to make short work of the putt by the bolting way, and have an end of it. At home that evening he did more putting practice on the carpet, and did not hole them quite so well. Lady Strand, who understands her husband thoroughly, and is the sweetest, gentlest sympathiser, coaxed him to telling her the trouble, for she saw that one existed. With perfect wisdom she suggested that he should wipe the fourteen guineas from the current account as already lost, and face the task as one who had all to gain and nothing to lose. Of course, her husband said, it was not the money, but the frightful jackass he would look if he missed the putt.

He went to his club in town the next day instead of going to golf, and took with him a book containing a chapter on putting, by Willie Park. He stretched himself out on a Chesterfield in a corner of the library, and gazed at two spots on the carpet which he had measured as being two-feet from each other. Eventually, he decided that that was not good enough for him, since equal distances in furnished rooms, as is well known, look longer than they look outside. He lunched with a few friends, and brought up the subject again.

"Give him the money and have done with it, Strand. You are sure to lose!" said the brutish Martin.

"I wish I had not to wait for a fortnight," murmured Strand.

"Ah! He knew! The other man knew!" rejoined Martin.

"He knows the game of golf! What I cannot understand is why he did not give you a year and make it 365 guineas. You would have sold out in six weeks at 200 pounds."

Sir Archibald wrote a letter to Mr. A. that evening, intimating that he would probably have to leave town the week after next. He hinted that it might be convenient if they got their wager out of the way beforehand, and if he putted a week from then. Mr. A. replied that he was sorry it would not be convenient for him to attend then, and that the signed terms of the contract had better be abided by.

Sir Archibald bought two new putters on the following day, and in the afternoon he had Taylor out for an hour, and they went practising on the putting lawn just outside the garden gate. Sir Archibald was putting very well then; but he insisted that it would be a good thing to change the ball he was using, which was rather lively. After he had done with Taylor, he went to look at the place on the eighteenth green where he would have to putt, and it seemed that the coarse grass had fattened up considerably with the rain that had fallen, and that the sand below it was distinctly gritty. It began to seem that he would have to run the ball in at the right side of the hole. He asked Lees some questions about the grasses on that green, and was sorry he could not take a little Mid-Surrey turf home with him. He was feeling a little tired when he reached his home that night, and as it was Thursday he suggested to Lady Strand that they should go to Folkstone for the week-end, and not bother at all about golf, which they did accordingly. He found it delightful to linger on the leas and not be worried with the game.

This kind of thing continued and became worse and worse again during the days that followed. There was practice, thought, and purchase continually, and unfortunately the proportion of missed putts at two feet, both on the carpet, on the practice lawn, and on the greens at Mid-Surrey, Coombe Hill, and Woking, began to increase. At putts of three feet, four, and five, Sir Archibald was marvellous, and, of course, he never missed the very little ones; but the two-feet putts bothered him all the time. He attributed it to his liver; and he was certainly looking worn. Matters were not improved by such inconsiderate remarks as were made by Martin, Evans, and others, whenever he had a two-feet putt to make, such as "Now, Strand, that's just your distance!" It was only a joke; but in the circumstances it was not perhaps in good taste.

On the evening of the twelfth day Strand, after deliberation, wrote a letter to A. in which he said he feared he would not be able to go down to the course at the appointed time, and intimated that, according to the terms of the wager, he would hand over the fourteen guineas to him when next they met. Before posting this letter he went and did a little practice in the dusk on the lawn outside the house. He seemed to get them down with some confidence on this occasion, and Lady S., watching him, called out cheerily, "Silly boy! as if you could really miss! Now what shall I buy with the fourteen guineas?"

So Strand tore up the letter and went to bed for a rest.

On the night before the appointed day he slept badly. He was putting in his mind until three o'clock in the morning. Then he rose, went in his pyjamas into the study, made a line on the top of his aluminum putter indicating the striking point, and went back to bed, but did not sleep. For some time he tried an imaginary humming of the "Jewel Song" from *Faust*, and repeated a few lines from Scott's "Lady of the Lake" — old dodges of his for assisting distraction and sleep — but they did not serve, nor did a fixed vision of millions of balls falling in an endless stream from the mouth of a pump and disappearing instantly through a golf hole in the ground.

At five-thirty he rose again and took his bath. He hesitated as to what golfing suit he should wear. Finally, for the sake of complete ease, and that there should be nothing to attract his eye from the ball, he put on some dark-blue flannels.

He looked at his breakfast, pecked at a sole, and at nine-fifteen, feeling distinctly unwell, he took a taxi for the course. He had one great consolation upholding him. At five minutes past ten it would all be over. He felt that he knew how glad a condemned criminal must be that at five minutes past eight on a certain morning — or a minute or two earlier with a little luck — a black flag would be hoisted on the prison pole.

At seven minutes to ten he drank a large brandy and soda and went out to the eighteenth green. Mr. A. and a few others were there to see the business properly carried out. Taylor placed the ball exactly two feet from the hole, which was cut in the proper place. He had his watch in his hand.

Sir Archibald bent down and examined the putt with great care. He essayed to pick up what seemed to be a "loose impediment" on his line, but saw that it was not loose. The putt seemed very difficult now, and he wished he had brought his plain putting cleek out with him, but it was too late.

At ten o'clock exactly, Taylor said, "Now, Sir Archibald, will you kindly putt?"

Sir Archibald Strand looked like a man who had been hunted down. He made one swift glance around him, but saw no escape, so he pulled himself together, smiled a little sadly, and said to himself, "Don't be a fool, Archie!" Then he faced the putter to the ball; the club was trembling slightly. He swung it back much too far, checked it in the return swing, and came on to the ball in a nervous, stupid way, doing little more than touch it. The ball took a line to the right of the hole, and did not run more than fourteen inches.

You may have thought that Sir Archibald used unfortunate words and was dismayed. He did not. A look of established happiness and placid contentment spread upon his countenance, as a streak of sunlight might flash across a plain. "Ha!" he sighed in relief. He took from his pocket a cheque for fourteen guineas already made out, and handed it to Mr. A., and then joyfully exclaimed: "Thank heaven, it is finished! Now, my friends, we will honour this unusual occasion in a suitable manner at your convenience, and this afternoon I leave for Sandwich for a week of golf. And no letters are being forwarded."

The Way it Ought to be Done
Patrick Campbell

In January, 1961, an exhibition match took place between Sam Snead and Harry Weetman, to celebrate the opening of Israel's first golf-course at Caesarea.

It also marked the first occasion upon which a match was followed by a gallery of two thousand people only twelve of whom — by my own personal estimate — had ever seen the game played before.

A brisk breeze was blowing up the first fairway, touching at times, I should say, fifty miles an hour, as Snead and Weetman tossed for the honour.

Sneed won, teed up his ball and then stood looking at the audience with an appearance of patience which anyone knowing him would not have trusted an inch.

What the audience was doing was commenting in Hebrew, German, Polish, French, Spanish and a variety of Scandinavian languages upon the force of the wind, the magnificence of the new club-house, the political situation *vis-à-vis* Jordan, Colonel Nasser and half a hundred other matters including Snead's Palm Beach straw hat. The babel of sound was tremendous, and only partially dissipated by the gale.

None of those present, of course, could have been expected to know that death-like silence should have been their portion, that Snead had been known to threaten legal action against people dropping pins half a mile away while he was trying to hole a four-foot putt.

As the Master continued to remain inactive, save for an ominous tapping of the right foot, the noise became even greater. I was able to identify enquiries in English, French and German as to whether he had already, perhaps, done it and if so where had it gone, and if he hadn't, what was he waiting for and would it be possible for him to get on with it now?

Snead then made a suggestion which some of the stewards carried out in part, waving their arms and asking politely for silence. This had the immediate effect of redoubling the noise, people asking one another in genuine bewilderment how silence on their part could possibly contribute to whatever Snead was trying to do. In the end a comparative hush was achieved, Snead stepped up to his ball and with that long, beautifully timed, power-packed swing slashed one straight down the middle, quail high into the wind and all of 280 yards.

Deathlike silence fell upon the gallery, for the first time. They'd seen him hit it, but no one was prepared for the result. No one, in fact, had seen where the ball had gone. It had simply passed out of their ken and so they remained silent, rather than appear at a disadvantage by applauding where, perhaps, no applause had been earned.

They were more ready for Weetman, as he stood up to it. Word had gone round that perhaps the ball went rather farther than anyone could have a right to expect. They saw every inch of Harry's tee-shot, an obviously apprehensive right-handed bash that took off like a bullet, turned sharp left and finished on the far side of the ninth fairway, about 150 yards off the line.

A great roar of applause went up, a thunderous clapping of hands. Snead's expression, never too sunny in action — or even in repose — would have frightened the lives out of a platoon of armed Algerian terrorists in broad daylight.

Subsequently, there was even worse to come. Many of the stewards got tired of the labour of lugging ropes around, seeing that the gallery paid little attention to them, and knocked off, leaving the ropes where they lay. At one moment, round about the seventh, Snead found himself trying to play a wedge shot over or around three splendidly bearded old gentlemen who stood directly in front of him, watching whatever he was trying to do with lively interest. Later, a pretty girl in khaki shorts picked Harry Weetman's ball out of a bush and helpfully placed it in his hand.

But how, as I say, could anyone who had never seen golf played before know any better? And how can anyone who has never seen Snead hit a golf ball guess that that is the way it ought to be done?

Crying Towel
Robinson Murray

When I chanced upon Seymour Snivvel, he was slumped on a bench near the Clubhouse, head in hands. A weeping willow bent its quivering branches over him in sympathy. All nature sorrowed while Seymour indulged in his weekly wail.

Being a manufacturer of crying towels, I sensed at once that here was a prime prospect for my Grade-A, Triple-Sec variety. I sat down beside him and threw a sympathetic arm over his quaking shoulders.

"Well," I said, holding out my own towel, king size, already slightly damp from use (after losing a ten-dollar match on the last hole because a leaf fell right in my line of putt as I hit the ball), "Well, what seems to be your trouble?"

Seymour accepted the towel silently and submerged his face in it.

"Bob, you know I'm not one of those fellows who always moans about hard luck," he began with a pathetic catch in his voice. "What I mean, when I run into hard luck, it's —" his voice broke again, "— it's — hard luck!"

"Yeah, I know. You never use more than four crying towels on a round —"

"Aw, now, wait, Bob," he choked. "Lemme tell you about this. It's the hardest luck you ever heard of, the most unbelievable kick in the pants a guy ever got. I —"

"You mean like the fellow who was up the creek with no means of propulsion and —"

"My heart is breaking, and you make a joke of it," he said bitterly. "It's this way. You know I've got a fifty-dollar bet with old Judge Whoppit that I'll break 100 this year. Well, there I was on the 18th green in 96, with three putts in hand to win my bet."

"All you have to do is play your normal game and you're into the judge for fifty," I nodded.

"Right. Well, sir, just as I bend over to putt, along comes a damnation bee and rams about six inches of stinger into my —"

"Oh, so that's why you're sitting sideways."

"That explains the overhand," he admitted. "I jumped so hard my putter knocked the ball off the green into the thick rough. I lost my bet and my ball and my God-given right to sit down comfortably, all at one fell swoop of a damnation —"

"That's pretty fell," I admitted, "but speaking of our insect friends, did I ever tell you about how a butterfly played it dirty on a guy I read about? Seems the other fellow's ball died on the edge of the cup, which left this guy with a short putt for a half. Just then along came a butterfly and landed on the other fellow's ball and it fell into the hole for a win! And another time I saw in the paper where a pheasant came whooshing across a green in England right in the path of Henry Cotton's shot and wingtipped his ball into the hole. What d'you think the other feller had to say about that?"

"Stop, stop!" wailed Seymour. "Now you've got me crying for the other fellow, and I've got my own sorry tale to tell. Ouch!" He shifted the position of his sorry tail a little, and I left him weeping alone in the wilderness.

Every Club has its chronic moaners, and a first quality line of crying towels is now a necessary adjunct to golf. I advocate special styles for special purposes: a small one for a three-putt green and a big one, double-thick, the size of a bed sheet, for the shot that hits the tree on the far side of the pond and bounces back in. If you'd like to see the towel I manufacture for bemoaning a shank, come over to my sail loft sometime.

The only man worse to play with than the man who laments his every lapse all around the course is the perpetual grinner who guffaws every time anyone in the foursome has bad luck or dubs a shot. He hasn't even the grace to get peeved when he blows one himself. He should die of laughing gas, that one.

Iffy golf can drive a man nuts. "If I hadn't taken three in the trap . . . if I hadn't just barely dribbled into the rough . . . if I'd known that worm cast was there . . . if my ball hadn't taken that lousy kick to the right . . . if that tree had only been six inches over . . ." Only God can make a tree, and it's His business where He puts them, but you'll never make an iffy golfer understand this.

Other games have their trials. The big ones always get away. The easy grounder takes a bad hop. But for sheer vindictive cussedness I'll pick golf. They say a miss is as good as a mile, but it's shaving things too close when a ball rims the cup and still stays out.

As the minister said after missing a short putt, "I don't swear, but where I step, no grass grows!"

The Wide, Wide World of Double Bogey Golf
Hollis Alpert, Ira Mothner, and Harold Schonberg

The first nationally televised double bogey golf tournament was held in May of 1971 at the Dread Dunes Country Club near Las Vegas, Nevada. The last of the four rounds was covered by ABC's Wide World of Sports, with Chris Schenkel, Byron Nelson, and Frank Gifford as commentators on the suspenseful action. The following remarks by these commentators were extracted from the videotape recording of the final three holes:

SCHENKEL: Well, here we are at the 16th hole of Dread Dunes, and I'd say it was anyone's tournament at this point, wouldn't you, Frank and Byron?
GIFFORD: Oh yes, definitely, Chris, with the possible

exception of Tom Zehner, who has just taken 14 strokes on the 14th. Four of his tee shots went into the water, and he took three more out of the trap at the left of the green.

NELSON: I wouldn't say that puts him out of it, Frank. Let's see, he's 122 over par at this point, which only puts him back six strokes with four holes to play. Anything can happen in double bogey golf. If he could manage to bogey the last three holes he'd be right back in it.

SCHENKEL: Right now it's a free-for-all, with Burkmiller, Popkin, and Derwint tied for the lead at 116 over par. Shh — Burkmiller is at the tee of the 16th, a par four with a dogleg to the right. What club has he selected, Byron?

NELSON: A four wood, I'd say. He should be able to clear that first 100 yards of rough stretching from the tee.

GIFFORD: Wow! Just did make the fairway.

SCHENKEL: With a few yards to spare, too. How would you describe Burkmiller's swing, Byron?

NELSON: I'd rather not, Chris.

SCHENKEL: Popkin's at the tee now. There's a rumour that he wears a brace of some kind. I've never seen anyone swing like that before.

GIFFORD: Ever seen me swing, Chris?

NELSON: Too bad. Never cleared the rough. That'll cost him a stroke or two.

SCHENKEL: Shhh — Derwint's hitting —

GIFFORD: Nice drive. No, it's slicing. Did the ball hit someone?

NELSON: Yes, looks like a caddie, over there on the 15th.

SCHENKEL: Does that put him out of bounds?

NELSON: There'll have to be a ruling by the tournament director.

SCHENKEL: We'll take a commercial break now. Don't go away, folks. There are fireworks ahead.

(Commercial Break)

SCHENKEL: Here we are at Dread Dunes for our coverage of the first nationally televised double bogey golf tournament, and word has just reached us that Tom Zehner has done the all but impossible. He has *parred* the 15th!

GIFFORD: That's only the third par of the entire tournament, Chris.

NELSON: That lets him stay at 122 over, with still three holes to play. I'd say he's definitely in it. Especially with the ruling made on Popkin's out-of-bounds tee shot on the 16th. He had to hit another tee shot, and right now is lying four in the rough, and he still hasn't reached the edge of the fairway. I must say, the excitement is mounting.

GIFFORD: There's more word in on Zehner's amazing par four on the 15th. His third shot hit a power line about 40 yards from the green. He used a wedge for his fourth shot, scuffed it, and it hit the bank of the trap guarding the green, bounced on the green and trickled in. There was some commotion. Seems Zehner fainted and had to be revived with smelling salts. He's definitely okay now, though. That's him, waiting to hit on the 17th tee. I'd say he's exuding confidence, wouldn't you, Chris?

SCHENKEL: Certainly would Frank. He's holding up two fingers in a V-for-victory sign. Getting applause from the onlookers, too. He's one of the crowd favorites. Who's he remind you of, Byron?

NELSON: Ted Williams?

GIFFORD: Forgive the correction, Byron, but he looks to me more like Monte Irvin of the old New York Giants.

NELSON: Yes, now that you mention it.

SCHENKEL: Oh, oh, Burkmiller's third shot hit the trap on the left side of the green.

NELSON: His next shot should be interesting.

SCHENKEL: Why do you say that, Byron?

NELSON: Watch what he does.

GIFFORD: Well, I'll be — He played it back to the fairway.

NELSON: Yes, he'll chip up from there, and settle for a seven. He'll be a stroke behind, but in a tournament like this, one or two strokes doesn't mean anything.

SCHENKEL: Zehner's on the fairway with his tee shot. He really boomed one. About 160 yards, it looks to me.

NELSON: Derwint hits farther, but he's not as accurate.

SCHENKEL: We'll have to break for another commercial, fellows.

(Commercial Break)

SCHENKEL: Here we are at the 17th of Dread Dunes, folks, and this is how we stand. Derwint and Popkin are tied for the lead at 119 over par for four rounds, and right behind them is Burkmiller at 119 over. Meanwhile, Zehner is thrilling the crowd with his driving finish. He has just bogied the 16th, after a fantastic par on the 15th. He's now at 123 over, with two holes left to play.

GIFFORD: He was on the green in four, about 100 feet from the pin. He has a really unique putting style. He runs his hand along the club shaft and sort of bunts the ball.

NELSON: And it went for the hole as though the ball had eyes. One thing you can say about Zehner; he doesn't fold under pressure.

GIFFORD: He fainted again, though.

SCHENKEL: But he's back on his feet, and holding up those two fingers again. Ever hear such a roar from the crowd?

NELSON: Not since Arnie won the Open in 1960.

SCHENKEL: The 17th here at Dread Dunes will be the key hole, I think. It's a par three, and you have to carry 140 yards over water. Yep, it's happened. Derwint's in the drink.

GIFFORD: So is Popkin.

NELSON: Burkmiller's safe. He hit sideways to the fairway of the 17th. Hold it, the shot may be out of bounds. They're consulting the rule book.

SCHENKEL: It is! Burkmiller must hit over from the tee. He's hitting three!

NELSON: So are Derwent and Popkin. This is a battle royal, if I've seen one. Derwint took his driver, and — He's in the water again.

SCHENKEL: What club is Popkin using, Byron?

NELSON: I believe he's chosen his graphite shafted, thick headed two iron, with tungsten inserts.

SCHENKEL: He should be able to make it with that.

NELSON: Bad luck! He cleared the water by a foot, but he's lying in mud.

SCHENKEL: SHH — Burkmiller is hitting. He's using his four wood, I believe. The crowd is quiet, tense — Unbelievable! He's on the green!

GIFFORD: Forty feet from the pin, but he's on the green! If he can get down in two —

SCHENKEL: Sorry to interrupt, Frank, but it's commercial time again.

(Commercial Break)

SCHENKEL: Here we are at Dread Dunes, for the 18th hole of the fourth and final round of the first nationally televised double bogey golf tournament, and do we have a finish for you! Derwint and Popkin took quadruple bogeys on the 17th, while Burkmiller took a triple bogey. That puts the three all even at 123 over par for the tournament. Meanwhile — and sit tight, folks — Zehner achieved *another* bogey at the 17th, and is at 124 over. There's been a delay while the marshals are attempting to keep the crowd, estimated at 15,000, within the boundaries. There hasn't been as much excitement in golf since Bobby Jones completed his grand slam at Merion, Pa., in 1928. And here's the situation: Derwint, Popkin, and Burkmiller are on the green of the par-five 18th in five strokes each, all in nice position for their double bogeys. Zehner is out on the fairway, about 80 yards from the green, lying only three. Derwint is putting now, an 18 footer —

GIFFORD: And it slides past the hole by about five feet.

NELSON: Popkin is putting, a 16 footer. Nice putt. He's now lying three feet from the hole. Should be able to sink that.

SCHENKEL: Burkmiller has a 12 footer. He's lining it up. If he makes this —

GIFFORD: The pressure was too much for him. He barely

touched the ball, and he's still 10 feet away.

SCHENKEL: Burkmiller is putting again. Oh, tough luck! It rimmed the hole and failed to drop. He finishes with a triple bogey, and a total of 126 over.

NELSON: Derwint is putting. The ball is heading for the hole, it's in — No, it popped out. A triple bogey for him, too.

GIFFORD: If Popkin can sink his three footer — He does, he does, and he's gotten his par — I mean, his double bogey for a score of 125 over par, a record, I daresay, that will be hard to beat in future tournaments.

SCHENKEL: And, with excitement like this, you may be sure that ABC's "Wide World of Sports" will be there to cover all the thrilling action.

NELSON: Zehner is about to hit.

SCHENKEL: What club has he selected, Byron?

NELSON: Seven iron, Chris. Good strategy.

GIFFORD: Here it comes. It's a high shot, it's hitting the fringe of the green on the left, it's rolling down, there's a trap there. No it stopped short. He's still on the fringe, but I doubt that he can use his putter. Isn't he lying four now, Byron?

NELSON: That's right, Frank. He's lying four, and he still has a chance to tie, if he gets down from where he is in two. Pretty tough assignment, though.

SCHENKEL: I'll say it is, and you can hear a pin drop. Not a sound from these 15,000 awed spectators surrounding the green. What club is he selecting, Byron?

NELSON: I've never seen one like it before, Chris. It has a club head that seems a combination of a wedge and a putter, and a shaft very much like the handle of a baseball bat. The tournament director is examining it — He's ruled it legal.

GIFFORD: Zehner is taking his time, and I don't blame him. Now he's looking at his caddie. What's the caddie up to?

SCHENKEL: He's touching his cap, slapping his right thigh, and plucking at his shirt. Reminds me of a coach at third base.

GIFFORD: Yes, the caddie is definitely giving him signals. All right, he's laying down the bunt, no, it's more of a little chip shot. Oh, it's too long, straight for the flag, but five feet too high.

NELSON: No, it hit the flag at the top of the pin. It seems caught in the folds, now it's dropping down the pole, it's hovering right on the edge of the cup and . . . and . . . it dropped in! It dropped in! Unbelievable, fantastic! I wouldn't believe it if I hadn't seen it with my own eyes! An absolutely amazing par five.

SCHENKEL: Zehner is lying face down on the green. I think he fainted again.

GIFFORD: Popkin is down, too. He thought he had it won. They're both being carried to the clubhouse.

SCHENKEL: Which is where we'll talk to them, Frank and Byron, after they've been revived, of course. What a tournament! Ever seen anything like it, Byron?

NELSON: Beats the Masters all hollow, Chris.

A Caddy's Diary
Ring Lardner

Wed. Apr. 12

I am 16 of age and am a caddy at the Pleasant View Golf Club but only temporary as I expect to soon land a job some wheres as asst pro as my game is good enough now to be a pro but to young looking. My pal Joe Bean also says I have not got enough swell head to make a good pro but suppose that will come in time, Joe is a wise cracker.

But first will put down how I come to be writeing this diary, we have got a member name Mr Colby who writes articles in the newspapers and I hope for his sakes that he is a better writer than he plays golf but any way I cadded for him a good many times last yr and today he was out for the first time this yr and I cadded for him and we got talking about this in that and something was mentioned in regards to the golf articles by Alex Laird that comes out every Sun in the paper

113

Mr Colby writes his articles for so I asked Mr Colby did he know how much Laird got paid for the articles and he said he did not know but supposed that Laird had to split 50-50 with who ever wrote the articles for him. So I said don't he write the articles himself and Mr Colby said why no he guessed not. Laird may be a master mind in regards to golf he said, but this is no sign he can write about it as very few men can write decent let alone a pro. Writeing is a nag.

How do you learn it I asked him.

Well he said read what other people writes and study them and write things yourself, and maybe you will get on to the nag and maybe you wont.

Well Mr Colby I said do you think I could get on to it?

Why he said smileing I did not know that was your ambition to be a writer.

Not exactly was my reply, but I am going to be a golf pro myself and maybe some day I will get good enough so as the papers will want I should write them articles and if I can learn to write them myself why I will not have to hire another writer and split with them.

Well said Mr Colby smileing you have certainly got the right temperament for a pro, they are all big hearted fellows.

But listen Mr Colby I said if I want to learn it would not do me no good to copy down what other writers have wrote, what I would have to do would be write things out of my own head.

That is true said Mr Colby.

Well I said what could I write about?

Well said Mr Colby why dont you keep a diary and every night after your supper set down and write what happened that day and write who you cadded for and what they done only leave me out of it. And you can write down what people say and what you think and etc., it will be the best kind of practice for you, and once in a wile you can bring me your writeings and I will tell you the truth if they are good or rotten.

So that is how I come to be writeing this diary is so as I can get some practice writeing and maybe if I keep at it long enough I can get on to the nag.

Friday, Apr. 14

We been haveing Apr. showers for a couple days and nobody out on the course so they has been nothing happen that I could write down in my diary but dont want to leave it go to long or will never learn the trick so will try and write a few lines about a caddys life and some of our members and etc.

Well I and Joe Bean is the 2 oldest caddys in the club and I been cadding now for 5 yrs and quit school 3 yrs ago tho my mother did not like it for me to quit but my father said he can read and write and figure so what is the use in keeping him there any longer as greek and latin dont get you no credit at the grocer, so they lied about my age to the trunce officer and I been cadding every yr from March till Nov and the rest of the winter I work around Heismans store in the village.

Dureing the time I am cadding I genally always manage to play at lease 9 holes a day myself on wk days and some times 18 and am never more then 2 or 3 over par figures on our course but it is a cinch.

I played the engineers course 1 day last summer in 75 which is some golf and some of our members who has been playing 20 yrs would give their right eye to play as good as myself.

I use to play around with our pro Jack Andrews till I got so as I could beat him pretty near every time we played and now he wont play with me no more, he is not a very good player for a pro but they claim he is a good teacher. Personly I think golf teachers is a joke tho I am glad people is suckers enough to fall for it as I expect to make my liveing that way. We have got a member Mr Dunham who must of took 500 lessons in the past 3 yrs and when he starts to shoot he trys to remember all the junk Andrews has learned him and he gets dizzy and they is no telling where the ball will go and about the safest place to stand when he is shooting is between he and the hole.

I dont beleive the club pays Andrews much salery but of course he makes pretty fair money giveing lessons but his best graft is a 3 some which he plays 2 and 3 times a wk with Mr Perdue and Mr Lewis and he gives Mr Lewis a stroke a hole and they genally break some wheres near even but Mr Perdue made a 83 one time so he thinks that is his game so he insists on playing Jack even, well they always play for $5.00 a hole and Andrews makes $20.00 to $30.00 per round and if he wanted to cut loose and play his best he could make $50.00 to $60.00 per round but a couple of wallops like that and Mr Perdue might get cured so Jack figures a small stedy income is safer.

I have got a pal named Joe Bean and we pal around together as he is about my age and he says some comical things and some times will wisper some thing comical to me wile we are cadding and it is all I can do to help from laughing out loud, that is one of the first things a caddy has got to learn is never laugh out loud only when a member makes a joke. How ever on the days when theys ladies on the course I dont get a chance to caddy with Joe because for some reason another the woman folks dont like Joe to caddy for them wile on the other hand they are always after me tho I am no Othello for looks or do I seek their flavors, in fact it is just the opp and I try to keep in the back ground when the fair sex appears on the seen as cadding for ladies means you will get just so much money and no more as theys no chance of them loosning up. As Joe says the rule against tipping is the only rule the woman folks keeps.

Theys one lady how ever who I like to caddy for as she looks like Lillian Gish and it is a pleasure to just look at her and I would caddy for her for nothing tho it is hard to keep your eye on the ball when you are cadding for this lady, her name is Mrs Doane.

Sat. Apr. 15
This was a long day and am pretty well wore out but must

116

not get behind in my writing practice. I and Joe carried all day for Mr Thomas and Mr Blake. Mr Thomas is the vice president of one of the big banks down town and he always slips you a $1.00 extra per round but beleive me you earn it cadding for Mr Thomas, there is just 16 clubs in his bag includeing 5 wood clubs tho he has not used the wood in 3 yrs but says he has got to have them along in case his irons goes wrong on him. I dont know how bad his irons will have to get before he will think they have went wrong on him but personly if I made some of the tee shots he made today I would certainly considder some kind of a change of weppons.

Mr Thomas is one of the kind of players that when it has took him more than 6 shots to get on the green he will turn to you and say how many have I had caddy and then you are suppose to pretend like you was thinking a minute and then say 4, then he will say to the man he is playing with well I did not know if I had shot 4 or 5 but the caddy says it is 4. You see in this way it is not him that is cheating but the caddy but he makes it up to the caddy afterwards with a $1.00 tip.

Mr Blake gives Mr Thomas a stroke a hole and they play a $10.00 nassua and niether one of them wins much money from the other one but even if they did why $10.00 is chickens food to men like they. But the way they crab and squak about different things you would think their last $1.00 was at stake. Mr Thomas started out this a.m. with a 8 and a 7 and of course that spoilt the day for him and me to. Theys lots of men that if they dont make a good score on the first 2 holes they will founder all the rest of the way around and raze H with their caddy and if I was laying out a golf course I would make the first 2 holes so darn easy that you could not help from getting a 4 or better on them and in that way everybody would start off good natured and it would be a few holes at lease before they begun to turn sour.

Mr Thomas was beat both in the a.m. and p.m. in spite of my help as Mr Blake is a pretty fair counter himself and I hear him say he got a 88 in the p.m. which is about a 94 but any way it was good enough to win. Mr Blakes regular game is about a 90 takeing his own figures and he is one of these cocky guys that takes his own game serious and snears at men that cant break 100 and if you was to ask him if he had ever been over 100 himself he would say not since the first yr he begun to play. Well I have watched a lot of those guys like he and I will tell you how they keep from going over 100 namely by doing just what he done this a.m. when he come to the 13th hole. Well he missed his tee shot and dubbed along and finely he got in a trap on his 4th shot and I seen him take 6 wallops in the trap and when he had took the 6th one his ball was worse off then when he started so he picked it up and marked a X down on his score card. Well if he had of played out the hole why the best he could of got was a 11 by holeing his next niblick shot but he would of probly got about a 20 which would of made him around 108 as he admitted takeing a 88 for the other 17 holes. But I bet if you was to ask him what score he had made he would say O I was terrible and I picked up on one hole but if I had of played them all out I guess I would of had about a 92.

These is the kind of men that laughs themselfs horse when they hear of some dub takeing 10 strokes for a hole but if they was made to play out every hole and mark down their real score their card would be decorated with many a big casino.

Well as I say I had a hard day and was pretty sore along towards the finish but still I had to laugh at Joe Bean on the 15th hole which is a par 3 and you can get there with a fair drive and personly I am genally hole high with a midiron, but Mr Thomas topped his tee shot and dubbed a couple with his mashie and was still quiet a ways off the green and he stood studing the situation a minute and said to Mr Blake well I wonder what I better take here. So Joe Bean was standing by me and he said under his breath take my advice and quit you old rascal.

Mon. Apr. 17
Yesterday was Sun and I was to wore out last night to write as I cadded 45 holes. I cadded for Mr Colby in the a.m.

118

and Mr Langley in the p.m. Mr Thomas thinks golf is wrong on the sabath tho as Joe Bean says it is wrong any day the way he plays it.

This a.m. they was nobody on the course and I played 18 holes by myself and had a 5 for 76 on the 18th hole but the wind got a hold of my drive and it went out of bounds. This p.m. they was 3 of us had a game of rummy started by Miss Rennie and Mrs Thomas come out to play and asked for me to caddy for them, they are both terrible.

Mrs Thomas is Mr Thomas wife and she is big and fat and shakes like jell and she always says she plays golf just to make her skinny and she dont care how rotten she plays as long as she is getting the exercise, well maybe so but when we find her ball in a bad lie she aint never sure it is hers till she picks it up and smells it and when she puts it back beleive me she don't cram it down no gopher hole.

Miss Rennie is a good looker and young and they say she is engaged to Chas Crane, he is one of our members and is the best player in the club and dont cheat hardly at all and he has got a job in the bank where Mr Thomas is the vice president. Well I have cadded for Miss Rennie when she was playing with Mr Crane and I have cadded for her when she was playing alone or with another lady and I often think if Mr Crane could hear her talk when he was not around he would not be so stuck on her. You would be surprised at some of the words that falls from those fare lips.

Well the 2 ladies played for 2 bits a hole and Miss Rennie was haveing a terrible time wile Mrs Thomas was shot with luck on the greens and sunk 3 or 4 putts that was murder. Well Miss Rennie used some expressions which was best not repeated but towards the last the luck changed around and it was Miss Rennie that was sinking the long ones and when they got to the 18th tee Mrs Thomas was only 1 up.

Well we had started pretty late and when we left the 17th green Miss Rennie made the remark that we would have to hurry to get the last hole played, well it was her honor and she got the best drive she made all day about 120 yds down the fair way. Well Mrs Thomas got nervous and looked up

119

and missed her ball a ft and then done the same thing right over and when she finely hit it she only knocked it about 20 yds and this made her lay 3. Well her 4th went wild and lit over in the rough in the apple trees. It was a cinch Miss Rennie would win the hole unless she dropped dead.

Well we all went over to hunt for Mrs Thomas ball but we would of been lucky to find it even in day light but now you could not hardly see under the trees, so Miss Rennie said drop another ball and we will not count no penalty. Well it is some job any time to make a woman give up hunting for a lost ball and all the more so when it is going to cost her 2 bits to play the hole out so there we stayed for at lease 10 minutes till it was so dark we could not see each other let alone a lost ball and finely Mrs Thomas said well it looks like we could not finish, how do we stand? Just like she did not know how they stood.

You had me one down up to this hole said Miss Rennie.

Well that is finishing pretty close said Mrs Thomas.

I will have to give Miss Rennie credit that what ever word she thought of for this occasion she did not say it out loud but when she was paying me she said I might of give you a quarter tip only I have to give Mrs Thomas a quarter she dont deserve so you dont get it.

Fat chance I would of had any way.

Thurs. Apr. 20

Well we been haveing some more bad weather but today the weather was all right but that was the only thing that was all right. This p.m. I cadded double for Mr Thomas and Chas Crane the club champion who is stuck on Miss Rennie. It was a 4 some with he and Mr Thomas against Mr Blake and Jack Andrews the pro, they was only playing best ball so it was really just a match between Mr Crane and Jack Andrews and Mr Crane win by 1 up. Joe Bean cadded for Jack and Mr Blake. Mr Thomas was terrible and I put in a swell p.m. lugging that heavy bag of his besides Mr Cranes bag.

Mr Thomas did not go off of the course as much as usual

but he kept hitting behind the ball and he run me ragged replaceing his divots but still I had to laugh when we was playing the 4th hole which you have to drive over a ravine and every time Mr Thomas misses his tee shot on this hole why he makes a squak about the ravine and says it ought not to be there and etc.

Today he had a terrible time getting over it and afterwards he said to Jack Andrews this is a joke hole and ought to be changed. So Joe Bean wispered to me that if Mr Thomas kept on playing like he was the whole course would be changed.

Then a little wile later when we come to the long 9th hole Mr Thomas got a fair tee shot but then he whiffed twice missing the ball by a ft and the 3rd time he hit it but it only went a little ways and Joe Bean said that is 3 trys and no gain, he will have to punt.

But I must write down about my tough luck, well we finely got through the 18 holes and Mr Thomas reached down in his pocket for the money to pay me and he genally pays for Mr Crane to when they play together as Mr Crane is just a employ in the bank and dont have much money but this time all Mr Thomas had was a $20.00 bill so he said to Mr Crane I guess you will have to pay the boy Charley so Charley dug down and got the money to pay me and he paid just what it was and not a dime over, where if Mr Thomas had of had the change I would of got a $1.00 extra at lease and maybe I was not sore and Joe Bean to because of course Andrews never gives you nothing and Mr Blake dont tip his caddy unless he wins.

They are a fine bunch of tight wads said Joe and I said well Crane is all right only he just has not got no money.

He aint all right no more than the rest of them said Joe.

Well at lease he dont cheat on his score I said.

And you know why that is said Joe, neither does Jack Andrews cheat on his score but that is because they play to good. Players like Crane and Andrews that goes around in 80 or better cant cheat on their score because they make the most of the holes in around 4 strokes and the 4 strokes includes their tee shot and couple of putts which everybody is right there to watch them when they make them and count them right along with them. So if they make a 4 and claim a 3 why people would just laugh in their face and say how did the ball get from the fair way on to the green, did it fly? But the boys that takes 7 and 8 strokes to a hole can shave their score and you know they are shaveing it but you have to let them get away with it because you cant prove nothing, But that is one of the penaltys for being a good player, you cant cheat.

To hear Joe tell it pretty near everybody are born crooks, well maybe he is right.

Wed. Apr. 26

Today Mrs Doane was out for the first time this yr and asked for me to caddy for her and you bet I was on the job. Well how are you Dick she said, she always calls me by name. She asked me what had I been doing all winter and was I glad to see her and etc.

She said she had been down south all winter and played golf pretty near every day and would I watch her and notice how much she had improved.

Well to tell the truth she was no better than last yr and wont never be no better and I guess she is just to pretty to be a golf player but of course when she asked me did I think her game was improved I had to reply yes indeed as I would not hurt her feelings and she laughed like my reply pleased her. She played with Mr and Mrs Carter and I carried the 2 ladies bags wile Joe Bean cadded for Mr. Carter. Mrs Carter is a ugly dame with things on her face and it must make Mr Carter feel sore when he looks at Mrs Doane to think he married Mrs Carter but I suppose they could not all marry the same one and besides Mrs Doane would not be a sucker enough to marry a man like he who drinks all the time and is pretty near always stood, tho Mr Doane who she did marry aint such a H of a man himself tho dirty with money.

They all gave me the laugh on the 3rd hole when Mrs Doane was makeing her 2d shot and the ball was in the fair way but laid kind of bad and she just ticked it and then she asked me if winter rules was in force and I said yes so we teed her ball up so as she could get a good shot at it and they gave me the laugh for saying winter rules was in force.

You have got the caddys bribed Mr Carter said to her.

But she just smiled and put her hand on my sholder and said Dick is my pal. That is enough of a bribe to just have her touch you and I would caddy all day for her and never ask for a cent only to have her smile at me and call me her pal.

Sat. Apr. 29

Today they had the first club tournament of the yr and they have a monthly tournament every month and today was the first one, it is a handicap tournament and everybody plays in it and they have prizes for low net score and low gross score and etc. I cadded for Mr Thomas today and will tell what happened.

They played a 4 some and besides Mr Thomas we had Mr Blake and Mr Carter and Mr Dunham. Mr Dunham is the worst man player in the club and the other men would not play with him a specialy on a Saturday only him and Mr Blake is partners together in business. Mr Dunham has got the highest handicap in the club which is 50 but it would have to be 150 for him to win a prize. Mr Blake and Mr Carter has got a handicap of about 15 a piece I think and Mr Thomas is 30, the first prize for the low net score for the day was a dozen golf balls and the second low score a ½ dozen golf balls and etc.

Well we had a great battle and Mr Colby ought to been along to write it up or some good writer. Mr Carter and Mr Dunham played partners against Mr Thomas and Mr Blake which ment that Mr Carter was playing Thomas and Blakes best ball, well Mr Dunham took the honor and the first ball he hit went strate off to the right and over the fence outside of the grounds, well he done the same thing 3 times. Well when he finely did hit one in the course why Mr Carter said why not let us not count them 3 first shots of Mr Dunham as they was just practice. Like H we wont count them said Mr

Thomas we must count every shot and keep our scores correct for the tournament.

All right said Mr Carter.

Well we got down to the green and Mr Dunham had about 11 and Mr Carter sunk a long putt for a par 5, Mr Blake all ready had 5 strokes and so did Mr Thomas and when Mr Carter sunk his putt why Mr Thomas picked his ball up and said Carter wins the hole and I and Blake will take 6s. Like H you will said Mr Carter, this is a tournament and we must play every hole out and keep our scores correct. So Mr Dunham putted and went down in 13 and Mr Blake got a 6 and Mr Thomas missed 2 easy putts and took a 8 and maybe he was not boiling.

Well it was still their honor and Mr Dunham had one of his dizzy spells on the 2d tee and he missed the ball twice before he hit it and then Mr Carter drove the green which is only a midiron shot and then Mr Thomas stepped up and missed the ball just like Mr Dunham. He was wild and yelled at Mr Dunham no man could play golf playing with a man like you, you would spoil anybodys game.

Your game was all ready spoiled said Mr Dunham, it turned sour on the 1st green.

You would turn anybody sour said Mr Thomas.

Well Mr Thomas finely took a 8 for the hole which is a par 3 and it certainly looked bad for him winning a prize when he started out with 2 8s, and he and Mr Dunham had another terrible time on No 3 and wile they was messing things up a 2 some come up behind us and hollered fore and we left them go through tho it was Mr Clayton and Mr Joyce and as Joe Bean said they was probly dissapointed when we left them go through as they are the kind that feels like the day is lost if they cant write to some committee and preffer charges.

Well Mr Thomas got a 7 on the 3rd and he said well it is no wonder I am off of my game today as I was up ½ the night with my teeth.

Well said Mr Carter if I had your money why on the night before a big tournament like this I would hire somebody else to set up with my teeth.

Well I wished I could remember all that was said and done but any way Mr Thomas kept getting sore and sore and we got to the 7th tee and he had not made a decent tee shot all day so Mr Blake said to him why dont you try the wood as you cant do no worse?

By Geo I beleive I will said Mr Thomas and took his driver out of the bag which he had not used it for 3 yrs.

Well he swang and zowie away went the ball pretty near 8 inches distants wile the head of the club broke off clean and saled 50 yds down the course. Well I have got a hold on myself so as I dont never laugh out loud and I beleive the other men was scarred to laugh or he would of killed them so we all stood there in silents waiting for what would happen.

Well without saying a word he come to where I was standing and took his other 4 wood clubs out of the bag and took them to a tree which stands a little ways from the tee box and one by one he swang them with all his strength against the trunk of the tree and smashed them to H and gone, all right gentlemen that is over he said.

Well to cut it short Mr Thomas score for the first 9 was a even 60 and then we started out on the 2d 9 and you would not think it was the same man playing, on the first 3 holes he made 2 4s and a 5 and beat Mr Carter even and followed up with a 6 and a 5 and that is how he kept going up to the 17th hole.

What has got in to you Thomas said Mr Carter.

Nothing said Mr Thomas only I broke my hoodoo when I broke them 5 wood clubs.

Yes I said to myself and if you had broke them 5 wood clubs 3 yrs ago I would not of broke my back lugging them around.

Well we come to the 18th tee and Mr Thomas had a 39 which give him a 99 for 17 holes, well everybody drove off and as we was following along why Mr Klabor come walking down the course from the club house on his way to the 17th green to join some friends and Mr Thomas asked him what had he made and he said he had turned in a 93 but his handicap is only 12 so that gave him a 81.

That wont get me no wheres he said as Charley Crane made a 75.

Well said Mr Thomas I can tie Crane for low net if I get a 6 on this hole.

Well it come his turn to make his 2d and zowie he hit the ball pretty good but they was a hook on it and away she went in to the woods on the left, the ball laid in behind a tree so as they was only one thing to do and that was waste a shot getting it back on the fair so that is what Mr Thomas done and it took him 2 more to reach the green.

How many have you had Thomas said Mr Carter when we was all on the green.

Let me see said Mr Thomas and then turned to me, how many have I had caddy?

I dont know I said.

Well it is either 4 or 5 said Mr Thomas.

I think it is 5 said Mr Carter.

I think it is 4 said Mr Thomas and turned to me again and said how many have I had caddy?

So I said 4.

Well said Mr Thomas personly I was not sure myself but my caddy says 4 and I guess he is right.

Well the other men looked at each other and I and Joe Bean looked at each other but Mr Thomas went ahead and putted and was down in 2 putts.

Well he said I certainly come to life on them last 9 holes.

So he turned in his score as 105 and with his handicap of 30 why that give him a net of 75 which was the same as Mr Crane so instead of Mr Crane getting 1 dozen golf balls and Mr Thomas getting ½ dozen golf balls why they will split the 1st and 2nd prize makeing 9 golf balls a piece.

Tues. May 2

This was the first ladies day of the season and even Joe Bean had to carry for the fair sex. We cadded for a 4 some which was Miss Rennie and Mrs Thomas against Mrs Doane and Mrs Carter. I guess if they had of kept their score right the total for the 4 of them would of ran well over a 1000.

Our course has a great many trees and they seemed to have a traction for our 4 ladies today and we was in amongst the trees more then we was on the fair way.

Well said Joe Bean theys one thing about cadding for these dames, it keeps you out of the hot sun.

And another time he said he felt like a boy scout studing wood craft.

These dames is always up against a stump he said.

And another time he said that it was not fair to charge these dames regular ladies dues in the club as they hardly ever used the course.

Well it seems like they was a party in the village last night and of course the ladies was talking about it and Mrs Doane said what a lovely dress Miss Rennie wore to the party and Miss Rennie said she did not care for the dress herself.

Well said Mrs Doane if you want to get rid of it just hand it over to me.

I wont give it to you said Miss Rennie but I will sell it to you at ½ what it cost me and it was a bargain at that as it only cost me a $100.00 and I will sell it to you for $50.00.

I have not got $50.00 just now to spend said Mrs Doane and besides I dont know would it fit me.

Sure it would fit you said Miss Rennie, you and I are exactly the same size and figure, I tell you what I will do with you I will play you golf for it and if you beat me you can have the gown for nothing and if I beat you why you will give me $50.00 for it.

All right but if I loose you may have to wait for your money said Mrs Doane.

So this was on the 4th hole and they started from there to play for the dress and they was both terrible and worse then usual on acct of being nervous as this was the biggest stakes they had either of them ever played for tho the Doanes has got a bbl of money and $50.00 is chickens food.

Well we was on the 16th hole and Mrs Doane was 1 up and Miss Rennie sliced her tee shot off in the rough and Mrs Doane landed in some rough over on the left so they was clear across the course from each other. Well I and Mrs Doane went over to her ball and as luck would have it it had come to rest in a kind of a groove where a good player could not hardly make a good shot of it let alone Mrs Doane. Well Mrs Thomas was out in the middle of the course for once in her life and the other 2 ladies was over on the right side and Joe Bean with them so they was nobody near Mrs Doane and I.

Do I have to play it from there she said. I guess you do was my reply.

Why Dick have you went back on me she said and give me one of her looks.

Well I looked to see if the others was looking and then I kind of give the ball a shove with my toe and it come out of the groove and laid where she could get a swipe at it.

This was the 16th hole and Mrs Doane win it by 11 strokes to 10 and that made her 2 up and 2 to go. Miss Rennie win the 17th but they both took a 10 for the 18th and that give Mrs Doane the match.

Well I wont never have a chance to see her in Miss Rennies dress but if I did I aint sure that I would like it on her.

Fri. May 5

Well I never thought we would have so much excitement in the club and so much to write down in my diary but I guess I better get busy writeing it down as here it is Friday and it was Wed. a.m. when the excitement broke loose and I was getting ready to play around when Harry Lear the caddy master come running out with the paper in his hand and showed it to me on the first page.

It told how Chas Crane our club champion had went south with $8000 which he had stole out of Mr Thomas bank and a swell looking dame that was a stenographer in the bank had elloped with him and they had her picture in the paper and I will say she is a pip but who would of thought a nice quiet young man like Mr Crane was going to prove himself a gay Romeo and a specialy as he was engaged to Miss Rennie tho she now says she broke their engagement a month ago but any way the whole affair has certainly give everybody something to talk about and one of the caddys Lou Crowell busted Fat Brunner in the nose because Fat claimed to of been the last one that cadded for Crane. Lou was really the last one and cadded for him last Sunday which was the last time Crane was at the club.

Well everybody was thinking how sore Mr Thomas would be and they would better not mention the affair around him and etc. but who should show up to play yesterday but Mr Thomas himself and he played with Mr Blake and all they talked about the whole p.m. was Crane and what he had pulled.

Well Thomas said Mr Blake I am curious to know if the thing come as a surprise to you or if you ever had a hunch that he was libel to do a thing like this.

Well Blake said Mr Thomas I will admit that the whole thing come as a complete suprise to me as Crane was all most like my son you might say and I was going to see that he got along all right and that is what makes me sore is not only that he has proved himself dishonest but that he could be such a sucker as to give up a bright future for a sum of money like $8000 and a doll face girl that cant be no good or she would not of let him do it. When you think how young he was and the carreer he might of had why it certainly seems like he sold his soul pretty cheap.

That is what Mr Thomas had to say or at lease part of it as I cant remember a ½ of all he said but any way this p.m. I cadded for Mrs Thomas and Mrs Doane and that is all they talked about to, and Mrs Thomas talked along the same lines like her husband and said she had always thought Crane was to smart a young man to pull a thing like that and ruin his whole future.

He was geting $4000 a yr said Mrs Thomas and everybody liked him and said he was bound to get ahead so that is what makes it such a silly thing for him to of done, sell his soul for $8000 and a pretty face.

Yes indeed said Mrs Doane.

Well all the time I was listening to Mr Thomas and Mr Blake and Mrs Thomas and Mrs Doane why I was thinking about something which I wanted to say to them but it would of ment me looseing my job so I kept it to myself but I sprung it on my pal Joe Bean on the way home tonight.

Joe I said what do these people mean when they talk about Crane selling his soul?

Why you know what they mean said Joe, they mean that a person that does something dishonest for a bunch of money or a gal or any kind of a reward why the person that does it is selling his soul.

All right I said and it dont make no differents does it if the reward is big or little?

Why no said Joe only the bigger it is the less of a sucker the person is that goes after it.

Well I said here is Mr Thomas who is vice president of a big bank and worth a bbl of money and it is just a few days ago when he lied about his golf score in order so as he would win 9 golf balls instead of a ½ a dozen.

Sure said Joe.

And how about his wife Mrs Thomas I said, who plays for 2 bits a hole and when her ball dont lie good why she picks it up and pretends to look at it to see if it is hers and then puts it back in a good lie where she can sock it.

And how about my friend Mrs Doane that made me move her ball out of a rut to help her beat Miss Rennie out of a party dress.

Well said Joe what of it?

Well I said it seems to me like these people have got a lot of nerve to pan Mr Crane and call him a sucker for doing what he done, it seems to me like $8000 and a swell dame is a pretty fair reward compared with what some of these other people sells their soul for, and I would like to tell them about it.

Well said Joe go ahead and tell them but maybe they will tell you something right back.

What will they tell me?

Well said Joe they might tell you this, that when Mr Thomas asks you how many shots he has had and you say 4 when you know he has had 5, why you are selling your soul for a $1.00 tip. And when you move Mrs Doanes ball out of a rut and give it a good lie, what are you selling your soul for? Just a smile.

O keep your mouth shut I said to him.

I am going to said Joe and would advice you to do the same.

The Charm of Golf
A.A. Milne

When he reads of the notable doings of famous golfers, the eighteen-handicap man has no envy in his heart. For by this time he has discovered the great secret of golf. Before he began to play it he wondered wherein lay the fascination of it; now he knows. Golf is so popular simply because it is the best game in the world at which to be bad.

Consider what it is to be bad at cricket. You have bought a new bat, perfect in balance; a new pair of pads, white as the driven snow; gloves of the very latest design. Do they let you use them? No. After one ball, in the negotiation of which neither your bat, nor your pads, nor your gloves came into play, they send you back into the pavilion to spend the rest of the afternoon listening to fatuous stories of some old gentleman who knew Fuller Pilch. And when your side takes the field, where are you? Probably at long leg both ends, exposed to the public gaze as the worst fieldsman in London. How devastating are your emotions. Remorse, anger, mortification, fill your heart; above all, envy — envy of the lucky immortals who disport themselves on the green level of Lord's.

Consider what it is to be bad at lawn tennis. True, you are allowed to hold on to your new racket all through the game, but how aften are you allowed to employ it usefully? How often does your partner cry "Mine!" and bundle you out of the way? Is there pleasure in playing football badly? You may spend the full eighty minutes in your new boots, but your relations with the ball may be distant. They do not give you a ball to yourself at football.

But how different a game is golf. At golf it is the bad player who gets the most strokes. However good his opponent, the bad player has the right to play out each hole to the end; he will get more than his share of the game. He need have no fears that his new driver will not be employed. He will have as many swings with it as the scratch man; more, if he misses the ball altogether upon one or two tees. If he buys a new niblick he is certain to get fun out of it on the very first day.

And, above all, there is this to be said for golfing mediocrity — the bad player can make the strokes of the good player. The poor cricketer has perhaps never made fifty in his life; as soon as he stands at the wickets he knows that he is not going to make fifty to-day. But the eighteen-handicap man has some time or other played every hole on the course to perfection. He has driven a ball 250 yards; he has made superb approaches; he has run down the long putt. Any of these things may suddenly happen to him again. And therefore it is not his fate to have to sit in the club smoking-room after his second round and listen to the wonderful deeds of others. He can join in too. He can say with perfect truth, "I once carried the ditch at the fourth with my second," or "I remember when I drove into the bunker guarding the eighth green," or even "I did a three at the eleventh this afternoon"— bogey being five. But if the bad cricketer says, "I remember when I took a century in forty minutes off Lockwood and Richardson," he is nothing but a liar.

For these and other reasons golf is the best game in the world for the bad player. And sometimes I am tempted to go further and say that it is a better game for the bad player than for the good player. The joy of driving a ball straight after a week of slicing, the joy of putting a mashie shot dead, the joy of even a moderate stroke with a brassie; best of all, the joy of the perfect cleek shot — these things the good player will never know. Every stroke we bad players make we make in hope. It is never so bad but it might have been worse; it is never so bad but we are confident of doing better next time. And if the next stroke is good, what happiness fills our soul. How eagerly we tell ourselves that in a little while all our strokes will be as good.

What does Vardon know of this? If he does a five hole in four he blames himself that he did not do it in three; if he does it in five he is miserable. He will never experience that happy surprise with which we hail our best strokes. Only his bad strokes surprise him, and then we may suppose that he is not happy. His length and accuracy are mechanical; they are not the result, as so often in our case, of some suddenly applied maxim or some suddenly discovered innovation. The only thing which can vary in his game is his putting, and putting is not golf but croquet.

But of course we, too, are going to be as good as Vardon one day. We are only postponing the day because meanwhile it is so pleasant to be bad. And it is part of the charm of being bad at golf that in a moment, in a single night, we may become good. If the bad cricketer said to a good cricketer, "What am I doing wrong?" the only possible answer would be, "Nothing particular, except that you can't play cricket." But if you or I were to say to our scratch friend, "What am I doing wrong?" he would reply at once, "Moving the head," or "Dropping the right knee," or "Not getting the wrists in soon enough," and by to-morrow we should be different players. Upon such a little depends, or seems to the eighteen-handicap to depend, excellence in golf.

And so, perfectly happy in our present badness and confident of our future goodness, we long-handicap men remain. Perhaps it would be pleasanter to be a little more certain of getting the ball safely off the first tee; perhaps at the fourteenth hole, where there is a right of way and the public encroach, we should like to feel that we have done with topping; perhaps —

Well, perhaps we might get our handicap down to fifteen this summer. But no lower; certainly no lower.

Who Wants to Marry Money?
Glynn Harvey

It was around ten o'clock on a Friday morning and I was hurrying around the corner of the clubhouse, head down, when I ran square into Roger Bartholdy. I mumbled an apology and was about to go on when I realized who it was.

"Tallyho!" I said. "I didn't recognize you without your horse."

This was a logical observation. The sight of Roger Bartholdy patrolling the terrace of the Pinehurst Country Club in golfing clothes was worth at least a notice in the Pinehurst newspaper. After all, Roger was master of the Moore County hounds and went around with the horsy set. You could put it down as a fairly accurate rule of thumb that the fox-chasing mob regarded golf as a footling pursuit, followed by idlers with overlapping arteries and interlocking brain cells.

In fairness, you might also put down that the Pinehurst golf crowd regarded the county cavalry — if at all — as a gang of eccentric stable swipes who dressed up in pink coats two mornings a week to go chasing foxes before breakfast. In short, never were two worlds farther apart.

When I barged into him, Roger reared back, nostrils flaring and eyes rolling wildly. For a moment I thought he might drop the putter he was holding and start pawing the air with his forelegs. Skittish was the word.

"Whoa," I said softly. Roger began to quiet down and even managed a cold smile.

"Oh," he said. "It's you."

I backed off and studied his haberdashery. Roger Bartholdy was certainly dressed to the nines, whatever that means. He was wearing a fancy red cap, and his golf shoes were so new they creaked even when he was standing still.

"You're beautiful this morning," I said, nodding approval.

"But I think we ought to remove the price tag from the putter."

Roger flushed and peeled off the marker and muttered something I didn't quite get. I thought I detected a general air of petulance and, as he glanced toward the door of the ladies' locker, a faint suggestion of impatience.

"Well," I said, after a decent pause. I made a show of looking at my wrist watch. "I've got to get into town and back before our foursome tees off at noon, but I have time to listen to any kind of plausible explanation."

There's something about old Yale crewmen that annoys the hell out of me, and Roger Bartholdy was a real prototype. They have a generic tendency to be brusque and opinionated. That isn't just my own private observation; other Harvard men have remarked on it.

Roger was in one of his Napoleonic moods. He stared me up and down with a gaze that can only be described as steely. Then he pushed past me and strutted off. At the putting green he was joined by Mimi Elverson, and together they headed for the first tee.

I continued to watch, bemused by the scene, while Mimi teed off. As befits the perennial champion of the Pinehurst Women's Open, she whipped one well down the fairway. Then the master of the hounds, after nearly decapitating himself with his first effort, plopped one neatly onto the bowling green.

"View halloo!" I shouted and pointed to the bowling lawn. Mimi waved in reply, but Roger Bartholdy only glared and then trudged off behind his caddie. I noticed that the razor-sharp crease in his slacks was already losing its edge.

I sighed for Mimi. If Roger was going to trail the ball through bush and bracken without his horse, it would be a long afternoon for her. Just watching that kind of game can be pretty boring for a good golfer, and Mimi shot in the low eighties. There are those who argue that she ought to — she has nothing else to do since her father passed on and left her his millions.

As I turned back toward the clubhouse I saw Link Dreyer standing on the porch, watching Mimi and Bartholdy with a faint suggestion of a frown on his brow.

Dreyer was a big, easygoing guy who might have been a great golfer if his life hadn't been complicated by the fact that he had to earn a living. He might have been a good salesman too, if his craving for golf hadn't brought him in off the road like a homing pigeon every Thursday. As it was, he couldn't perfect his golf game; he had to waste too much time working. And he put in too many days playing golf to make any serious dent in the Carolina sales market.

Under the circumstances, of course, we all felt that the ends of justice and humanity would best be served if Mimi Elverson and Link Dreyer would quietly pair off and withdraw to some convenient rectory for the wedding. Then Link wouldn't have to waste Monday, Tuesday and Wednesday on the road. And Mimi could go about her golf with a high heart and a clear conscience, serene in the knowledge that she was serving society and not just reaping the fruits of compound-interest accounts.

Some astute observers of the social scene were inclined to believe that all this would one day come to pass. And certainly Link Dreyer was in there pitching to the pin; he was sensible enough to realize that he was missing a lot of fine golfing days. Mimi, on the other hand, was inclined to practice evasive tactics — but it was the consensus in the village that she just wanted to be chased a little bit. Women, I'm told, are like that.

Consequently, the sight of Link Dreyer watching his social security tack off down the fairway with Roger Bartholdy was most interesting. "It looks like somebody is playing your ball," I said gently.

Link turned to face me. A dark flush started up from his collar line. Perhaps that's why everyone was so genuinely fond of Link; he was such a total oaf; he even could blush.

"Isn't that Roger Bartholdy, the horse guy?" he said. Behind his horn-rimmed glasses, his eyes blinked in disbelief.

"Uh-huh."

Link turned this piece of intelligence over in his mind. "But he doesn't play golf," he said at length and rather suspiciously, as if testing the statement for a secret loophole.

I looked off down the fairway where Roger was emerging from the brush for the fourth time. "No," I said, "he sure doesn't."

Link frowned and pursed his lips. "Then," he went on stubbornly, "what's he doing out there with Mimi?"

"Well," I said airily, "he's not playing golf. We both agree on that point."

Link stared hard at me, and as he began to get the point his jaw dropped in astonishment. But I'll say this for Link Dreyer: Once he comes to grips with the subject he goes right to the mat. He looked quickly over his shoulder and then pulled me aside behind a pillar. "But Bartholdy's got lots of dough," he said hoarsely. Then, a bit anxiously, he added, "Hasn't he?"

I nodded. "They tell me his stable-boys make mops out of dirty old twenty-dollar bills and use 'em to clean the stalls," I said. "What's that got to do with it?"

"Well —" Link gestured weakly down the distant fairway.

I tapped him confidentially on the arm. "Don't let this get around town," I whispered, "but out there, in the world, people are still marrying for love."

Link stiffened and clenched his jaws. Poor guy. All his life he had either been in a bunker or under a shower when Dan Cupid posted the starting times. He recognized the word "romance" when he saw it, but he associated it vaguely with perfume advertisements.

"Love?" he said. And then he repeated it softly, over and over. I backed him to a wicker chair and gave a slight push. Then I shrugged and started off for town. Empires might totter and dynasties fall, but if I wasn't back by tee time, I'd have to spend the afternoon at gin rummy.

As luck would have it, whom do I meet on Broad Street but Victoria Nelson, the editor of the Pinehurst Pilot. After exploring the customary conversational gambits, I casually passed along the bulletin about Bartholdy and his new diversion. Victoria took it standing up.

"I'm not surprised," she said. "I heard he was selling his horses."

"How come?" I asked. "Did he bow a tendon or something?"

Victoria looked at me queerly. "He's broke," she said flatly. "And the government's put a plaster on his paint business up North until he kicks through with two years' back taxes."

I tipped my hat to her, accomplished my errand and hurried back out to the country club.

I found Link Dreyer there hovering weakly on the fringe of a gin game, still convalescing from the effects of the blockbuster. I dragged him out onto the porch and fed him the 11:00 A.M. newscast.

Righteous anger is beautiful to behold. Link gripped his hamlike hands into fists and the muscles of his forearms twitched convulsively. His normally cherubic face seemed to harden strangely. I was hoping that a small vein in his forehead would begin to throb, like it does in the movies, but nothing developed there except a few beads of perspiration. "Why, the lousy —" he began.

I cut him off. "Ah-ah," I chided him. "Temper never won the match. We've got to be cold and calculating, like Ben Hogan . . ."

Hogan's name worked magic. For a moment I thought the mention of Link's personal golfing deity would bring him to his knees. Instead he simply bowed his head momentarily. When he looked up again, the fury of the moment was gone. Gone, too, was the coiled-spring tenseness, though his eyes, behind the spectacles, were still glacier-cold.

He took my hand in a firm grip. "Thank you, Kelsey," he said humbly. "You're right. We must think." Then a look of panic came over his face. "But I'm not very good at that."

I poked his shoulder reassuringly. "Leave it to Kelsey," I said. . . .

Some people practice perfidy; others have conspiracy

thrust upon them. I can't take full credit for what followed. The scheme was tossed into my lap, smoking hot, almost as soon as I got home: Jane, my wife, reported that her sister Margaret was en route for a visit.

Now, normally, a visit from Margaret fills me with the same sense of exhilaration as a ball out of bounds. Margaret is a schoolmarm of fairly formidable spirit who toils at her educational forge in distant Texas, hammering out sturdy little minds that someday will complete the winning of the West.

That is, if Margaret doesn't get impatient and decide to finish up the job herself.

"Margaret?" I said blankly. "What happened? Did she flunk out?"

My spouse seared me with a look. "It's spring vacation," she said. "She's flying here for the week."

She waited for me to return to the attack, but a nasty little idea was seeping into a dark corner of my brain. I carried it gingerly out to the porch, where I sat quietly with it through the full incubation period. Ten minutes later, the plot fully hatched and scratching, I went to the telephone.

With my helpmeet eavesdropping, I unfolded my scheme to Link Dreyer. When I hung up she was standing in the doorway, staring at me as if I were something that had just wriggled out of the kitchen faucet.

"You're insane," she announced without any preamble. "Do you think Margaret is going to stand for such nonsense? Imagine! Masquerading as the widow of a wealthy Texas oilman, looking for a place to settle in the Sandhills . . ."

She snorted. "And a horsewoman, at that," she went on. "Why, the idea! Margaret probably thinks a snaffle is the past tense of sniffle."

Under Jane's withering barrage my bold project began to look shabbier and shabbier. "You don't think she'd go along with the gag, huh?" I asked glumly.

To my surprise Jane began to laugh. "Go along with it?"

she exclaimed. "If I know Margaret, she'll dress it up so even you won't recognize it!"

It just goes to show you about women. Like I say, they're balky as jennies ordinarily, but rig up a scheme to ease some poor goof into matrimony and no piece of knavery is too foul, no plot too diabolical.

And Margaret, sure enough, went along with the idea. She sniffed suspiciously at first, but with Jane and me both working at her, she began to thaw. Then a formidable glitter crept into her eye and she began to embroider on her role with growing enthusiasm.

"And you want me to lead the hounds off on another scent," she said finally. "Is that it?"

"Just the one hound — Roger Bartholdy," I explained. "A pretty mangy cur, if you ask me. But if you can get him baying after you, just for a few days, Link will move in and win the championship by default."

A strange little smile softened the strong line of Margaret's mouth. "Sounds like it might be fun," she said dreamily.

I'll say this for Margaret: she isn't bad looking. I came to the conclusion that it was just those steel-rimmed spectacles that gave her the appearance of a drill sergeant.

In fact, when she arrived at the Moultons' cocktail party the next evening, squired by Link Dreyer, I began to think I had misjudged her — either that, or else Texas does something for women.

Jane had done a good job of planting her propaganda stories. When Margaret entered the room the clatter of tongues stopped as if somebody had snapped of a switch. There's something about a million dollars when it walks into a room that seems to focus attention. Everyone at the party looked Margaret over as though she were a six-foot sidehill putt.

Me, I was watching Roger Bartholdy — who was there, of course, with Mimi Elverson. When Margaret came in, he lifted his head like a hound catching the scent of a fox. I noticed he lingered over their introduction — getting quite a brisk run out of it, as we say around the tackroom.

Bartholdy would like to have carried on the conversaiton the rest of the evening, but Link broke it up by dragging Margaret off just as Mimi, a trifle grim, reminded Bartholdy that her glass was empty again. I caught Link's eye in passing and winked. He grinned happily. . . .

Sure enough, on Sunday afternoon there was a telephone call for Margaret — from Bartholdy. But Margaret wasn't there to receive the call. She had driven up to Chapel Hill with Link Dreyer to see the state university and they didn't get home until rather late. In fact, Jane and I had gone to bed when Link's old sedan turned into the drive.

"Say," I said to Jane, "don't you think you'd better tell your sister to concentrate a little more on Roger Bartholdy?"

She muttered something I couldn't make out. "What?" I said.

Jane's voice was muffled and fuzzy when she spoke again, but I'm pretty sure I understood her clearly. "Don't forget," she said, "that the backswing is just as important as the follow-through."

I didn't see Link during the next three days. He was rocketing around the Carolinas, selling just enough kitchen crockery to pay for his weekend golf losses. But on Thursday, when he showed up at the country club, I was able to announce important advances all along the front.

"Bartholdy had Margaret up to look at his farm Monday," I told him.

Link tugged reflectively at his ear.

"And he took her to the hunt breakfast Tuesday," I added, a little disappointed by his lukewarm reaction.

Link took off his glasses, held them up to the light, and then began polishing the lenses thoughtfully.

"And they went up to his farm again yesterday," I said peevishly. The guy's total lack of response irked me. We were standing in front of the pro shop and I turned away and strode over to the putting green, where I dropped a couple of balls and began batting them furiously around and about.

I suppose that's why I didn't notice when Roger Bartholdy came up. The first inkling I got was when I heard Link's voice, choking with anger: "Bartholdy, I want to see you."

I looked up as Link charged past me and I turned my head in time to see Roger advancing with a dark gleam in his eyes.

It was a pretty pallid battle and both principals would have been thrown out of the ring at the Garden. I don't know who opened fire first. Link threw a right over Roger's head and then Roger retaliated with a right hook that missed by two feet. Link jabbed twice with his left and didn't connect, and Bartholdy uncorked a haymaker that tore a gaping hole in thin air. After that they grappled and began to roll around on the lawn.

By the time we bystanders had got the warriors separated, unhurt but breathing hard, the affair had attracted quite a gathering from the club and the pro shop. It was the first time anything of the sort had ever happened in the staid purlieus of the Pinehurst Country Club, and oldsters who interpreted all disputes in the light of the rules of golf were shaking their heads and clucking their dismay.

It was Link Dreyer who first recovered his breath. "That'll teach you," he gasped, "to play around with other men's women."

Bartholdy glared venomously at him, but before he could reply Mimi Elverson pushed her way through the spectators and stepped up beside him. She stared coldly at Link. "For your information, Mr. Dreyer," she said, "I don't appreciate being made the subject of a common street brawl."

Dreyer blinked and readjusted his spectacles.

"And for your further information," Mimi went on, turning to wipe a tiny smudge of dirt off Roger's cheek, "Mr. Bartholdy and I have reached an understanding. Your brutal attack has only confirmed my judgment." She leaned forward and planted a light kiss on Roger's cheek.

Link gaped at her, and then he glanced at Roger and back to Mimi again. "You mean" — he pointed from one to the other, his forefinger swinging like a metronome — "you and him? You mean, you and he are —"

Suddenly Link lunged toward them. Roger Bartholdy, in alarm, started to assume the appropriate Marquis of Queensberry defense, but Link merely seized his hand and shook it excitedly. Then, before Mimi could fend him off, he swept her up and kissed her loudly on the cheek.

"Congratulations," he cried. "Congratulations to both of you. I didn't realize. I thought —" he stopped and turned abruptly to me.

"Where's Margaret?" he said.

"Home, I suppose," I said, puzzled by his giddy behavior.

Without another word, Link darted through the ring of spectators and ran toward the parking area. In a few moments his old sedan careened down the driveway like a hot rod. I turned to Doc Kerrins.

"What do you make of it, Watson?" I asked.

Doc shrugged. "A clear case of a mixed foursome," he said as he drew me off toward the cardroom. "Anyone for gin rummy?"

It was a quiet wedding, Margaret and Link's — nothing as elaborate as the one Mimi Elverson and Roger Bartholdy staged the following week. And Margaret made a handsome bride. She left her steel-rimmed spectacles at home.

She and Link are living now at the old Bartholdy place, which they bought from Roger. Margaret has opened a private school. Of course, we don't see much of Link these days. He's just a Saturday-afternoon golfer and his iron shots lack that old crispness; but they say he's a crackajack salesman — he's even taken on a couple of new lines.

We miss Link in the regular foursome. But Roger

Bartholdy plays with us quite a lot, and he's not too bad if you give him a couple of strokes a side. He can't putt, though. Personally, I think those bowlegs of his have something to do with it.

But he's turning out to be a pretty fair gin player — for a Yale man.

Excerpts From
How to Talk Golf
(A to Z of Golfing Terms)
David Langdon

"Am I in your way?" A question asked on the green by a player whose ball appears to be in line with another player's putt (*see* Stymie, now archaic). If affirmed, the player lifts his ball, marks its position and replaces it after the other player's putt is taken. A useful ploy (The Langdon Gambit) is to put the question when your ball is geometrically nowhere near your opponent's line of putt. Addressing his ball, his mind will be focusing on the absurdity of your suggestion rather than on the putt, and the result could well be a foozled shot.

Backspin A motion imparted to a ball by an expert, causing the club-head to come into contact with it when moving in a downward direction, arresting the ball's run on the green towards the hole. More effective than any amount of shouting "Whoa!," "Stop, you blighter!" or "Sit!"

Committeeman A chap who is quite normal and friendly but once appointed to a committee suddenly turns all toffee-nosed and nasty when you complain about the greens or the food.

"Do please carry on" A plea lacking in sincerity made by a player who has struck his ball into deep rough, to those helping him search for it, after a decent interval. Silent umbrage, however, is taken by the player if his helpers actually take him up on his offer and walk off leaving him to look for his ball on his own.

"Effortless" Description by a friendly partner of one of your rare good shots into which you have poured every ounce of effort.

"Fantastic!" Description of any good but flukey shot made by a RABBIT, usually by an opponent who stands rooted, arms akimbo, looking at you with insulting incredulity.

Grip The way you arrange your hands to hold a club, varying between the overlapping to the interlocking and the two-handed. Whichever you use and are used to, some busybody will encourage you to switch to the other, with dire results.

"Head up" The all too common fault of lifting the head during the striking of a ball, resulting in a poor SHOT. Usually followed by an agonized shriek from the player as though stung by a passing wasp.

"Justice" As in "There's no justice in this game." A comment made when a player's ball, in his own judgement well-struck, finds its way into a bunker or runs through the green. Or more to the point, when his opponent's ball, badly struck, finds its way through the same bunker and on to the green. (Cf. "Luck.")

"Luck" That elusive quality needed in the performance of most games but more especially in golf, judging by the frequency with which it is invoked. Balls which are struck wildly into trees and ricochet safely on to the fairway, flukey chip shots off the green which find their way into the hole, are examples of Luck's bounty. Putts which drop and then pop out of the hole, and straight, long shots on the fairway which kick malevolently into the rough, are examples of bad, or lack of, Luck. A statistical study of a round of golf will prove incontrovertibly that every player has an equal share of both good and bad breaks, but the latter are invariably remembered to the exclusion of the former.

Marker 1. A movable black and white painted post set in the ground with a metal roundel atop, indicating the direction of a green unsighted from the tee. Often hit with bull's-eye precision by players whose direction of shot anywhere else on the fairway is rarely accurate. 2. A scorer in STROKE play appointed by the committee to record a competitor's score. 3. A small plastic disc like a large drawing pin used for marking a ball on the green. Very difficult to find if kept in the same trouser pocket as your assortment of tees, but makes its presence felt sharply if kept in the back pocket when you are sitting in your car on your way home from golf.

"Nobbut a minute" In MATCH play a player faced with a miniscule but perhaps decisive putt, may arch his eyebrows enquiringly at his opponent hoping to have the putt conceded. The latter, ignoring the mute appeal, and using the vernacular to temper the rebuff, may say "It'll take nobbut a minute" (i.e. "It won't take a minute to sink it"). Der. hard-headed Yorkshire.

"Only a game" A general comment on the game of golf made by a player to comfort an opponent who is having a bad round. Seldom accepted in the spirit in which it is offered.

Partner The chap who plays on your side in a FOUR-BALL, FOURSOME or GREENSOME. (He becomes your "opponent" in a SINGLES or THREEBALL.) You use his Christian name when the game is going in your favour, and fall back on the impersonal "Partner" when his bad play loses your side the hole. Thus, "Oh, *bad* luck, Partner," said with barely concealed venom.

"Rub of the green" This is said to occur when a ball in motion is stopped or deflected by an outside agency, i.e. anyone not part of a competitor's side, including a marker, a referee or forecaddie. Used now colloquially to mean *C'est la vie.*

Shank A short stabbing or socketing shot made by hitting a ball other than with the face of the club-head, sending the ball at an acute and alarming angle to the right. Pros are terrified of shanking, even of discussing the aberration, and consider that it should be a notifiable contagious disease.

Through the green Official description of "the whole area of the course except the teeing ground and putting green of the hole being played, and all the HAZARDS on the course." To the average golfer "through the green" simply means his ball running across the green into the rough beyond.

Wedge An open-faced club used for short pitches around the green (pitching-wedge) or in bunkers (sandwedge). The request "Pass me a sandwedge" runs the risk of the witty reposte "The ham or the cheese?"

Zaharias, Mrs. Mildred "Babe" Famed American woman golfer who won the British Women's Amateur Open in 1946. Also the 1954 US Women's Open Championship with a prodigious score of 291 for four rounds. She is included here not only to record her prowess, but to conclude an A-Z glossary with a Z.

Cowboy on the Green
Max Green

THE LAZY F RANCH harbored three men, several horses, and dozens of bulls. The men were as hard-working a crew as you'd find on any ranch. The horses were well-fed and gentle-broken. As for the bulls, they were something again. Yes, sir, definitely an animal of a higher order: registered bulls from great herd sires. And creatures so pampered and worried over; so washed and brushed for hours on end; so scrupulously fed, you probably never saw this side of the moon.

But old Matt Sikes knew just what he was doing. Matt, and Pete, his boy, and Bulldog Barnes, his foreman for as far back as Matt could remember. The three of them were a devoted team.

Old Matt, not much bigger than a peanut, was a flinty and determined little man. It was he who made the stock shows and supervised generally. Bulldog, strong as a fat percheron horse, did the heavy labor. Pete was right in there when it came to dolling the bulls up. He could gentle a bull so, you'd think it was a tame dog rather than a beast of vast anti-social potentialities.

Pete was old Matt's one and only known relation. Pete's ma gave up the ghost the night he was born. It almost killed old Matt, but he pulled through. From then on, he spent a lot of time with his boy, and after twenty-three years, there wasn't a man anywhere knew more about the raising and care of bulls than young Pete.

Their ranch prospered with the years, their animals fattened and flourished.

When fall came, the old man once again made his annual trip to Kansas City for the stock show. Matt sighed contentedly when Fat Boy II, their top bull, took the blue ribbon. It was clear easy.

Some Big Boys, representing a packing outfit, made a deal with him immediately, and Fat Boy brought a record price. By this time, Matt was something of a celebrity. They dined him at the Beefsteak Club, invited him out for a few rounds of golf, a game he'd only heard about till now. The old man naturally felt flattered.

He had wired Pete and Bulldog the good news, and they could hardly wait for his return. But now, several days went by, and they heard nothing further. They were a little worried. They jumped into the pick-up and started for town. Another wire was waiting for them there. "DELAYED STOP BIG DEAL STOP LEARNING SOME NEW ANGLES STOP MATT."

They went to town every day for a month. Matt never failed with a good reason for delaying his return. Soon Pete was rearing and tearing at the halter. One day he had reached his limit and was about ready to pitch off to Kansas City, when a final wire came, saying something about *high fever but cooling off and would be home day after tomorrow.*

Pete and Bulldog were waiting at the station for Matt when the train pulled in. Their greetings were just a little short of hearty, for the boys were too eager to get the news. But old Matt volunteered nothing, only saying, "Pick up the trunk, boys, and load her in the pick-up." Pete stared at Bulldog and Bulldog at him. Matt wasn't one to be travelling with much baggage, ordinarily. "Mebbe it's presents," muttered Bulldog. Pete shrugged his shoulders.

Matt did open up about the big show on the way home, and for a moment they shared a common warmth. But though they waited for him to come to the part about the Big Deal, and kept glancing at the trunk, Matt did not let on a word.

They soon drew up at the ranch. Old Matt jumped out, limber as a cottontail rabbit, and without blinking an eye, asked them to carry the trunk into the bedroom. When they had got it there, they set themselves stubbornly to wait. But Matt was not going to hold out any longer. He attacked the lock of the trunk, and there was a peculiar excitement in his expression as he raised the lid.

There, before their eyes, was a scene Pete would never forget .... thousands of golf balls scattered over an underbrush of countless clubs, golf clubs!

The whole perverse rigging must have looked like a Christmas scene to old Matt, for his eyes opened on the display in loving admiration. He scarcely noticed the others. Pete just managed to keep himself from exploding as he stamped out of the now suffocating room. Bulldog, blubbering like a foundered calf, followed him quickly.

From that day on, old Matt was like a man bewitched. All day long, and with an eerie intensity of energy, he would run up and down the surrounding hills, club in hand, sending the little white balls racing before him.

It was too much for Pete and Bulldog to grasp, but they hoped the mania would run its course. Indeed, the ranch atmosphere finally began exerting its quieting influence on the old man, and the animals once again knew his sure touch. But Matt continued to play his endless game in the cool of the evenings. Once he tried to get Pete to go out and join him at it. Pete refused in no uncertain terms. Matt appeared hurt, but didn't say anything more.

Pete continued working with the bulls through the year, and they were soon ready for another show. The Lazy F entry pulled only third place this time. Matt was gone three months. Pete and Bulldog heard from him only once.

Pete confided to Bulldog, "I'm worried about Matt. He's been failin' pretty fast the last few years, and I'm afraid this golf craze is gonna finish him off."

When Matt returned, he looked surprisingly better than he had for years. The trip seemed to have renewed him. Pete didn't mind so much after that.

Five years went by, and Matt played golf and sold bulls. Pete and Bulldog worked a little harder, and kept the animals in shape. Then one night, amid the splendor of dreams which left a shadow of a smile on his lips, Matt came to rest in the tireless gathering arms of old Father Time.

Chapter II

Pete and Bulldog felt lost for a while after Matt's death. But the old man in his grave left them no peace.

It started with the reading of the will. Pete had to have the lawyer read it three times to make sure his ears were not playing foul tricks on him.

The general run of Matt's last testament was that he had bought a little island off the Gulf of Mexico. Pete — so it specified — was to spend one year and a day out there before he could become owner of the Lazy F Ranch. There was a sizable bank account involved.

Pete, almost driven outside himself, hauled up every slanderous word he knew or could invent. The lawyer only shrugged blandly. Bulldog, staring at him with sad puppy-eyes, finally ventured a meek explanation. Pete only humped his tall frame like a freshly-saddled bronc. It took days before it subsided. Bulldog was finally able to tell the lawyer that it was all right — Pete would go.

There were a lot of preparations to be made. The ranch was finally leased to a neighbor with whom they made a deal to care for the bulls. The lawyer had told them they would not need to take anything except a few clothes . . . . all other arrangements had been made.

They boarded a train for Galveston, and not many hours hence were on a boat headed for Matt's Island.

Pete had little time to relish his remaining anger. The tossing boat soon turned him sea-green. Bulldog followed suit. They went down like axed saplings. After what seemed years, they were hoisted to their feet by the skipper.

"Here we are, boys, Matt's Island. Your supplies have been unloaded. I'll be back in a year and a day." Just like that, and he was gone.

The two weaving, wobbly figures did not attempt an answer. They simply fell over on the sandy beach and slept from weakness. They slept right on through what was left of the day, and all the night.

It was Bulldog who first opened his eyes at dawn. He jerked into a sitting position and looked out across the expanse of water which was turned pink and gold by the rising sun. The beauty of the scene was somehow lost on him. His stomach felt as if it had been trampled by a herd of buffaloes. Besides, it was cold. Bulldog struggled to his feet and strolled inland, looking for something with which to build a fire. He needed the sight of some pieces of driftwood to remind him that it was wood he was looking for. His next inspiration was an ax, which he found among the supplies unloaded from the boat.

As soon as the fire was blazing warm, he called to his companion. "Hey, Pete, get up. It's time to milk, and old Jersey is bawling in pain." Bulldog had not yet remembered the trip across the water. He was still a mass of shivering instinct.

It was doubtful if Pete understood any of this. He did roll over and groan. Bulldog shook him. Pete suddenly bolted upright, and stood there swaying and rubbing his eyes. "Boy," was all he could say. He dashed for the fire.

Bulldog found some sowbelly and quickly had a skilletful sizzling over the fire. There was a big old tin coffee pot which he soon had perking with the fragrant black liquid. The two shivering men consumed almost the whole pot before they could look at each other. They took moments out now and then to down a chunk of sowbelly.

The hot food and drink were producing their effect. When the sun came up and began warming their skins, the world seemed suddenly to brighten for them.

They were now glancing about them between swallows, not without suspicion. "Let's look this place over," Pete said.

The island proved to be about a mile long, very narrow, rocky and rough in the center, smooth and sandy around the border. There was very little vegetation except for some sort of bush that was unknown to them. It would supply them with plenty of firewood.

After their tour of the island, they were a little nearer their normal selves. There was a big tent to pitch, cots to prepare for sleeping, and various utensils and implements to sort. They stayed busy all day and by nightfall had everything in shape except two wooden crates which they hadn't opened.

Bulldog declared, "I'm ready to hit the hay, Pete. How about you?"

"Me, too," answered Pete. "I feel like I'd climbed every mountain in the Rockies today." With that, they went to bed.

The two islanders slept late the next morning. The sun had already warmed the sand of the beach when they arose. Breakfast over, Pete announced, "I think I'll take a look in these . . ." motioning to the two unopened wooden crates.

"I'll help you," replied Bulldog.

They found a small prize bar among the supplies. Pete soon had one end of the crate loosened. He pulled the boards up one at a time. When the last board was raised, he stopped dead still. A blank look covered his face. Slowly he reached into the crate and pulled out a piece of paper. Bulldog was watching him anxiously. He didn't have to ask what it was, for Pete was reading it aloud. "Son, here are some articles I wish you would learn to use, and when you do, play in the Southwestern Open. You don't have to do this unless you want to. Good Luck, Matt."

Pete folded the note and put it in his pocket. They were both emptying the contents of the crate. It held at least two dozen golf clubs. They looked glumly at each other.

"Let's try the other crate," meekly suggested Bulldog. His throat was dry. The Old Man was certainly having his joke. Pete gritted his teeth. He seemed to have heard Bulldog's thought.

The two worked the top off the other crate deliberately. Balls. That same vision had affronted their eyes once before. Impulsively, they both tipped the crate over, sending forth a Niagara of these diabolical pellets over the ground in all directions. This seemed to relieve them. They both roared out in a seizure of laughter that left them weak. Both Pete and Bulldog had expended every grimy word of execration pent up within them all these weeks since the will had been read. They felt much better.

"Say," Pete observed, "didn't the Old Man have a lot of different clubs — different heads and . . . . built different, you know?"

"Yeah, as I recall," wondering what Pete had in mind.

"Well, look at these." Pete strode over to the first crate, Bulldog following him. "Look . . . all the same . . . No. 2 . . . No. 2 . . . No. 2," he was reading off the clubs. "All the same heads," he summed up, fingering one of them, glancing over the others. "Thought I heard the Old Man say something about needing a different one for different things . . ."

Pete looked blankly at him. They both sat down, staring across the water.

They stared, walked, puttered about for two weeks, aimless and undirected. One day, when Bulldog was straightening things up a bit, something smacked him in the middle of the back. He whirled, and saw a sight that, if he had to confess it, eased him a lot. There was Pete standing out there swinging wildly at a golf ball. At least, the stalemate was broken.

From then on, Bulldog had to stay on his toes to avoid accidents. Pete was no sharpshooter. He had an unbiased affinity for all directions.

Pete's native thoroughness, and the inevitability of their droll situation, wrought on him gradually. Day after day, their few chores disposed of, Pete took to his pastime, his curiosity whetted by each failure, each half-success. They were both amused by his new interest.

By the end of the first week, Pete could hit the balls intentionally, if not with foreordained accuracy. He rarely missed the ball, but had a harder time controlling its direction. Perversely enough, most of them would sail out into the gulf and with a little splash sink from view. This didn't seem to matter, much, until Pete realized what was happening — his store of balls would give out in no time. Less drastic but not less vexing was the way in which the soaring balls sank into the densest part of the brush in mid-isle. He spent hours searching for them, often in vain.

After a couple of months, Pete seldom got one off the beach. He played without tees, laying the ball out on the sand and whamming it. The challenge of inadequate equipment sharpened, perfected his senses. Pete realized by now that something must have gone wrong with the supplies his father had gotten for him. Playing against the difficulties of the terrain, he got to know why this strange little useless game required such a variety of clubs. He now began recalling the different kinds he'd seen his father using.

But he was glad that on this barren island he was not going to have it made easy for him. It was better without the trimmings.

His long arms made quite an arc with the club as he knocked one somewhat better than two hundred steps. The beach had a slight curve to it, and Pete was unconsciously putting a hook on the ball so that it curved with the beach

154

right around the edge of the water. He seldom now lifted the ball aloft — just sort of drove it in a line, like some fellows do in baseball.

The sea gulls that inhabited the island afforded Pete and Bulldog considerable entertainment for a while. They would follow the ball in its flight, and pounce on it when it stopped. Laying hold of the missile, they would fly out into the gulf and drop it. It was amusing for a while, but again Pete caught up with what was happening. The balls would not hold out at this rate. One day he impatiently aimed a whizzer into their midst. It sent them squawking in general confusion high into the air. Pete could hardly credit his senses. His accuracy surprised him.

They were resting after one of the noon meals, when he said, "Wonder if maybe we shouldn't figger out a way for me to judge distance on the shots. I noticed Matt used to practice different distances. And shoot them into holes, too," he recollected. "Ought to dig some holes and start rolling them in."

"Might split up a piece of that driftwood there into thin sticks, and put 'em down in places," offered Bulldog. "Yeah, along one side of the island," they both added, the same thought coming to them. Pete elaborated. "If I went along the other side and started shooting at the sticks . . . well, it's wider in some places, and you could get your distances that way." Bulldog assented, adding, "You'd have to lay 'em right on the peg to keep 'em from going out into the gulf."

From the day the sticks were up, Bulldog became target man. He would station himself a little way back of each, offering his bulk to Pete's vision, for lining up the shots. When the balls came over, Bulldog would signal where they had fallen. Pete would shoot just high enough to clear the brush in the center, sending them straight toward the sticks. His trouble came from dropping the balls too short, so that they sank into the rough, or else overshooting them into the gulf.

Every morning brought the flying balls a little nearer to the sticks. Pete would soon be able to call his distance. The island gave him a variety of widths to master, from fifty to two hundred yards.

His afternoons, he used for putting. He had already dug a series of holes in the sand for this purpose. The putting gave him more trouble than ever. He had to learn to hit the ball while bending forward at an angle to equalize the angle of his number two iron. Fortunately, his tough rancher's body stood him in good stead, for he was able to keep a solid stance even in this uncomfortable posture. Before long, he had learned to sink them with great accuracy. He was effective at all distances.

He grew so sure of himself, that he was able to direct his shots at clusters of gulls and their young ones, dropping the balls lightly down in their midst so as not to hurt them. They would scatter in flight, screaming, only to return in a wide arc, as if the sport amused them.

The two men had lost all track of time after the first month or so. They had learned to make the best of their isolation. By this time, they had built themselves comfortably in, displaying a great deal of unsuspected ingenuity at the work. Their daily chores disposed of, they were free to pick up where they had left off at golf. Their idle evening hours were spent in reminiscing, in planning. At times they ached for the feel of saddle leather against their haunches, for the smell of a hard-run horse. They looked forward to the day when they could return to ranch life.

To his surprise, Pete found himself relishing the thought of matching his golfing skill against that of others. He suspected he would make an odd figure striding across golf links such as he had seen pictured in some periodicals somebody had once left at the ranch. "Cowboy on the green," he grimaced. Still, he'd like to try it . . .

One warm and balmy day, Pete was just drawing back to take a cut at a ball, when Bulldog, down by the water's edge, let out a roar. "Hey, Pete . . . . Pete! Look off there . . . . to the northwest. A boat!" A year and a day had gone over the far rim of time.

Chapter III

The trip to Galveston wasn't bad. Only a slight queasiness overtook both of them when they were about a half-hour out, but it settled quickly, and they were able to shout, "Good fishing, Skipper," when the boat finally left them ashore at their destination. With the exception of a few number two irons and some golf balls which Pete wanted to have with him, they made a deal with the skipper to take over all their supplies.

A couple of days later found them near the scene of the Annual Southwestern Open. They were settled in a tourist cabin when Bulldog announced, "I'm goin' out to the course to find out what I can about this deal. Be back after a while."

Pete was dozing when Bulldog stamped in from his scouting tour. He sat up. "Looks like we've got a lot to learn in the next few days, Pete. The Open's only two weeks off. You've got to shoot a qualifying round before you can play."

"What's that?"

"It's a preliminary round of the course. You have to shoot a low-enough score to where the officials figger you are qualified to play the big game. I talked with some of those fellows out at the . . . . country club," he sniggered at the name, "and most of them have been playing for years. From the way they talked, I figger you concentrated five or six years in that year and a day. I went around nine holes with a couple of local professionals. The only chance you've got is your straight shootin'. No use tryin' anything new."

They were out on the course every day after that. It was the seventeenth hole that gave Pete some trouble. This was a short hole and had to be shot downhill. The island had been almost level from one end to the other. Pete tended to overshoot in spite of everything he tried.

He shot a two under par on the day of the qualification round, and so made it. But the seventeenth had almost wrecked his chances.

Word got around about a man in high-heeled boots and

big white hat who played only with a number two iron and had qualified for the open. The press got hold of the story and boomed it lovingly. When they ran a follow-up column on Bulldog, curiosity burst all limits.

Bulldog was certainly an indispensable part of the setting. He had volunteered his squat form to caddy for Pete. A miniature gallery gathered to watch the powerfully built caddy carrying one little spare iron around on his shoulders. They had a time of it.

The attraction of the pair was irresistible on opening day. Most of the spectators followed them — not at all intent on practicing good manners. One fellow asked Pete why he hadn't brought along his post-hole digger. Set himself up that way, with private golf holes. Another wanted him to sing "Home on the Range" at every hole. The crowd took this up boisterously.

Pete didn't say much, offering a grin to their remarks. But before long, they had calmed down. To everyone's amazement, including that of Pete himself, he was leading the pack at the seventeenth. Remembering his tendency to overshoot, Pete pulled himself in nervously. He was short by fifty yards. He took a one over par, dropping behind Barney Otter. He parred the eighteenth, and carded a score of sixty-nine for the first round.

When the evening papers came out, they listed Pete tied with two others for second, and Barney Otter in the lead with sixty-eight.

The second round started off with the biggest gallery in the golf history of the Southwestern Open. The city police were out in force and had a rough time keeping the crowd back far enough for Pete to shoot. A golfer wearing cowboy clothes was undeniably a strange sight. The "tee-off" fascinated them especially. Pete didn't use a wooden tee. He simply tossed the ball to the ground unceremoniously and took his stance at an impossible angle. His legs would buckle as if he were coming apart at the joints. His long arms would flash through the air, bringing the iron down as if he were chopping wood. The ball would hook, turn off the fairway, then curve right back almost to center.

The crowd went wild when Pete completed a putt. He would lean over like a windblown hollyhock, and with gentle persuasion settle the pill softly into the cup.

Pete shot unbelievable golf. But the seventeenth pestered him up to the last round. He and Barney Otter were tied for the lead, with the nearest contender four strokes behind. Barney was red in the face and suffering a lot of teasing from the onlookers.

Bulldog lay awake most of the night before the final round, his mind turning and turning on the same irrepressible worry. Just before dawn, he sighed and wished he were rid of it. He was too tired to think any more. Then he dozed off. At about 7:30, he awoke with a start. Crows . . . . crows! By . . . . ! That was it! The crows out there! The idea had come up at him from the restless twilight of his over-tired brain. Pete's only chance, by . . . . ! He arose quickly, dressed, left the cabin quietly, his strained face unwashed. He headed toward the course. A cab, motor stirring awake with the morning, picked him up on the way.

When he returned, Pete was up and dressed. "Couldn't sleep, went out for a walk," muttered Bulldog, answering the other's silent query. Pete nodded. He himself had slept soundly, but his naturally easy spirits had a fine edge of dread to them this morning. He went to the window. The air was clear and sweet. He breathed deeply, stretching his arms widely aloft.

Their taxi carried them to the course amid a continuous stream of cars all heading the same way. Ranchers and cowboys from all over the countryside were there, piqued to curiosity by the vision of one of their own on this strange terrain. Pete started when he saw them gathered. He smiled broadly. It was like a rodeo crowd. The dudes thought so, too, and enjoyed it.

As they "teed off" on number one, Bulldog thought there wasn't much left to do now but pray. Out there, at the seventeenth, the crows were whirling and circling in the air like a big revolving funnel.

Pete and Barney were both keyed to top form. Barney was outdriving Pete a little by using woods. Pete, however, was laying his second and third shots right by the cup. Pete was taking one hole, Barney the other.

The cowboys, enjoying the dude game no limit, had squalled like mountain lions at every critical play. The crowd joined them good-naturedly. But by the 17th, everyone had grown solemnly still. Pete and Barney were tied.

Bulldog's heart was almost pounding out of his chest while the two were putting on the sixteenth. He looked up nervously. The birds were still there, darting down now and then to the green and sweeping up again into the whorl.

Pete walked up, had the same tremor of uncertainty he'd always felt here. He poised himself for the shot. Barney's heart eased out. He'd feel better with the small lead Pete would give him after this hole. He tensed expectantly as Pete unlatched for the shot, letting go with what looked like a pile drive.

Pete put into it every ounce of controlled strength he had in his body. Yet the onlookers sensed he had pulled in somewhere, mastering, shaping, his power. The ball seemed to hang in the air, spinning in a slow line toward its goal. Like an object under a spell, it glided into the funneling whorl of the birds, seemed to hang on their wings, was lost to sight.

Nobody knew what had happened. Pete, spent, could hardly catch his breath. Then suddenly they all stampeded toward the seventeenth. The pellet was only a half-dozen inches from the hole. Barney, unnerved, raised a row, claiming the crows had broken the ball's flight and funneled it down toward the cup. This was too fantastic for anybody to believe.

It was pure bedlam now. Barney went to pieces. He overshot by about twenty yards, fumbled the putting, broke down on the last hole. Pete took the match three under.

The last car was starting up, getting into speed. It had been a great holiday for the crowd. On the quiet green, two or three capped men were combing through for litter. Pete and Bulldog had taken all the congratulations, all the queries. Now they were alone, waiting for a taxi. They had been offered a lift into town by several people, but wanted their independence. They'd be heading for the ranch soon.

"Wonder whether the crows did have anything to do with it, Bulldog?"

"Dunno," Bulldog shrugged. "Was some yellow corn around there kept 'em hoverin'. Mebbe you were just lucky." Bulldog was straight-faced.

Pete looked at him, but didn't seem to notice.

Golf and the POO Muscle
Mervyn J. Huston

Golf, that ancient and honourable game, has been played for centuries by mankind with, in general, indifferent results. A great deal of attention has been paid to improvement of equipment and to development of skill and muscles. Recent research in our laboratories has demonstrated that insufficient attention has been given to the most important factor of all — the POO muscle.

We were brought to a recognition of this phenomenon when a colleague who is an ardent golfer returned from a sabbatical leave in Mexico where he had found that it was impossible to play golf while in the throes of the Montezuma syndrome. Exploratory tests verified our hypothesis that the alimentary tract plays a basic role in golf and that the power of a golf swing is directly proportional to the puissance of the back door thereof. The mechanism involved is the Posterior Orifice Obturator device which is referred to in our laboratories as the POO muscle. The empirical recognition of the importance of this device is to be found in golfing folklore in the expression "to cut washers" when exerting oneself very hard. When a golf pro exhorts a student to "get your ass into the ball" he has arrived intuitively at a fundamental truth.

An analysis of a golf swing discloses that in the back swing the club is raised with the muscles relatively relaxed, then with the down swing all hell breaks loose physiologically and anatomically. The POO muscle synchronizes and co-ordinates all the viscera in a synergistic recruitment of the ancillary abdominal structures. The key device and limiting factor in a powerful swing is the power and finesse of the POO muscle.

The POO muscle is a truly remarkable device. It can accommodate itself to various postures; it can distinguish between the three states of matter; and it can adjust to different social occasions. Since the device is muscular in nature, there is no doubt that it can be strengthened by exercise, as can other muscles of the body such as that of the arm or leg. The strength of the handgrip can be increased by squeezing a spring contraption, so possibly something along this line would be effective, or lifting weights — the whole field is wide open. In the meantime, until more refined techniques have been developed by physical education departments in universities, a golfing enthusiast should introduce the POO muscle into his isometric exercises — very cautiously.

Our research group decided that the first step in our analysis of the role of the POO muscle in golf should be an effort to quantify the change in power from a resting state to that engendered during a swing. Our golfing colleague (hereinafter designated as the "Subject") was recruited as the experimental animal.

The power of the resting state was determined rather simply by measuring the force necessary to pluck a daffodil from the experimental area. We used a daffodil to add a touch of elegance to what might otherwise have been a rather vulgar performance. Our group feels that the niceties of life are frequently ignored by researchers, so we are spearheading a move to add some class to biological investigations.

162

The experimental set-up required a somewhat more elaborate protocol. The Subject, after preliminary connections had been made in the clubhouse, was escorted to the practice fairway by a procession of scientists wheeling along a portable myodynamometer, a respirometer, a cardiograph, a multi-channel recorder, a computer, a set of golf clubs, and a bevy of children. After much fussing about testing connections and so forth, we waited with baited breath for the denouement of this historic event. The Subject wiggled and waggled interminably and then finally smote the ball two hundred and thirty yards down the fairway.

That part of the experiment went well. Unfortunately, we had not reckoned with the magnitude of the power of the phenomenon we were dealing with. The internal unit was extruded with such force that it ripped the seat right out of Subject's pants. This dramatic result caused much excitement, confusion, and consternation. The team conferred on ways in which to adjust to this new difficulty. Someone came up with the obvious suggestion that the internal device would have to be anchored in some fashion. The Subject, after examining the disaster to his pants, vetoed the proposal, fearing some sort of implosive contrafissura. After considerable more palaver, we shooed the children away and trundled the whole experimental unit off to a secluded part of the course where we continued the experiment minus pants.

After the various attachments had been reassembled and checked, Subject again took a great swipe at the ball with everybody standing well back. Our worst fears were realized — he blew the whole attachment into the top of a nearby pine tree. Our team again entered into heated discussion which eventually became rather acrimonious. Subject remained adamant in his rejection of an anchoring system. It seemed for a while that the whole project would go down the tube.

Eventually, our theoretician came up with a solution. With an eye on the pine tree, he gave us a dissertation on Newton's third law of motion and recommended that we use a golf ball as the recording instrument. His proposal was as follows: a golf ball would be placed in the experimental area (hereinafter referred to as the POO ball); Subject would hit a drive (hereinafter referred to as the shot ball); the distance travelled by the drive would be compared with the distance travelled by the POO ball. This arrangement would provide an excellent opportunity for mathematical correlation between the power of the drive and the power of the POO muscle.

The first test was a resounding success. The shot ball travelled two hundred yards, and the POO ball one hundred yards. We were elated. We began to discuss a new type of tournament but decided the world was not ready for this yet. Subsequent tests were less well correlated; the standard deviation of the mean for both balls became rather large. In some instances the POO ball travelled farther than the shot ball. Apparently, it is difficult to concentrate on a golf shot with a golf ball up your POO. One variable we had failed to take into account was the matter of diet. There was strong evidence that diet played a role in our experiments and may have accounted to some extent for our remarkable results.

We discovered that the placing of the POO ball *in situ* had a considerable effect on the results. On one shot the POO ball was directed inward rather than outward and had to be retrieved with a putter. At this point the Subject resigned. All of our entreaties based on sacrifices in the interests of science were to no avail. He was adamant. Our quantitative experiments, therefore, are at a standstill at the present time. It is to be hoped, however, that this preliminary report will encourage others to carry on this important work.

All Golf is Divided into Three Parts
Harry Leon Wilson

Golf consists of exercise and emotion, in parts of one to nine respectively. The exercise is often said to be salutary. The emotions are frequently devastating.

The game has three grades: Supergolf, golf and subgolf.

164

The first is too serious to be talked much of here. It is hushed and tense and holy. An ever-widening area of silence surrounds the shrine from which the supergolfer drives. If he takes as many as two practice swings or stops to put down his pipe it has widened to the tee back of him and the one before him. The other supergolfers cease to breathe and the one with a wrist watch hastily removes it and throws it away. The breeze dies, birds still their songs, and the man driving a mower far down the fairway stops to roll a noiseless cigarette.

But when the supergolfers have reached the putting green a real silence ensues. The tension is tightened; the expensive, trained grass stops growing, the ants quit their uproar, the little worms beneath the sward cease their clamor; a pair of loud golf stockings would be instantly hissed to a quiet gray. The silence becomes positively noiseless.

Nor is this solemnity relaxed when the putting is done and the supergolfers pose on the green, leaning sportily against their putters, while an awe-stricken photographer snaps them for the front page of "Golf, Craps and Farming." The stillness is broken only at a distance by some common or subgolfers who blasphemously wish to use that green for their own contemptible putting. The supergolfers remain properly unaware of these loathsome insects.

They eventually leave, however, to be photographed on the next green in some more golf attitudes for the doublepage center of "Golf, Pole Vaulting and Dentistry in the Home."

And so it goes. The supergolfer need be followed no further. Besides, he is always annoyed by a gallery. He says so himself. Anyway he has nothing in common with the lesser species save an unconquerable tendency to miss three-foot putts. Let us observe, therefore, those of the lesser sort with whom golf is still an adventure.

Golf, the plain sort, is played by more or less tired businessmen who are off their game today. They hope sometime to become supergolfers. They know perfectly well they never will; still, they hope to. They can't help it. They dream, in secret, of some day blushing modestly on the White

House front porch while President Harding in a few fitting words confers upon them a two-gallon silver mug with three handles, hardly big enough to hold umbrellas and too big for anything else. They already have a few smaller cups, suitable for holding lump sugar, won in the Allied Metal Trades and Drugs tournament with a handicap of twenty-two, but nothing you would really call attention to except in a spirit of jolly good fun.

This big affair, from the hands of the President, is a different matter. And if only they could cure that slice and get some distance with the wood and some more distance with the iron and learn the chip shot and quit topping them and acquire the right putting stance — because, of course, if you have to take three putts on every green, look what it does to your score! So they prevail upon good old Angus McAngus to come out with them twice a week in the hope of working these little miracles. Their clubs are religiously cleaned after each round, and their cards are preserved to be studied in the long winter evenings when practice is confined to a few perfect swings in the library, and too bad the rose jar happened to be just a the point on the mantel! Why couldn't it have been kept on the hall stand? Then nothing would have happened.

Well, no good talking about it. It's gone, isn't it? Anyway, that was the right idea, the club head passing through a flattened arc into and past the ball, just the way it does in the diagram. Like this, now. Gee! Well, then keep the children out of the room. It's past their bedtime anyway. Now let's see — he says it's a flick of the wrists that turns on the juice. Oh, I'm not hurting the old rug, am I? Now, wait — let's see that diagram a minute.

And so forth.

Besides various bibelots in the home, this golfer has twice broken ninety on an actual course. Of course he didn't break it beyond repair; still eighty-nine isn't so rotten, is it, for a man that took up the fool game only eight years ago?

And there lies the chief of the plain golfer's delusions. He believes sincerely that he took up the game. But it was nothing so gentle or so voluntary as that. He was stricken with it and will never recover. He will pass out at last, still visioning himself modestly erect, the three-quarter view toward the photographer, while the President tells him that he is a credit to American sport and here is this splendid trophy, and so forth. He will be viewing a halftone of this scene in "Golf, Poultry and Beadwork," and on the opposite page another halftone in which his defeated opponent is warmly wringing his hand. The defeated opponent is seen to be Chick Evans.

On the bedside table among the medicine bottles will be a copy of "Golf Croquet and Osteopathy" lying open at How to Correct Your Faults with Plenty of Diagrams, by Angus McAngus. In his last lucid moment he will recall that one time or another — but not in the same round — he has made every hole in his course in par, with a birdie on the hard sixth on August 3, 1918. But no one else will remember this of him; no one in all the wide world.

His playmates will remember him kindly, no doubt, but if they recall any birdies it will be their own. They will say that Bill was a good scout, but they will be much more likely to recall that spell when he had such hard luck with the dice and had to sign the lunch check for the gang nine times running. They will never say that he had the makings of a finalist. They will more probably say that he certainly put that pipe-and-fittings concern on its feet after he once got control of the stock. The closest they will come to golf in their chat about him will be to remark in reverent tones that he died worth over fifty cases of Scotch. Yet no golfer will be dismayed by the brutal realism of this picture. It would do him no good if he were. He has been stricken. Dismay wouldn't help him. Nothing will.

And that is golf.

We now come to the rest of us, or subgolfers. The supergolfer has style and hence is called a stylist. The golfer has form, but is not hence called a formist. For some reason this word has not yet been invented. But the subgolfer has neither form nor style and is never called much of anything worth repeating. Yet, let it be said at once that we are the only class of golfers of any real importance to the game. We are its spine and sinews, comprising ninety-two per cent of its players.

Lacking us, the supergolfer could not play his tournaments nor be photographed for "Golf, Pastry and Plumbing." Lacking us, the golfer could never dramatize that tender little scene before the executive mansion. For there would be no links to perform on. You might see one link here and there, but not more. It is we who pay the bills for the lush spread of land that would otherwise be producing rutabagas, shotes and other table delicacies. Lacking us, golf-ball makers would not be thinking up catchy new names for balls that will give more yardage than any other ball on the market, nor thinking up machines to etch your name into the ball's surface.

As if that did any good! Shall I not today play with a ball into the surface of which has been deeply bitten the meaningless inscription "Geo. S. Garritt" or something? What of it? The name didn't prevent its being knocked into the far rough by unspeakably clumsy dub playing, did it, nor prevent me from finding it when I happened to be over there, did it?

And lacking us subgolfers, where would golf literature be? Answer: it wouldn't. I have omitted to point out that for the subgolfer golf consists largely of literature. The mere golfer plays by book now and then, but not steadily, as we do. And the literature of golf came about in this way: The subgolfer, coming to the game with a fresh, unspoiled mind, is cursed with a belief that much may be learned about it from a printed page. So he demands reading matter.

And so good old Angus McAngus writes a nice thick book on how to play golf. That is, not exactly. His name is on it and the photographs are all of Angus; a close-up of his right elbow at top of swing, his left ankle at the same tremendous crisis, the sole of his left shoe and the mole on his chin when nearest his right wrist; also his famous interlocking grip, looking like a bunch of severely twisted bananas. These photographs are all authentic and are labeled Fig. 1, Fig. 2, and so forth. But the book is written by a friend of Angus who knows how to spell a lot of words Angus has never had any occasion to use, including the word "pronate," and who imagines the way Angus would tell how to play golf if only Angus knew himself.

Perhaps Angus after reading the book will begin to think he does know how he does it, but he will be wrong there. All he really knows about his game is that he was sanctified to it at the age of nine and has never done anything but play it, not being vexed with a pipe-and-fittings concern. He actually knows that he can catfoot up to the ball and clout it on the nose right. But there he gets off.

Nevertheless here is the book, a beautiful creation costing five-fifty, with about two hundred glimpses of different bits of Angus in action. He has easily learned, after a few lessons, to stand still while being photographed. And the subgolfer pays and pays and pays, believing his worries are over. The book is cordial and reassuring, yet stern; stern enough to keep the subgolfer thinking he must have got his money's worth. It begins this way:

"It is of the utmost importance that the tyro should early grasp the three prime essentials of the game, which are — first, the stance; second, the grip; and third, the swing. There are golfing authorities who will maintain, with some shadow of plausibility, one must concede, that the swing is more prime than any of the other essentials, but a long study of the essentials of the game has convinced me that the other two essentials are fully as prime as this one.

"Having grasped the prime essentials, the tyro will do well to next put himself in the hands of some competent professional, who will see that he is outfitted with the right clubs. Much depends on this.

"Next in order for the tyro are the lessons from some good professional. A good deal may be obtained from a book like this, but lessons are a prime essential. They are almost one of the primest essentials there is."

And so forth.

Follows instructive comment, enlivened with Figs. 1, 2, 3, up to Fig. 186, which is merely a photograph of Angus not doing anything but having his photograph taken after shooting the home course in sixty-seven.

This is what keeps the subgolfer up nights: "It is hardly necessary to tell the tyro," says Angus, "that the first step is to get the correct line from ball to hole — the straight line." Of course it is hardly necessary, old top, but if you didn't tell him a lot of hardly necessary things, where would your book be? So the subgolfer reads on, fascinated by the things that are hardly necessary to tell him, enthralled by the halftones of Angus' right hip and the diagrammed relation of his left ear to his left shoulder at top of swing. On he reads, to How to Avoid Slicing Your Putts, with a spirited portrait of Angus engaged in avoiding a sliced putt. And then back to the grip: "I bring my left hand over," confides Angus, "until I can count all my knuckles." The subgolfer rejoices in this. It seems to him that if Angus counted up and found a couple of his knuckles missing he would be hiking back to the last tee to look for them. He resolves always to count his own knuckles carefully.

But Angus is never dogmatic. There is a nice feeling among these golf writers. Angus may admit that, after years of deep study, he has become convinced that the interlocking grip is the ideal grip; still, he doesn't say it is the only ideal grip, and the tyro must remember that Sandy McHaggis is strong for the open grip, while good old Cluny McWhoosh has for years obtained brilliant results with the merely over-lapping grip. "It is, after all," warns Angus, "a detail that must be decided by the individual player for himself."

The subgolfer wishes Angus would be a little more positive. But he buys the McHaggis and the McWhoosh brochures, with more photographs of grips and right elbows and left ankles and teeth and pipes and moles and hair and spiked shoes. He is hoping one of them will tell him the only right way to hold his club so he can go on with the rest of his education, but this never happens. Only another subgolfer can tell him the only right way. Any subgolfer after six lessons can tell him the only right way to do everything from driving to putting.

But the tyro, as he is never called outside golf books, keeps on reading. He buys more books and subscribes to "Golf, Brewing and Basket Weaving," to get those bully articles on the chip shot, with photographs showing the feet fairly close together so one is not likely to pull the shot, and so forth.

He never wearies of studying the picture of Davy Macdivot's follow through, nor of reading underneath it the beautiful words, "I use the Vardon grip with the little finger of the right hand overlapping the index finger of the left." And he is captivated by the picture of Davy in "Golf, Checkers and Beadwork," playing out of trouble. This shows a minor ditch, a blur-r-r of club shaft and the ball starting out for the green, followed by a fine mess of sand, like a comet trailing its tail. If he gets into a hole like that tomorrow he will try to recall just what it was that Davy seemed to be doing with his wrists and his feet and his knees and his club.

There is other literature in which the subgolfer rejoices. He follows all the big matches. He loves to read how Hagen laid his mashie second dead and chipped off a birdie on the notoriously hard twelfth at the Chicago Stockyards course. How Jock sent the ball away with a crisp snap on a straight line and proved unbeatable on all short shots from a chip to a long pitch. How Barnes made a sensational recovery, nabbing a two-hole lead. How Mitchell dashed out in thirty-three and how though under a racking strain due to trouble on the fifteenth and seventeenth, nevertheless came romping in with a thirty-eight. And how Chick took his opponent for a merry walk for the full thirty-six-hole route.

Also, if nothing more exciting offers he will read about golf being splendid exercise. He believes in this reading. He undoubtedly believes in this reading. He undoubtedly believes that Angus McAngus became the man he is among us today by studying a book. He pictures the bleak moorland with fairways stretching to every horizon, broken only by bunkers that add a touch of grimness to the wild scene. It is midnight. Standing not far from the ninth green is the

171

humble burn, or crofter, that was the childhood home of Angus, and inside the laddie is studying his lesson by the light of a simple tweed knot. Outside he hears the mournful call of the upland kiltie to its mate. A fur-bearing haggis lurks along the bank of the claymore, seeking its prey. Just beyond the pibroch, a faithful old byre is smoking a few last pipefuls of peat for the adjacent distillery.

The boyish impulse to be a part of this night life is manfully stifled. He knows he will never shoot a sixty-eight unless he studies. He kindles a fresh tweed and brings his page nearer to the wavering flame. The room is chill and he pulls closer about his boney knees the rug he has crocheted from the pure heather. His eyes are heavy with sleep, but he must master this photograph, Fig. 19, showing about one dozen fingers and thumbs jammed into the interlocking grip. Before sleep can come he must master this to the last detail, or some day he might get up on a tee and forget how to count his knuckles. He kindles a fresh tweed from the dying one and studies on.

This is the way the subgolfer undoubtedly sees the beginnings of Angus. If he didn't he would buy fewer golf books.

But after all his reading practice, how does the subgolfer actually play? Of course that is different because he only took up the game to get out into the open. And a foursome of subgolfers is further distinguished by the circumstance that not one of them should have tried to play today.

Yet in spite of it all, few victims ever wholly recover. Now and then one of exceptional strength of mind will pass from the acute to the merely chronic stage, but no case is known where the virus, once in blood, has been wholly eliminated; it remains a permanent menace, and the sufferer is never freed from the fear of relapse. My own case is in point. For may careless years I was immune apparently. I frequented contagion zones in fancied security. I had analyzed the game. I said pithily that golf was too much of a walk for a good game and just enough game to spoil a good walk.

Then I took up golf, as I lightly said. I took it up the way people take up smallpox or the black plague, which is the only way anyone ever takes up golf. The initial attack was most severe. It was diagnosed as the black, or confluent golf. As Mrs. Etta Schwartz, of Macon, Georgia, confides to the press, I suffered untold agonies and my friends gave me up. With a temperature running eight over par I would say that golf was a great game because it took my mind off my work. I deluded myself with this thought until it became all too plain that I must find some new kind of work to take my mind off golf. The old work simply wasn't doing it. I was swept on by the tide. And only bulldog determination ever saved me; bulldog determination and the final bitter knowledge that the day would never come when I could be safely entrusted with a loaded mashie. I admit that this last item helped me lower the temperature back to par. Anyway, I am looking for something else to take my mind off my work. Golf no longer does it. I can now take golf or let it alone. If I feel the old fever rising I have only to go out and try a few mashie shots.

Lately, there were three whole days when I never went near the course. Playing in oilskins is ruinous to the swing. Of course I haven't given the game up. There's the exercise, and it gets one out into the open, even if there isn't the slightest hope of ever shooting a decent round. And I will say that I am not always so bad on some holes, not for one who has only played a year.

Of course I'm not through with the game, by any means. It is an excellent diversion for one who can play it temperately. Besides, Bill tells me that the interlocking grip is, after all, the only sure one to cure a slice. A friend of his who is chummy with the pro up at Lakeside has shown him precisely how not to slice with this grip and Bill is going to show me the little trick. Of course with that slice out and a few lessons with the mashie, my game would be different. And this new book of Davy Macdivot's has a bully lot of photographs on the chip shot. You can see just how the iron comes down, going from A to B on the flattened arc, and not from A to C, which gives the ball a nasty hook. Probably I've been going from A to C without knowing it. And there is that new driver with ivory diamonds set in the face. That ought to make a difference. And I hear there's a putter just published that you simply can't miss with. You never can tell about this game. Lots of those scratch men were dubs not so long ago. And do I ever really expect to break into the eighties? Well, yes and no. But, of course, there's the exercise and everything.

And that is golf.

Four-Balls, Two-Balls, and Mixed Foursomes
Rex Lardner

Golf is a social game. By this I mean that you normally play it with other human beings. You neighbor, perhaps, or your neighbor and his wife with you and your wife. For wife you may read girlfriend, if neither player is married.

The two-ball game, when two men or two women play each other, is usually a far more grim experience than golf when it is played with members of the opposite sex. The stag game often degenerates into a match of frayed nerves, curt words, and glances that can kill at more than six paces. When two women go over the course together and there is any rivalry between them at all, very much the same thing occurs. Sometimes, even more so.

Two men, when they go walking over the links, are, more often than not, friendly enemies. Each is out to show the other he can score lower than his buddy. To prove this, a man will stoop, at times, to an ethical code upon which he would frown with distaste in any other game or even in business.

This is where psychological warfare truly touches the peaks.

A player will often go to bed early (yeah, even on a Saturday night). He will be up earlier and with more pep in his step than on weekdays when he goes to the office on the daily business round. It is best for his wife to stay in bed on such mornings. Her mate will not be at his best. He will be too worried about the upcoming trials — his putting game or his iron play or perhaps that double sand trap that lies across the fairway on the eleventh hole and that he can never seem to clear without the loss of at least two strokes — to be in a friendly mood.

He may or may not eat.

Now, I always enjoy a good breakfast before I go out to play eighteen holes. By the time I reach the first tee, that breakfast will be pleasantly settled, ready to furnish me with the energy needed to play golf and psych myself and my partner around the links. It is bad enough to be on the eleventh green and feel your stomach tying itself in knots at the prospect of a twenty-foot putt without having already ill-treated your stomach by refusing it the only thing it really wants out of life: food.

So I eat well for starters. At least, my insides won't have *that* to complain about. Scrambled eggs, toast, and coffee always provide me with the necessary fuel. If it's a brisk fall or spring day, I cajole my mate into making me some pancake batter the night before so I can enjoy griddle cakes with sausage before I set foot outside the house.

I also drink several cups of coffee. Coffee warms the body, sets my blood to stirring, and assures me that all will be well with my game on this fine day.

Some players I know refuse to eat breakfast. This renders them utterly unsociable by the time they reach the tenth green. It also, I suspect, reduces their energy because they begin to lag thereabouts. Their drives are not so long; their putts are slightly off.

I encourage my opponents to fast. It's part of my golf game, which means that if I can con some poor sucker into tottering around the course on the last five or six holes by talking him into not eating anything since dinnertime the night before, I can maybe make up in strokes what I have lost in the early going.

An empty stomach also means that when you finally reach the club bar, a martini or a manhattan will produce an effect like a depth bomb in your insides. These are the golfers who have to call their wives to come and get them.

But with a full breakfast under your belt, you can go out and give that ball a good, healthy whack. You aren't worrying about how you'll feel, come the sixteenth tee. You may even feel so good after a fine breakfast that you'll go upstairs where your wife is wisely curled up in bed and give her a good-bye kiss, at which she will sleepily wish you good luck. This makes your wife realize you really love her and scores brownie points in your marital relations.

It is very smart at this time to make sure you have your good-luck charm in your golf bag. If you don't have one, invent it.

I am reminded of the story they tell about Gene Sarazen and how he always attributed his success at winning the first Masters Tournament he had ever entered, held on the Augusta National, to a good-luck ring that had been given him by a friend. Of course, it was his superb play that won it, but the ring didn't hurt. Maybe it gave him that little extra measure of confidence just when he needed it most. I like to think so.

Be that as it may, I suggest that you obtain a good-luck object. It needn't be anything more or less than an old cap, a neckerchief, a rabbit's foot, an old battered club. Anything at all.

It will help you if you really do have good luck with it, but even if you don't, you can always use it against your opponent.

You lift the half-dollar (we'll say) out of your pocket right when you need it most, to sink a twelve-footer. You toss the coin in the air, catch it, and remark, "This is the time I need you, old buddy!"

You try to sink the putt. If you do happen to do just that, you will have badly shattered your opponent. You have a good-luck symbol working for you. He doesn't, and it will worry him. Just enough, let's hope.

If you don't sink the putt, you say, "Well, that 1923 half-dollar can't be expected to do it all the time." Then very cheerfully (never show dismay at a moment like this), you turn a smiling face to your opponent and murmur, "Nine times out of ten, it really does work for me."

He will think about that for the rest of the game. He will wait for you to drag out that half a buck, and if you ever should sink that putt or hit that wonderful two-iron shot onto the green, he will be convinced.

A note on sartorial elegance will fit in nicely here. A very colorful sweater or a psychedelic sort of shirt, if you can ignore it and play your normal game, may be something of a weapon in the psychology department, especially if you are playing against a gentleman who believes in a drab sport shirt and plain sweater as the proper links attire.

If something bright and colorful bothers you, however, if you are more conscious of the socks you wear than of the socks you give the ball, ignore this advice. The main idea of the game is to make your opponent uncomfortable, not you. But sometimes a paisley-print knit shirt will so distract your opponent, especially if you stand where he can't help but notice it, when he is in the middle of a swing, that he will commit a few bad blunders. You don't have to move, even. Just make sure you're where his eye — which should be on the ball — is on your shirt.

It helps if a wind is blowing. The wind will ruffle the shirt, sort of waggle all those wild colors, so that it will seem as if somebody is wigwagging with signal flags on the edge of your opponent's peripheral vision.

There are numerous other gambits you can practice that can throw your opponent off stride. You might try jingling some coins in your pocket until the last second or two before he lunges at his tee shot. He's bound to hear that infernal jingling, and the noise will creep in just enough to take some of the edge off his concentration.

You might try blowing your nose while he's going into his preliminary waggle or do a little discreet humming under your breath, then cut it off at the last minute and murmur an apology, "Oops, sorry, Fred. I didn't realize you were ready to hit." You can substitute a belch or a cough for a nose-blowing session, but do it with finesse. Of course, you can't do these things too often. You've got to be cute about it.

Also, you can pretend you notice something about the guy's stance or his practice swing and stop him just as he's about to go into his backswing. "Oh, Fred, sorry — but I noticed you took an awful fast backswing. Better slow it up." Or: "Fred, you've got your feet very far apart. It's going to keep you from pivoting. Didn't mean to interrupt — but I don't want you to rush your shot." Not much!

If Fred's a reasonably nice chap, he'll grin a little tightly and murmur his thanks and start all over again. Hopefully, you've upset his rhythm, and he'll slice or hook his drive.

Here's another great idea: During the first nine holes of an important match you might routinely concede close putts to your opponent until he is so lulled by picking up the ball without putting out that you can really shake him up suddenly on the tenth hole when he putts the ball within a foot of the cup, looks to you for a nod of concession, and you reward him with a blank stare. Realizing he's got to stroke that ball into the cup, he'll tighten up, sweat a little, and nine times out of ten push the ball past the hole. Walter (the Haig) Hagen, famous for his psychological warfare in golf, pulled this stunt on Leo Diegel in the final round of the 1926 P.G.A. tourney played in Salisbury, Long Island, and wound up taking the title.

Another ploy used by the Haig on the putting green was to unnerve his opponent by making light of his own long putts. The trick was particularly effective if Hagen had a much longer putt than the other fellow. He would suddenly start to laugh and keep on chuckling until his opponent asked him what was funny. Hagen would then casually mention that he was thinking how much tougher the other fellow's shot was going to look after he'd sunk his longer shot. Time and again the Haig would hole out from five or six feet while the other player — only inches away — would flub his putt and lose the hole.

Accordingly, if you've got any kind of putting ability, you might try this bit of psychological maneuvering. Of course, it's not likely to work if you miss your shot and push it three feet past the cup.

All these little hints can be useful in playing four-ball foursomes, too, which is when you're playing a round with three other guys. Just be sure you don't try them when your partner, if you're playing partners, is addressing the ball. You want to give *him* all the help you can.

The mixed foursome is a cat of another color. Here, you and a man friend are playing golf with two ladies. They may or may not be wives.

Always flatter your opposing female.

If your wife is going around the links with you, make damn sure she knows in advance about this bit of psychology. It won't do at all to win the match and have the little woman in a towering rage because of all the attention you've been paying to Myrtle Hodges, or whatever her name is.

Make your wife understand at the outset that you are going to flatter Myrtle because you want to win the golf match. If she is the understanding sort, she may even join in the game by buttering up to Big Charley. However, a word of caution here. You don't want the gals to engage in a hair-pulling match on the thirteenth tee. Make sure Sylvia bats her eyes in such a way that Charley's wife won't see her.

I repeat, the main idea is to take your opponents' minds off golf, to the detriment of their game. And with those curvaceous creatures known as women around, this can be done quite easily.

Unless Big Charley is the jealous type, you can even offer to help his wife or girlfriend with her swing. This will necessitate your standing behind her and putting your arms about her, to guide her grip on the club. It will maybe make her think you are contemplating a play for her.

It may also make Big Charley think about you, too, which is all right if it disturbs his game, but not when it gets to the point of his thinking of wrapping a steel-shafted club about your neck. You have to play it by feel, here.

You must caution your wife against any such tricks by Big Charley. I wouldn't want to be the cause of a divorce in the family. But properly done, this bit of byplay is almost guaranteed to hurt the other fellow's game, even if it won't improve your own.

Girls are talkative creatures, in case you don't already know, so get Sylvia to yakk it up on the green when the other side is about to putt. A male golfer will overlook such a breach of etiquette on the part of a woman not his wife. He will seethe inside and maybe ask for silence, but he won't get to the point of apoplexy, the way he would if you had just spoken.

Tell Sylvia beforehand that it might be a great idea for her to talk fashions to Myrtle from time to time, so that Myrtle will be thinking about the new mink coat you have promised her (makes no difference if you have or not, except maybe to Sylvia). Myrtle will believe her and will start getting so mad at Big Charley, who is stingy with a buck when it comes to Myrtle's clothes, that she may even deliberately begin to waste strokes.

This will get Big Charley mad, in turn. And his game will go out the window.

Most men will trudge down the fairways in more or less complete silence. Their minds for the most part are intent on their next shots. But the women — bless them — think of a thousand and one other things besides the little white ball and what they are going to hit it with when they finally reach it. It is at times like this that Sylvia can mention the mink coat or the cute little nightie or the stunning new dress that will put Myrtle into a tailspin.

Some wives will not play this game. So you have to lie a little, even before you get to the first tee. "Honey, how'd you like that silver-fox jacket you've been talking about? If we have a good day today and beat the Smiths, I may be able to pick it up for you."

You will then explain that beating the Smiths means more than money to you. Your wife will have that silver-fox jacket in her eyes while she listens to your game plan. She may even agree to mention the jacket to Myrtle, but *not* the fact that it is obtainable only by beating her and Charley.

Winning this game must mean something to you, however.

You can't go around buying furs or whatever for your wife every time you go out to play golf. Golf costs enough all by itself, so save this one for a very special occasion.

There is also reverse psychology to be mentioned here. You are going to play at golf-downmanship. You are playing a very important client and his wife. You want your client to win. So you must coach your wife a little differently.

Assuming your darling is a very good player, and Mary and John Walker, your client and his wife, are duffers, you must get your wife to agree to throw the game. This may not be easy. Good golfers look on any such jiggery-pokery with jaundiced eyes.

But if the loss of the game may mean a big contract, then you hit your wife with the offer of the silver fox. If it is a very large contract, indeed, you may even go so far as to promise her that new car she wants. This all depends on individual circumstance and must be carefully thought out before the first word is spoken.

The same rule goes for your boss, though not on such a grand scale. You could probably get your frau's assistance by buying her a new dress or even a hat. The boss, or the client, must win at all costs, even if it shrinks your pocketbook momentarily. You can always make up the difference with a big contract or a nice raise.

You cannot be too obvious about these matters. You and your wife must appear to be playing to the best of your ability. However, this is where that good-luck charm comes in. You leave it home, and you mention this fact to the boss, so that he will think you are out to beat him, at least.

Now, there are many bosses who like to bend an elbow during the golf game. For this purpose they will carry with them small flasks, usually of sterling silver if they are very well-to-do bosses, and will pause from time to time to sample their contents.

You will be offered the flask. This is an important moment. A chill wind is blowing, and you happen to enjoy a nip of the sauce, which will warm you up. It is all very tempting. Willpower counts highly here. You accept the flask with a big grin, say thanks, and put it to your lips — and your tongue to the opening. This last bit is most important. Be sure the tongue fits closely. Never cheat at a time like this. Your job may depend on it. You need a clear head, because you have a tough row to hoe ahead of you.

Only when the flask if firmly stoppered by your tongue do you tilt your head back and pretend to have a sip. You do not swallow any of the Canadian Club or the Napoleon brandy or the twenty-five-year-old Ambassador scotch that your boss can afford. Not a drop.

However, you pretend to do so.

You take the flask from your lips with a long-drawn sigh of approval and hand it back. Now you have an excuse to make a lousy shot or two. If your boss can drink you under the table, this is all to the good. He will be thinking he has put one over on you, and this is just as it should be, since he is your boss.

Maybe you even say that you never drink on the job, but this is a fun time, and so you pretend to have another swig when he offers it. He will chortle to himself, or maybe out loud, because he is the guy who pays your salary or sees to it that the organization pays it, which is much the same thing.

You realize what you are doing, don't you? You are flattering the boss, in a very subtle way. You are letting him think he is doing you one in the eye, which makes him think he is a very smart fellow. You must never let him realize that you are not actually drinking.

If you have a boss who is not drinking but only pretending to, this poses a problem. If neither of you is actually drinking, the boss, when he goes home or maybe even before, will find that the liquor in his flask is not diminishing, and this could be very embarrassing.

So you must watch him closely. If you believe that he is not drinking, then you're going to have to. I see no other way out of this dilemma except to go whole hog and really let the stuff trickle down your throat. Your boss has beaten you at the game.

But because he is the boss, you may be doing yourself a favor by getting sloshed. You will lose the game to him, which you intended doing anyhow, and you will have been made the patsy for his small bit of skullduggery. I approve of this only when the boss is not drinking himself.

Weigh the flask gently with your hand when he hands it to you. If it feels perceptibly lighter, you know at once that he is downing the sauce. If the flask weighs just as much as when he first drew it out, I'm afraid there's nothing to do but swallow.

I must mention one facet of this particular bit of golf-upmanship. Never let your fuddled state permit you to play better because you are feeling the drinks. This is very bad form. Some men I know play far better golf when they are three sheets to the wind than they do when they are stone-cold sober. It serves to relax them. If liquor affects you in this way, all you can do is resort to your willpower.

You must conquer yourself, and by this I mean you must force yourself to make poor shots. This takes a lot out of you, I know. But it's better to do that than to beat your boss and have him glowering at you all week long and wondering if it might not be better to eliminate your job and you at the same time.

I mention this drinking bit because golf is basically a sociable game. When men hit a little white ball on the green grass and sniff the fresh air, it parches their throats and gives them a thirst that connot be quenched in any other way than by bellying up to the bar at the clubhouse after the game. Liquor loosens tongues and adds a piquant flavor to a game that had been adjudged by certain critics to be that of lunatics. It makes everybody feel he is a jolly good fellow. You may even feel this way yourself about the man who has just beaten you so badly.

Tomorrow will be another day. Or so the bottom of your glass will say.

While on the subject of drinking, another good ploy to use, particularly if you're involved in an important match you are really anxious to win, is to suggest stopping for a drink and a bite of lunch after the first nine holes. The thing to do is to urge your opponent to have a couple of martinis while you stick to beer. If he's just thirsty and not hungry, all the better. Two martinis on a fairly empty stomach can often produce some interesting results on a golf course. Your opponent may begin to see two or three balls instead of one when he's ready to take a poke at his next tee shot.

If the guy isn't a drinker, then urge some food on him — maybe a couple of big hamburgers with onions and tomatoes — anything to make him feel stuffed and loggy afterward (while you just order a hot dog or a lean corned beef on rye and only eat half of the sandwich), so that he begins to lose his competitive edge.

No other game I know seems to call for a nip every other hole or even more often. A tennis player will fall flat on his face if asked to hit swiftly moving tennis balls when he is drinking at the end of every game. But a golfer can walk and stand up and perhaps even manage to hit the ball when a large amount of scotch, rye, brandy, or gin nestles warmly in his middle.

Of course, if the boss is downing those shots regularly as he steps off the greens after his final putt, you have nothing to worry about. Sober, you can take an extra putt or two, or hook a drive when occasion demands it, so that the boss will win. Or a very important client, which amounts to much the same thing.

You will be blind to his cheating, too.

If he says he got a six on a hole when you know damn well he took an eight, you will make yourself smile and congratulate him. This is very important. Your boss — or client — must be made to feel that he is king of the hill. Man, your very living, and maybe your new set of wheels, depends on it.

I have never been able to figure out why golf practically forces a man to lie so much. I guess it's because a lot of us play it in the rough where nobody is around to count our strokes. Three becomes two or even one, at times when we know we are safe from discovery.

Vanity. That must be it. Nobody wants to be thought a complete duffer. One always wants to make a good showing in front of his fellowman. And so your golfer will lie and cheat — after all, it's just a stroke or two, so what does it matter? — as he wends his way from tee to rough and sand trap and that patch of sumac behind the green.

If you have a playing partner who walks with you to the lie of your ball and stands there as you swing, you must be very circumspect in your stroke counting. This is a very definite must. You must never, ever, be caught subtracting from your stroke total, or you will get a very bad name among your golfing buddies. And we just can't have that!

Subtlety is the first rule you must memorize.

Only when you are positive that you are safe from observation do you nudge the ball with your foot, moving it to a better lie. This is extremely difficult on the fairways when you are out in full view of everybody, unless, of course, you are playing winter rules, which permit you to improve your lie in the fairway by nudging the ball with the clubhead. It becomes downright impossible on the greens.

The rough affords you the best chance of all. Here you may be hidden by trees or underbrush and can kick the ball with a toe without its being noticed. You really need only a few of these to better your otherwise honest score.

I mention all these tidbits because I am talking about playing golf with other people. Naturally, if you go around alone, you can cheat to your heart's content. Only you will ever know.

But never brag about the 75 you scored when you were playing alone, because the handicapper may hear about it, and if you boast about enough of these rounds, your handicap will be lowered. This is very bad, indeed, in certain cases.

Furthermore, your golf friends will want to play around with you, and if you begin to shoot over 100 time and again where there are witnesses to see it, your 75 scorecard will become extremely suspect.

Brag if you must. But do it with other friends, friends who do not play golf and don't know any golfers who know you. If you can find such friends, that is. Otherwise, you must keep your mouth shut. There just isn't any way out of this bind.

I have certain golf buddies who keep two scorecards. One they show publicly to their acquaintances. The other, which records their true score, they are wont to stare at very disconsolately in the privacy of their own kitchens, late at night and with a fifth martini in their grubby little paws.

Oh, you can cheat a little, and it may not affect your handicap or your relations with your golf pals. If you normally card 100, and you bring in a score of 95, nobody is going to faint dead away. It may even earn you a few words of praise and an encouraging clap on the shoulder. What you have done here is ignore only five strokes.

There was that whiff on the second fairway when you took your eye off the ball and that extra stroke in the sand trap on the third. They weren't so bad, were they? Of course not. You can hardly even remember them. You talk to yourself like this, and pretty soon you have forgotten them, even in your subconscious.

Now you consider the ball you knocked into the water at the eleventh. You replaced your ball, but you didn't count a stroke, which you should have. Big deal, you sneer. And then there were the two strokes you took in the rough, only one of which you marked down. So what? It was the second shot you hit out of the rough that really counted, because it was a beauty. Ignore the first one.

And that stupid shank you hit when two-ironing your way toward the seventeenth green was just one of those practice shots you take from time to time. It shouldn't be counted against you that the ball got in the way of your club, should it? Certainly not!

Five little mistakes. Easy to dismiss from your mind; easy to say they don't matter. But they make a difference in your score.

So you just ignore those mistakes, nor does your conscience bother you. It is a mental game we golfers play, something like self-hypnosis. In my opinion we do this because golf is a game you play by yourself, no matter how many partners you have going around the course with you. It is so easy to lie and cheat a little. Why? Because you are lying to yourself.

And that is very different from lying to your fellowman, though this is also involved, eventually. You will find that you will be having a mild conversation with yourself, like so:

"I scored a five on this par-four hole," you mutter to yourself.

Your conscience digs you with, "Now wait a minute. There was that stroke in the rough, following which you hit that great seven-iron shot onto the lip of the green. You haven't marked it down."

"Ah, who's to know? Charley didn't see it."

"You saw it!"

"Yes, but I'm the one who says it doesn't count."

You write down a five.

This harms nobody, really, if you aren't playing for money. Every man alive has lied to himself at one time or another. So you lie to yourself at golf.

You aren't walking up to Charley and telling him you scored a five. You just mark it down on the scorecard that you are keeping for your own amusement. Of course, Charley will ask you what you shot, and you will show him your scorecard.

What this means is: This is the way you *think* you shot that hole. It's the way you play, in other words. If Charley doesn't care for the way you score your own game, that's his tough luck, unless Charley actually saw you take that extra shot in the rough, which you haven't put down. This will make a difference. There are some sticklers who will enumerate out loud the number of shots you took, telling you about each one in detail. Shun such spoilsports.

By and large, however, you will be off by yourself in the rough when you make the flub. Charley will be walking toward his own ball, or ought to be. It is always best to cheat when you know that Charley is off in another corner of the rough, having his own problems. The guy can't be watching you and hunting for his own ball at the same time, can he?

On putting greens, however, it is difficult to cheat. First, because everybody is staring right at you. The ball is right there, a round white pellet on green grass, and everyone can see you miss those three putts because the sun is shining and they all have twenty-twenty vision. So you admit your mistakes at putting. What the hell else can you do?

Still, sometimes you can concede putts to yourself (if your opponents will let you get away with it). Say, a putt of from four inches inward to the cup. Every golf player makes those easy ones, doesn't he? No, but you ignore this. You pick your ball up with an air of saying a putt like that is beneath your dignity. Or you casually one-hand the putt toward the cup indicating your opinion that it's an automatic "gimme." Even if the ball missed, your careless one-handed poke shows your opponent you figure he conceded the shot anyway.

If your fellow players scream about it, as they have been known to do, you must putt. There's no way out of that one. None.

A note about golf etiquette when on the greens: If your ball is lying in the path of another ball, you courteously lift it off the green and mark its position with a flat marker.

This marker can be individualized with your initials; it can be gold or sterling silver or just plain chrome. The idea is that the fellow farthest from the hole putts first and your ball may lie between his ball and the hole, thus constituting a hazard that may be removed.

Sometimes you can conveniently forget the position of your ball and drop the ball a little closer to the cup as you lift your marker to take your own putt, all in one deft movement. This may or may not help, because you really can't drop your ball so far from its original lie that nobody will notice. All these little details must be performed with extreme subtlety.

Of course, you can always kick your ball closer to the cup, pretending to stumble, but I don't recommend this to be done more than once in any eighteen holes. Golfers have been shot for less. It helps if you have been drinking, for then you'll have some sort of excuse. Otherwise, you have none at all.

Always remember, whether you are playing a two-ball or a four-ball game, that your opponents are reasonably intelligent people. Never insult that intelligence. They will resent it, and you, too.

Better to lose the game than have that happen!

On Diegeling
Bernard Darwin

I DIEGEL, thou diegelest, he or she diegels, we all diegel or are about to diegel; and I trust that no golfer needs telling that the verb which I am conjugating signifies to try to imitate the putting methods of the hero, on the American side, of the Ryder Cup match.

Leo Diegel did not win the Championship. If he had we should all have had cricks in our backs for the rest of our lives. Even as it is, when it has been published far and wide that for one fatal round his putting forsook him, I am sure that many backs have been broken and elbows crooked to the point of agony in the attempt to get the ball into the hole as he does. Not, of course, that these thousands of sincere flatterers all over the country will admit what they are doing. They will scoff at my statement should they chance to read it, and then they will sneak away to that little corner of the lawn screened by the laurel bushes, or to that spare bedroom floor over the kitchen, knowing that the cook will not understand all that rolling and tapping over her head, or that, at any rate, she will not tell tales in the drawing room if she does.

I will not myself be guilty of any such shiftiness. I will confess that I have been evicted from room after room in the house while openly and unashamedly diegeling. So far I have met with no conspicuous success, but then the Master himself is said to have taken a year and a half to perfect his method, and I have been at it for only a few days. Moreover, I am hampered by the fact that I do not possess a square yard either of floor or garden which is reasonably true; the ball regularly misses the hole when it ought, were there any justice in the world, to have gone in, and, just as regularly, it hits the table leg when it ought to have missed it. This leaves the student in a state of painful uncertainty as to how he is getting on. I have not felt my progress sufficient to justify diegeling in a real game on a real green. The other day, in an essentially friendly match, being three up at the fourth hole I announced my intention of doing so, but my courage failed me. First of all I thought that in the approach putt I had better lay the ball dead in the ordinary manner; and I did lay it dead, but when it was dead I utterly failed to indiegel it. Still I have a year and twenty-four weeks left.

I have assumed that everyone knows in what the great man's method consists. Many writers have described it and photographers depicted it. Still there may be some whom the knowledge has passed by; so perhaps I had better give a brief recipe. You take a putter, not outrageously upright in the lie, with a reasonably long shaft. You hold it at the very top of the grip with the left hand well under. You stand square to the line of the putt, the feet spread rather wide apart. A friend of mine, an instructor of innocent boyhood who ought to know better, suggests that the stance should be called the spread-eagle stance. You next crook the elbows, particularly the left elbow, till you feel that something will break if you crook them any more. You drop the nose — not the club's but your own — lower and lower, till the top of the putter shaft lightly brushes the stomach. Then with wrists perfectly rigid you take the club back a short way: you give the ball a stiff little push, apparently with the right hand, and in it goes.

I have guarded myself by saying "apparently with the right hand" because learned persons have argued in my presence, at almost excessive length, whether the motive power comes in fact from the player's shoulders or from his feet. I am sure I don't know which is right, but I also feel sure that for the elementary student it is essential to remember that the wrists are stiff. It is so particularly because the method has been described as a pendulum method, and to many people the word pendulum conveys the swinging of the club to and fro with flexible wrists. It was in that sense that Mr. Horace Hutchinson used the word in the beloved old *Badminton,* friend of my youth, when he wrote: "The clubhead will be swinging something after the manner of a pendulum, and if the golfer gets the hanging arrangements of this pendulum correct, it cannot very well swing out of the true line." Mr. Hutchinson's putter did not swing out of the true line. With what pitiful envy, what smoldering fury have I watched him pendulum-ing the ball into the hole on those curly greens at Forest Row! But, though he crooked his elbow to some extent, he kept an insolently free wrist. To putt thus is to have genius, but it is not to diegel and I am writing about diegeling.

We all laugh at our friends and sometimes even pretend to laugh at ourselves for imitating the styles of the eminent. Yet there is this to be said, that if we are going to do it at all, the imitation of a putting style gives much the greater satisfaction. When we attempt a champion's driving swing, nobody by any chance recognizes our rendering of it. No total stranger will ever come up to us and say, "I beg your pardon, my dear sir, but I cannot help noticing that you are copying the effortless grace and free pivot of Mr. John Ball. I hope you are making good progress." On the other hand, we have only to contort ourselves for a single minute in front of the clubhouse windows and a dozen kind friends will shout "How is the diegeling getting on?" The ball may not go into the hole, but recognition is something. It encourages us to go on and, by the way, there comes to me, as I write, a most encouraging sound. It is a pleasantly purring sound as of one mowing. The gardener has been told to mow a patch for me and afterwards to roll it. Then I shall really be able to get down to it.

Excerpt from
Golf the Loneliest Game
Roland Wild

Ivy Sludge, a nice girl in many ways, became a golfer. Married to Art Sludge for twelve years and mother of two, Ivy was a good housekeeper, gardener, churchgoer, and wife. She had only one weakness — bridge on Tuesdays — and her marriage seemed destined to be serene through the future, with the minimum of connubial spats and crises. Art was a weekend golfer.

Ivy's life at weekends was dictated by the routine of Arthur retiring early on Friday nights and off to the course at seven the following morning. He returned at two in the afternoon, and was usually in good shape for the Saturday night entertaining. The same procedure occupied Sunday. It was a routine familiar to tens of thousands of couples. Ivy was a golf widow, but could live with it. She even listened with patience to Art's hole-by-hole analysis of his rounds as they dressed for the party on Saturday nights, making appropriate sounds at appropriate moments, though if ever she were asked to give even a sketchy precis of the drama, she would have failed miserably. The partnership was therefore almost banal in its normalcy.

There is no known record of how Ivy was enticed away from her God-fearing domesticity. It may have been the sight one day of lady golfers on a sunny fairway, clad in gay plumage and obviously contented. It may have been the sound of the click of a driver against the ball on the tee. It may have been merely the spectacle, on a fall evening of a flag flying bravely on a sun-dappled green, empty and inviting. These things happen.

Whatever the cause, the urge came to Ivy Sludge, and like undetected criminals, she had to make a confession. She told a golfing neighbor she was "considering" taking up golf. Now it is well known that addicts must recruit other victims. The pot smoker needs company. The lush likes to clink glasses with other slaves of the grape. The golfer wants to seduce the world.

The neighbor thrust a club into Ivy's hands, adjusted her grip, told her to keep her head down and swing, and said, with the unctiousness of all who proselytize, "Why, Ivy, you'd be a natural . . ." Such is the insidious missionary work of the golfer.

Ivy went to a driving range in secret, and took a lesson. She played a few rounds on a public course, and, cheating a little on the household bills and raiding the savings that were to buy a fall outfit, bought a starter set of clubs, which she kept at her neighbor's home. But the day came when she had to tell Art. She chose a Saturday night when she had listened to his usual dissertation on how Cruel Fate, and the infamy of the course superintendent, had robbed him of the last, dollar-winning putt. "Art," she said quietly, "I'd like to take up golf."

If a chill tightened his throat muscles, Art showed no sign. Stiff upper lip. As casual as if his wife had said she thought the drapes were getting shabby. "Yes, dear," said Art. "Good idea . . ." He did not know, in that pregnant moment, that he had reached a watershed in his progress through life. Poor clot, he did not know that henceforth his beloved home would become a shelter to be used between rounds of golf.

So Ivy, instead of being a golf widow, became a golfing wife. She played bridge in the evenings now, for Tuesday was ladies' day on the course. She still went to church on Sundays, for there was no play for her at weekends. The garden, which had always given evidence of her loving care and long hours of work, began to show signs of untidiness. The local librarian, meeting her in the street, remarked that Mrs. Sludge seemed to be reading less. (Ivy agreed, concealing the fact that she now read even more — the biography of Sam Snead, the golf magazines, and a booklet "You too can putt like Casper.") She bought a book called "Cooking with a Can Opener," and on Mother's Day, her daughters bought her a golf glove and she told them, "No mother has more intelligent kids." The day came when Ivy joined her husband's golf club, and she told him, "Art, I'd like to play with you in the club's Mixed Two-Ball."

A man faces many turning points in his life. He has to leave his favorite town for a better job, he grows older, he moves to a more expensive home for reasons of status. Or his wife wants to play with him in a Mixed Two-Ball. "Yes, dear," said Art.

Now the Sludges were, it would seem, closer than ever in their interests and outlook on Life. This was Togetherness. Side by side, they would now face the challenge of a golf course. But at first sight, the results were not completely propitious.

Art Sludge, having accepted nemesis, seemed to welcome the plan with enthusiasm. He began giving hints to his wife, urged the necessity of an hour's putting practice a day, a systematic routine on the practice ground, a study of the course and a plan of strategy.

Though accepting her husband as obvious leader of their team, Ivy found herself wondering how she got into this. She betrayed small signs of impatience at his advice on her swing. Should husbands and wives play golf together? "Well," said her neighbor, "it's usually done in the Mixed Two-Ball . . ."

The great day came. The first tee was alive with the golfing couples, and Ivy and Art were congratulated on their first appearance together. Art drove from the first tee, a screamer down the middle, on the 355 yard hole.

"Now, Ivy," he said as they walked down the fairway, "just try and keep it in play. Carefully, just *towards* the green . . ."

A small fire of resentment smouldered in Ivy's breast. She topped the ball and it ran 75 yards. "Fine," Art said, and put his approach on the green. They putted out for a bogey five.

It would be too injurious to the nerves to relate in detail the course of this day's experiment in marital co-operation. It should be enough to say that before every stroke, Ivy was given a brief, one-sentence homily that stressed the need for

194

extreme caution and the unambitious performance. Driving at long holes, she must "just try to get the ball off the tee." On the fairway, she should "just keep out of the rough, at all costs." Approaching the green, "anywhere on the putting surface — anywhere. Don't try anything fancy."

Ivy burned. More than anything else in the world, she wanted to glare at the ball, twist herself up like a spring, and let fly. She had done so once at the ninth and hit the green in two to score a par. She had often hit the stick when she played boldly with an approach. She had sunk 20-foot putts when she went for the back of the hole. But now Art said, "Just lag it up there, Ivy. Anywhere within two feet, not too far . . ."

Yet oddly enough, the Sludge team made the turn in six over par, mainly because Art was sinking long putts, and they learned they were faring as well as anybody in the tournament. "Just keep going like this, Ivy," said Art. "Just take it easy . . ."

But there are limits to the restraint of every woman, even a golfing wife. Ivy was in torment, facing the fact that marriage was one thing, but a golf partnership was something else.

They edged their way over the back nine, Ivy biting her lip with frustration but forcing herself to obey her master's constant call for caution. They were ten over par at the 16th. Art made a quick canvass of the state of the game from other players, and learnt that the Martins, in the foursome ahead, were nine over par.

"Critical holes ahead, Ivy," said Art.

Something snapped in Ivy's brain. Years of restraint fell from her shoulders like a discarded cloak. The veneer of civilization was thin after all. This was primitive woman, fired by an emotion more powerful than jealousy. Ivy felt her status as a female was impugned.

Art drove on the 17th — 365 yards. The shot was topped, and short, perhaps because of Art's anxiety. He was morose and silent as they walked up the fairway. They saw that the Martins were on the green in two, now putting out. There would be a par four on their card, still nine over par.

"That does it," Art said at last. "Sorry about that. We go for second place, Ivy. Just get the ball going up the fairway, I'll put it on, and we get our five."

But it was fortunate that he did not see the glint in Ivy's eyes at this moment, the color that diffused the back of her neck. She hurried to the ball, pulling her two-wood from the bag. One preliminary swing, deceptively gentle, and she laid the clubhead behind the ball. One glance at the now-empty green ahead, and she glared at the ball, tightened up her left side, her left arm. Out the window went all the rules of slow back, smoothly through the ball and "don't try to hit the cover off." Ivy Sludge wound herself into a tight knot, every muscle in use, and unleashed, connecting with a click of faultless timing. She pushed through her right hand and her weight shifted to her left foot as the hands came through and the clubhead reached and gently touched the small of her back. She did not look up for a split second. She did not have to. Her husband's gasp of "Ivy!" told her all.

The ball hit the slope in front of the green, kicked right and headed to the big trap. A slight rise diverted its path, guided it, urged it onto the green. It had momentum still, imparted surely by the raw savagery of Ivy's follow-through if not by her indomitable will. Then the ball stopped — four feet from the pin.

After his cry of anguish, Art was silent. He did not look at his rebellious spouse. Her lips were pursed, but her eyes were brimming. Art putted out for the par, and they were still silent as they walked to the 18th tee. But then it was Ivy who spoke the obvious.

"Ten over," she said crisply. "Martins nine over. We need a bird."

She teed up. She had never been so happy. Life seemed to have reversed itself, but more than that, she knew that she herself had changed. There was a new Ivy Sludge on the golf course.

No longer did she conjure up the rage that had put power into her last shot. She wanted this thing over with, on this last long hole, par five, where they must get a four. The glare at the ball was there again, and the coil of the spring as she took the club back until the muscles on the left side were taut. She had no doubt about this. The same click on the screws of the clubhead, and the ball was away, on a telegraph-line course 190 yards up the centre.

"Great, Ivy!" said Art. But there was something in her husband's voice she had never heard before.

A man can break down at times under great emotion. There are some things that corrode his spirit. Art proved himself to be a man too weak to withstand the high tension of that moment. The breaking point had come.

His two-wood shot was a quick-fire explosion of muscular disaster. From the moment he took the clubhead away from the ball — but faster than the speed of light! — to the instant when his poor body crumpled into ruin and the ball was half-contacted and the turf flew, there was nothing that was right about Art Sludge's critical bid to redeem himself and, perhaps, save his marriage. The shot was an exhibition of unco-ordination, the type about which men say, "Your swing reminds me of my grandmother trying to dislodge the cat from under the bed with a broom" — such is the splendid imagery of golfers.

No sound escaped the white lips of Art Sludge in his darkest hour. Ivy felt no need for comment, walking up the fairway, thinking. The ball was now some 300 yards from the tee, and the hole was 490 yards. She saw the Martins on the green, and saw the short putt missed, the inevitable six. The enemy had finished ten over par. This shot of hers must lie dead by the pin for a birdie and the tournament.

There was never a woman so calm and confident. She noted there was a little gallery round the green, and she was glad. She knew the ball would roll right-handed to the pin if she hit the bank on the left, and she had picked her spot. The lie was good, and God was in His heaven. Ivy swung, connected, looked up languidly, and was unsurprised as she picked up the glorious flight of the ball, satisfactorily to the left flank, kicking right, rolling on and finishing two feet short of the pin. The gallery's roar came to her. She was already walking towards them. Everything was according to plan.

Art sank the putt, and was able to beat a way through the crowd and kissed her. She was pleased with him now, and somewhere in her heart there was room for pity. She revelled in the rest of that evening of triumph — the congratulations, the prize-giving, the drinks that made her a little tipsy, the slow and agonizing recovery by Art, from humiliation to acceptance of Life. As a married couple, they were never quite the same again, but they were happy. You can't blame the game of golf for that. They even played Mixed Two-Balls again.

There is no moral at all in this fantasy. But there is perhaps the footnote that golfers, both male and female, have read it and said, "There's a lot more in this game than just hitting the ball . . ."

And this really doesn't take us any further, does it?

Perils of the First Tee
Michael Green

> "The driving is like the driving of Jehu, the son of Numshi; for he driveth furiously."
>
> The Book of Kings

Like all Coarse Sport, golf is best enjoyed in fantasy. No one believes that a bald-headed wreck in the seventh team of some obscure London old boys' rugby club really enjoys spending his Saturday afternoons limping around a swamp. What he really enjoys is slaking his thirst after the game and talking about great matches of the past from the comfort of an armchair.

So it with Coarse Golf. The past games take on an aura of

pleasure and one forgets the time when you tried to snap your putter, the pitiful feeling of futility about it all. All that is remembered is the shot when everything went right. The conviction grows that the two holes you did decently were your normal game, and the other sixteen just an unfortunate aberration.

I always think that the Coarse Golfers who get most out of the game are those who have been compelled to give it up, or those who are always going to have a round next week.

The height of fantasy golf is Postal Golf. This was invented by Askew and myself for use during the depths of winter but some people might prefer it to the ordinary game even when the weather is good.

The rules are simple. A course is selected and each player has a card. The player who has the honour goes into his garden and drives a plastic practice ball, and on the basis of the stroke makes an estimation of what would have happened to the ball.

He then sends a postcard to his opponent, saying for instance, HAVE JUST DRIVEN TWO HUNDRED YARDS BUT SLICED INTO ROUGH GRASS ON FIRST.

His opponent replies, and then both go on to their irons. Putting is done in the dining-room, using a tumbler on the carpet.

This harmless and amusing game was, however, wrecked by the sheer egotism of Askew. While I honestly recorded each slice, hook or dunch (the penalty for slicing or hooking was the compulsory use of an eight iron for the next shot, with subsequent loss of distance), Askew's overweening sense of his own importance led him to make fantastic claims.

It all began with a postcard reading: HAVE JUST HIT THREE HUNDRED YARD DRIVE STRAIGHT DOWN MIDDLE.

When I replied: HAVE LANDED TWO FEET FROM PIN WITH THREE IRON, Askew started claiming a succession of birdies, first lulling me into a false sense of security by admitting that he was in a bunker and then claiming to have sunk the bunker shot.

We finally abandoned the game when, after I had clearly

won a hole, he sent a postcard: YOU ARE PENALISED TWO STROKES BECAUSE YOUR BALL STRUCK MINE ON THE GREEN.

We did not talk to each other for some time after that but I still think the game could be successful, provided it is not played between two psychopaths.

But however much the Coarse Golfer likes to indulge in fantasy the time must come when he has to face up to reality and march out on to the course.

The initial problem that will confront him is the first tee.

Driving from the first tee can be an ordeal even for a good player. For a Coarse Golfer it is a terrifying experience. This is partly because one's efforts are usually watched by a large gallery impatiently swishing their drivers.

It is some comfort, though, that those who do the most swishing while waiting invariably drive the worst (Law Six of Coarse Golf: "He who swisheth most driveth least").

When one is called to take the stroke, the arms, never fully under control, become like ramrods, the clubhead is seized with a life of its own, the hips lock and the wrists have all the strength and flexibility of a couple of overripe bananas.

In my own case, whenever I drive from the first tee, my left foot always twitches off the ground on the backswing, so I am left standing on one leg. This is quite uncontrollable, and short of spiking the foot to the floor I don't know what can be done.

The reason for this sort of thing is not only the fear of appearing a fool in front of the gallery, but also the First Tee Syndrome, an unreasonable fear that the patient will be thrown off golf courses. It can be very persistent and while it can be alleviated cannot be cured completely.

The fear is not entirely without basis as far as I am concerned. I was ejected from a golf course after my very first stroke in the game.

I had been hacking around secretly for some time with my old wooden-shafted clubs, when a friend suggested that the moment had come for me to spread my wings on a real course and he unwisely arranged to play the next Sunday morning.

200

There was a long queue behind us as I teed up in front of the clubhouse. Completely unnerved I took my courage in both hands, decided to cut out the address and struck savagely at the ball with the laudable intention of getting away from this lot as soon as possible.

A huge clod of earth vanished down the fairway and behind me came a low moan.

Again I swung desperately and this time came a satisfying click and a small dot hurtled towards the hole. It was the clubhead followed by what seemed a hundred yards of twine.

At the same time a man standing about fifty yards away gave a great shout, flung up his arms and fell senseless to the ground. I started to move towards the stricken man when my partner, who was a solicitor, stepped forward and put a hand on my arm.

"Say nothing, old chap," he muttered. "You are not obliged to make a statement and don't apologise in case that should be construed as an admission of liability."

"I'm not making a statement," I explained. "I want to retrieve the ball. It's the only new one I've got."

There was, however, no sign of the ball except for the words "Dunlop 65" imprinted upside down on the forehead of the club bore, who was being helped into the bar by his friends.

My attempts at apoligising without admitting liability ("I deeply regret the injury you appear to have suffered from some unknown person") merely resulted in a torrent of abuse and I returned to the tee. It seemed the only thing to do.

As I swung for my third attempt there was no gallery. The waiting players had all retreated to the verandah, and some to the bar, where their faces were pressed against the window. But before I could strike the ball the club secretary came running across to the tee.

"Leave the course immediately, sir," he bellowed. "The steward will refund your green fee."

"I'm sorry," I muttered humbly. "I didn't mean to hit that man on the head. It was an accident."

"I don't know what the devil you're talking about," said the secretary, "but I will not tolerate people who *wheel their trolleys over the tee.*"

I mention this to show that there are more hazards on a first tee than hitting the ball in all directions. Perhaps one day golf clubs will see reason and provide a first tee which is heavily boxed in with soundproof material, so that all spectators will see is the ball trickling feebly forth.

However, there is nothing that the Coarse Golfer can do but take the tee as he finds it, even though it will probably be different when he leaves it, having gained several deep indentations.

One of the essential precautions to take upon driving from the first tee is to make sure that you are on the right course and playing with the correct opponents.

This may seem rather obvious but I give the advice following an unfortunate incident last year when a complete stranger turned up for a meeting of the Warreners' Golf Society at West Herts and said he was a friend of Peter Brown who had asked him to play in his place.

"How thoughtful," we said, "good old Pete."

The stranger played a superb morning round, which looked as if it would win the cup.

At lunch we asked what was wrong with Peter.

"His old trouble," said the stranger. "Still, you've got to expect it at his age. We're lucky to have him still with us."

Since Peter was a virile twenty-two-year-old we pressed for further information as a result of which it turned out the stranger was a friend of a totally different Peter Brown and he was supposed to be playing on the *East* Herts course. He left hurriedly in a taxi and we never saw him again.

When driving from the first tee, a Coarse Golfer should also make absolutely sure that he is playing to the correct green. I have rarely known anything as embarrasing as when myself and a friend found after making our drives that we had played to the eighteenth. Fortunately our drives were so inaccurate that we were able to use them for the proper hole.

A Coarse Golfer would probably prefer to use an iron off

the first tee. He certainly ought to use an iron off every tee. Any Coarse Golfer could knock ten strokes off his game by taking a six iron off every tee and trying to hit the ball straight for a hundred yards, instead of swishing wildly with a driver and sending the ball underneath his trolley.

However, it is not considered good golf to use an iron on a long hole, although I suspect this idea is spread by the club manufacturers. Therefore, some sort of excuse must be made. Here are some suggestions:

"They say Palmer never touches his woods now."

"The pro said he hadn't sold a wood for six months."

"An old golfer told me I had the finest iron action he had ever seen."

"You don't need woods on a piddling little course like this."

"The doctor took one look at my wrist and said: 'No more woods until that tendon's cleared up'."

"Funny, you won't believe this, but I meant to play a wood and absent-mindedly took out a three iron." (To be used after the stroke only.)

Feeble though these excuses are, they at least give some sort of protection.

Strange how using an iron for a long hole is considered such a sin in golf, and it is typical of how the game upsets normal civilised values.

The biggest crook in town can be popular in a golf club provided he pays for his round of drinks. But if Dr. Barnardo himself used an iron off the first tee people would start whispering in corners of the bar, "He's not a bad chap but there's something sinister about him. Never uses his woods y'know."

A friend, Mr. Tony Owen, of Ealing, tells me he ruined his health through taking a three iron off the first tee at St. Andrews.

"It was the silence that got me down," he said. "Nobody said a word. But ever since then I've slept badly. I wake up after a nightmare, and I can still see them all staring at me, just standing there *staring*."

In all this I have made no reference to caddies. A Coarse

Golfer will not normally have any connection with these people.

I can say with perfect honesty that I had been playing golf for fifteen years before I saw my first caddy.

This event took place at Royal Wimbledon when I was playing in a society match. As my partner and I stood on the first tee I noticed a crowd of men eyeing us in a curious way and I whispered to my partner, "Who are those shabbily dressed people crowding round the tee? Shall I tell them the Labour Exchange is further down the road?"

"Those are caddies," replied my partner stiffly. "Haven't you ever seen one before?"

It then came to me that I hadn't — they don't have them in the sort of places where I usually play golf — and I favoured them with a good stare, which was returned with interest, rather insolently I thought.

As luck would have it, my drive was slightly sliced. Not to put too fine a point on it, it vanished off the toe of the club with a low humming sound and scattered the caddies in all directions. No one spoke. They all reassembled as if nothing had happened and simply looked at me with rheumy eyes.

It was one of the most terrifying experiences of my life (even worse than when our television set caught fire), and I made up my mind there and then that I would never have the courage to employ a caddy, even if I had the money.

But to return to the tee itself. It is in the interests of all Coarse Golfers that they should leave the first tee as quickly and with as little fuss as possible.*

For this reason no attempt should be made to interfere with an opponent's play on the first hole, for example by using the Sweets of Damocles. Both players should concentrate on getting as far away from the clubhouse as possible, as quickly as possible.

Only then may battle start in earnest.

*In an effort to do this Askew once threw the ball off the tee.

Excerpt from **Wide Open**
Dan Jenkins

Thus, one got used to an Open and knew exactly what to expect of it. Every year in mid-June didn't we read stories something like the following:

Open Field May Revolt

OYSTER BISQUE, N.Y. — A glittering field on the eve of the National Open golf championship agreed today that there is so much exotic plantlife bordering the narrow fairways of historic old Baltus Oak Country Club that only a malnourished hippie could walk down the middle of them without snagging his britches.

During today's final warm-up round two foursomes actually got lost in the foliage of the back nine holes and wound up at a Southampton lawn party.

Gardner Dickinson, chairman of the PGA tournament players committee, said he was withdrawing from the championship because he had never learned how to hit golf shots out of waist-high asparagus.

The irate Dickinson said, "If this kind of thing doesn't stop we might not have a spot on the tour for the USGA next year. The sponsors may have the tents, but the players have the dog acts."

Unknown Leads Open

OYSTER BISQUE, N.Y. — Jesse Ray Rives, an unheralded driving range pro from Hoot, Utah, grabbed the opening round lead in the National Open here today with a sizzling even-par 70 on historic old Baltus Oak, the course where Bobby Jones first wore knickers.

Rives, who wore coveralls and a straw hat with a band on it which said "Root for Hoot," birdied the first nine holes and blew out a full row of lights on the IBM scoreboard, and although he bogeyed the entire back side for a 44, his score held up against an array of glamorous challengers.

Incredibly, Rives took only six putts for the round, tying a record set by Bob Rosburg. He tied another Open record held by Don January when he holed out eight sand wedges.

Rives, 25, said he would feel better about his chances if he weren't so lonely so far away from home. "I wisht my uncle Clyde and my pet bobcat was here," he said.

Open Jolted By Second Mystery Man

OYSTER BISQUE, N.Y. — R.J. (Bo) Mackey, an obscure pro at a putt-putt course in Clump, Calif., seized the halfway lead in the National Open here tonight when he added a 65 to his first-round 81 for a 36-hole total of 146, only 6 over par on historic old Baltus Oak, the course where Walter Hagen had his first hangover.

Having teed off at 5:14 A.M., Mackey was one of the day's early finishers at 4 o'clock in the afternoon as the field of 150 moved along briskly despite the 101-degree heat. Sweating out his lead in Baltus Oak's non-air-conditioned clubhouse, Mackey had some anxious moments until shortly before midnight when defending champion Jack Nicklaus came in.

Nicklaus had threatened to overtake Mackey until the 17th hole. Jack finished with a horrendous 13 and then a 15 on the last green when his children persisted in clinging to his back when he swung the club. He failed not only to catch Mackey but to make the 36-hole cut.

"I'm tired of golf," Nicklaus said. "All I really want to do anymore is go to family reunions and take my kids to Astro-world."

First-round leader Jesse Ray Rives also failed to make the cut, largely because a lurking animal — believed by some to be a bobcat — swallowed his ball on the 10th fairway.

Mackey, who wore khakis and a tool dresser's helmet, confessed that he had received a lot of help in molding his game. He said he owed a lot to the crew on the B.W. Roberts No. 2 oil rig in Clump. They had encouraged him to leave town, he said. He also specifically singled out two men who had pieced together his compact swing: Ralph Tibitt, his ex-warden, and Roy Sangry, his parole officer.

Unknown Log Jam In Open

OYSTER BISQUE, N.Y. — Billy Tom Riddle, an assistant pro from Harper Valley, Tenn., playing in his first professional golf tournament, tied for the 54-hole lead in the National Open here today with four amateurs, all from the powerful University of Houston. Their score was 223, only 13 over par on historic old Baltus Oak, the course where Harry Vardon tripped on a dining room carpet.

Best known of the Houston collegians was Rex Zark, who has been the Western, Trans-Miss, Southern, North-South, Broadmoor, British and Idaho State amateur champion every year since the age of 9. The other talented members of the Texas team are Kermir Blank from Albany, N.Y., Babe Stimmett from Seattle, Wash., and Joel Wuthergrind from Worcester, Mass.

None of the leaders could rest easily, it appeared, for only 16 strokes off the pace, poised to make one of his patented stretch runs, was Arnold Palmer.

The championship was struck with an indelicate misfortune during Saturday's third round when R.J. (Bo) Mackey, the putt-putt pro, was disqualified on the first 9 holes of his round. A USGA spokesman said Mackey had been warned repeatedly since Thursday to refrain from making obscene gestures and comments to women in his gallery but that he had refused to heed the warning. "We had no other course of action to take," said T. Phillip Carter duPont Lawrence, a USGA vice-president. "This, after all, is the Open championship. Not Orlando."

Hogan Wins Unprecedented Ninth Open

OYSTER BISQUE, N.Y. — With the coveted National Open championship all but sewed up, Arnold Palmer caught his backswing in a flowering banyan today on historic old Baltus Oak, the course where Tommy Armour once bought lunch, and Ben Hogan, looking tanned and fit despite his 67 years, breezed past him to win an unprecedented ninth Open.

Palmer caught his swing in the tree at Baltus Oak's 17th hole and had to be rescued by a demolition team from the Corps of Engineers. Palmer was unable to complete the round and the tournament, and thus he will have to endure sectional qualifying again next year.

"It's pretty disheartening to know you can finish 10-10 and win, and then not even be able to play," said Palmer.

Hogan shot a flaming 67 in the final round for a 72-hole total of 301, only 21 over par. Hogan's round was the lowest since architect Robert Trent Jones had revamped Baltus Oak, placing a number of bunkers in the center of some tees and forcing carries of 280 yards or more over water.

There was a moment of pure drama at the final green after Hogan finished, flashing his familiar outgoing, quick-smiling expression. Hogan went over to Jones and shook his hand until the architect knelt down, uttering a bit of a whimper.

"I brought the monster to its knees," said Hogan.

Sam Snead, who mailed in his scores, again finished second.

None of the third-round leaders managed to finish. Billy Tom Riddle, tormented by the sight of his first gallery, picked up at the 3rd hole after striking his ball 21 times in a bunker. The entire University of Houston team, including Rex Zark, quit after 9 and mysteriously departed for West Lafayette, Ind., the site of next week's NCAA championships.

Palmer was one of several blowups as the Open pressure mounted late in the day.

Billy Casper needed only to play even bogey over the last 9 holes to tie Hogan, but he suffered a sneezing fit because of pesticides which had been sprayed on the fairways and shot an incoming 46. A man of great inner peace, however, Casper smiled and said, "Boy, it looks like the Lord got up on the wrong side of the bed today."

Miller Barber, who kept swallowing diet pills throughout the round, could have parred the 72nd hole for victory, but he hit a 5-iron an amazing 240 yards over the clubhouse and the massive marble statue on the veranda of T. Phillip Carter-Hughes Bentley McCarver duPont Lawrence, Sr. "Well, you get pretty revved up out there," said Barber.

Finally, Julius Boros, chewing on a weed and sipping a can of beer, nonchalantly tried to backhand 3 successive putts on the final green, missed them all, and lost by the same margin as Casper, 2 strokes.

As Hogan accepted the unprecedented ninth Open trophy in a moving ceremony at the putting green and in turn presented the USGA with his full set of clubs and his wife Valerie for the Golf House museum, some 30 players were still out on the course, completing the last 9 holes in the dark. Word circulated momentarily that one of them, Frank Clack, a driving range operator from Davenport Iowa, could tie Hogan with 2 birdies over the last 4 holes. Officials, however, dismissed the news as wild, malicious rumor.

In its only other action of the day the USGA announced that next year's Open had been awarded to the Upper Course at historic old Baltus Oak, the club where Jug McSpaden first wore sun glasses.

Goat Getting
Morie Morrison

Golfers might be said to fall into six separate emotional groups. Each group has its own weaknesses, and it is those weaknesses that unsportsmanlike "friends" study. They know that opponents who add special worries of their own to regular worries about their play will be easier to defeat.

(The author assumes, naturally, that readers will refrain from using this information to further their own selfish ends, except in cases of dire emergency.)

1. **The timid type:** Fearful of attempting unfamiliar tasks, afraid of failure, shuns competition.

2. **The irascible type:** Bitter about the success of others, complains of his hard luck, always wants another chance, is touchy.

3. **The aggressive type:** Frequently tries to cover inferiority, seldom has a planned attack, does things with a "grandstand" flourish, impulsive, somewhat emotional.

4. **The egocentric type:** Supremely confident because he doesn't realize how little he knows, likes to take bows for his good play, resentful of criticism that implies he is ignorant of the rules or customs.

5. **The perfectionist type:** Observes all the rules, intolerant of compromising standards, loves flattery, overreaches himself when complimented.

6. **The intense type:** Normally polite and considerate, prone to forget everyday golf courtesies and customs, oblivious of his golfing habits and traits that irritate others.

A golfer who likes to make wagers quickly spots the **timid** player who dreads failure and worries about competition. To the money players, the shrinking opponent is a wonderful prospect to whom he can sell worry and fear, and he loves to do it with not-too-helpful suggestions. He has in his repertoire such remarks as, "Now don't let that fast, sloping green bother you. You can roll into the trap, but I don't think you will," or "The sand in the traps is heavy, but don't let it worry you."

A timid person is easily upset when an opponent says casually, "We've got to keep moving. That foursome back there is breathing down our necks." Being a conscientious soul, he naturally becomes flustered if he thinks he is spoiling the foursome's fun. As he hurries his shots, he makes more than his normal quota of errors.

A sensitive player will fall apart completely when, after making a poor shot, his opponent gives him a look of pity. If a remark accompanies the scornful glance, such as "For gosh sakes, Harry, I don't know why you ever took up this game," it will short-circuit the duffer's entire nervous system.

A timid player will sometimes accept a higher than normal bet because he doesn't want to appear "cheap." Having made it, he will then worry about the sizable amount until he loses it.

If an **irascible** golfer is a methodical person, he will become nervous whenever his rival mixes fast play with delays. For instance, taking an extra-long time to find a lost ball will make him very impatient. Opponents who desire to dip into his pocketbook sometimes pair him with a boisterous, non-methodical partner who will exasperate the excitable gentleman so much that his stroke count will soar to the stratosphere.

When in a deep trap, an irritable player is particularly vulnerable. Because he is over-aggressive, he can be encouraged to risk a shot for the pin instead of shooting safely for the green. As often as not, his anger or concern will cause him to swing so furiously that he will muff the shot.

When playing with women, especially his wife, an impatient player is prone to mutter, "Playing with women always ruins my game." He becomes very touchy when an opponent intimates that a lady's drive almost equals his. In trying to drive the next shot a mile, he will find himself slicing onto the wrong fairway.

A golfer who "blows his top" generally seeks a scapegoat for his troubles and frequently focuses his venom on a caddy. Unsportsmanlike rivals know this and sometimes instruct a "green" caddy to be in the wrong place at the right time. A caddy whose shadow waves back and forth across the cup has a particularly devastating effect on an irascible player.

An **aggressive** person is one who long ago acquired the habit of depending upon himself for results. Consequently he approaches every adverse situation with grim determination. If his opponent says casually, "That's a tough shot. Why don't you play it safe?" it is a distinct challenge to the aggressive player to do just the opposite. He is in the habit of thinking that he can lick any situation, and he is inclined to swing with more bravado than sense.

When a determined player is having trouble with his game, he will sometimes find himself listening to suggestions, such as "Keep your head down. You're rolling your shoulders and head before you hit the ball." This will cause him to hunch his shoulders, lower his head, and tighten the muscles of his upper body. The greens' committee will be able to trace him by the blazed trail of divots he digs.

Remarks associating the aggressive player's style with something uncomplimentary are usually disturbing to him. If a rival suggests, for instance, that he wiggles his "fanny" like a wornout fan dancer, the aggressive type will begin thinking more about the movement of his posterior than his swing. This, too, can soon wreck his game.

The aggressive player prides himself on his ability to "take it." He thinks of himself as being physically superior to everyone else with whom he plays. He can be persuaded to hurry his play when he should be relaxing between shots.

The **egocentric** golfer is a self-centered person who thinks well of himself. An opponent can easily take advantage of the egocentric's self-satisfaction by asking him for advice. The know-it-all egotist will be flattered by this and happy to pass out his words of wisdom. He will often forget his own game and devote much of his time to encouraging his opponent.

The egocentric longs secretly to be mistaken for a low-handicap expert. During warm-up swings on the first tee, he will swing with so much elegance that one would think he was putting on a gala performance. In his rendition of the style-beautiful, he forgets swinging fundamentals, if he knows them, and with adequate encouragement can be persuaded to continue showing onlookers how beautiful a golf swing can be. This can ruin his game before he starts playing.

When practicing, the egotistical golfer devotes ninety per cent of his time to hitting drives. He likes to be called a long hitter, and he forgets that seventy per cent of a good player's shots are of the short variety. He will accept bets on his ability to hit occasional long balls, and he will lose wagers because he goes to pieces on the greens.

Since he is interested in himself, he is naturally interested in his score. With encouragement, he will dwell on the bad luck he had on a previous hole, and this can easily cause him to try too hard to regain lost strokes. On the other hand, if he is playing over his head, he is easy prey for that old line of reasoning, "If you keep this up, you will break ninety." This will usually boost his score back to normal as he begins to think about how well he is playing.

When the **perfectionist** is disappointed because something didn't work out as he had planned it, he will explain in detail the reason for his failure. If an opponent chooses this opportune time to belittle the alibis and say, "Aw nuts, with that wild shot of yours, you're lucky to be on the golf course," the precise player will be exceedingly upset. Frustrated because his drive was imperfect, on his next shot he may try a tricky hook to give the boys something to talk about, and five to one he will be in further trouble.

Flattering remarks please a golfer who strives continually to perfect his game. He glories in the appreciation for his skill. If he has been getting a string of pars, flattery will encourage him to shoot for birdies. This set-up in his game can be disastrous, because it can cause him to worry unnecessarily about slight mistakes. For this reason, a player who has good luck on the first nine holes will often throw his game away on the second nine.

The perfectionist takes his game seriously and addresses his ball in a painstaking manner. He regards his careful deliberation over each shot as a sort of holy ritual. As in the case of the timid golfer, he is easily disturbed by such remarks as "Are we going to let that foresome behind us go through, or are we going to continue to hold up the whole course?" In his case, this is especially lethal and his game will suffer because it is geared to a snail's pace.

A perfectionist is easily embarrassed by any implication that there has been some slight misunderstanding about his knowledge of the rules, etiquette of the game, or sportsmanship. This is particularly true if he is trying to make a favorable impression. A flustered golfer who finds himself concentrating on being a gentleman will usually pay off at the eighteenth green.

The **intense** player usually yells at his ball after each shot and then turns to the other members of the foursome to explain what did or did not happen. A casual inquiry, such as "Why do you always have to explain each shot?" will make him realize he may have been acting foolishly, and this can easily affect his composure and confidence.

When an intense golfer hits a shot, he often starts walking immediately. In his deep concentration he often forgets that his companions also have to shoot. A pointed remark, such as "Now where are you going?" can have a bombshell effect. It will blast his composure and break his intense concentration on the game. As soon as this happens he is a goner, because his winning instinct has been deadened.

On a putting green an intense golfer can become so wrapped up in his own problems that he is honestly unaware he is bothering others while he continually moves around to study his ball's lie. Calling him a "Jingle Foot," a "Nervous Nellie," or any other uncomplimentary nickname will surprise him so much that he will become intensely apologetic and determined to make amends. This will unconsciously change his routine and perhaps upset his timing.

A golfer who strains for perfection on every shot frequently becomes so intense that he takes an unusually long time to address his ball. Such a player can be driven to distraction by an opponent who is obviously worried about completing the round before sunset.

Flattery is Expensive

As old King Henry IV of France remarked back in 1602 or thereabouts, "One catches more flies with a spoonful of honey than with twenty casks of vinegar." With a philosophy of this kind, His Royal Highness would have made a superlative weekend golfer. There is no more foolproof way to undermine a rival's game than to make syrupy and flattering remarks about his performance.

Compliments stir a person's ego, and in a game like golf they make a player acutely conscious of his swing. This self-consciousness is in itself dangerous, but a complimentary remark or two can flatter a player so much that he will be encouraged to go all out to show off his specialty and to share his pleasure with others by telling them how he does it. This establishes a one-way path to self-destruction, because as he performs, describes the reasons for his skill, and answers questions as to why he is so good, he becomes conscious of his different motions. The first thing he knows, he is slamming his shots out of bounds. As it is with a blonde cutie who flatters a butter-and-egg man into thinking he is Mr. Muscles, so it is on a golf course where an ordinary 90 shooter can be flattered into thinking he is another Lloyd Mangrum.

There are different type of flattery that work best on different types of individuals. For instance, the gregarious, full-of-personality golfer who enjoys talking continually is a sucker for any type of flattery that suggests he really knows his golf. He is secretly convinced that this is true, and when others imply that they, too, realize it, naturally he feels very good about it. Little does he know that in sharing his secret

215

he is paving the way to the scene of his downfall. In his case, praise takes his mind off the game. It makes him conscious of his movements, which can affect the smoothness of his swing. He is vulnerable for a well-timed gibe which may suddenly shatter his confidence.

The ex-athlete is also particularly susceptible to flattery. His early training taught him to believe that he can always perform best when the chips are down. The ex-hero doesn't need much encouragement or praise to be persuaded to accept unfair odds, swing too hard, or overestimate his skill. He thinks he is still an all-around athlete and forgets that he is older and less skillful than he was in the old days. Consequently he is often inclined to hit with hope instead of skill.

A long hitter can be thrown off his game if he is asked consistently how he does it. A sensitive man who wants to look like an expert can be flattered into swinging with so much nonchalance that he sacrifices precision for elegance.

Despite the fact that flattery is pleasant to hear, it is one of the most effective tools in a clever golfer's bag of tricks. A few complimentary remarks aimed at the ear of a week-end player can revive weaknesses he has almost forgotten. It takes very little to bring them to life again.

There are a thousand and one phrases, such as "You have powerful wrist action," or "You shift your weight beautifully," that are highly complimentary but may cause a man's game to blow sky-high. They are the statements a man always wants to hear, and a flatterer uses them for bait as the housewife uses cheese to attract a mouse to a trap. A golfer is heading for trouble when he gobbles the flattery his rival proffers, because actually it is merely another form of cheese.

Beware of Friendly Rivals

The average week-end golfer harbors a wee bit of legal larceny in his heart. One of the reasons he likes to play golf is that the game offers many opportunities for making small wagers. By winning more than his share of these bets he is able to prove to himself that he is really not such a dull, plodding sort after all.

The cagey money player figures that his opponent always regards the poor round yesterday as a matter of bad luck. Lack of skill had nothing to do with it. More often than not a golfer will forget the high score of yesterday and accept a bet based on what he hopes to shoot today. He never expects to three and four putt again, and he tees off determined to hit every shot down the middle and avoid the rough or traps.

Keeping all these human frailties in mind, the "friendly" week-end money player loves to offer a tantalizing assortment of bets. He does this, not because he is in need of money, but rather because money is a symbol of victory. As he sees it, the more money won from a variety of bets, the greater the victory. During the match he may be genuinely helpful to an opponent and make constructive suggestions or concede long putts; but regardless of courtesies or comradeship, he will always have his mind on the wagers he can win.

He may suggest bets on the first nine, the second nine, and the match. Perhaps he wants a syndicate at ten cents a hole, with double for birdies. He frequently recommends paying twenty-five cents to the man nearest the pin and fifty cents for the longest ball. He will offer a string of handicap bets that he knows his opponent will consider it folly to refuse. For instance, he may suggest three different wagers and offer to give his opponent one-up, two-up, and three-up for the eighteen-hole round, at fifty cents a bet. His rival will think automatically and gleefully of the highest three-up handicap and accept all three bets on that basis. This is questionable business judgment on the part of his opponent, because the money player will proceed to knock him off on the one-up bet, begin gaining ground on the two-up bet, and soon he will have his opponent fretting, and sometimes losing, the three-up wager.

The "friendly" golfer who likes to play for fair-sized stakes begins planning his strategy long before game time. He enjoys exploring ways and means of building up the amounts to be played for. In the locker room he may talk casually of sizable bets and how they help to make a good game. This is especially effective at country clubs where certain games of chance are available for members and guests. The money player uses this informal atmosphere to advantage while conditioning his prospects. Dice games such as "Ship, Captain, and Crew," "Bull," and "Liar's Dice" are typical of the sociable activities to which a player is introduced while he is being "prepared." The betting connected with these games gives a prospect the habit of winning and losing quarters and half dollars, something the prospect doesn't intend to do, he thinks, on the golf course. But it is surprising how quickly he responds to good fellowship, laughter, and a slap on the back as he shakes the dice, makes small wagers, and hears such remarks from his host as "You lucky stiff, I'll never beat you at golf today." In no time at all he may even be leaving the dice games momentarily to drop coins into a slot machine in the hope of winning a golf ball. At this point, the fact that it may cost two dollars to win a ninety-five cent ball is not even considered of importance. The poor fellow is too full of good will toward men to worry about crass things like pieces of silver. Little does he realize that already he is well on his way toward reaching for his folding money.

From the dice tables, the prospect is led to the luncheon table for further treatment. Here an extravagant luncheon is ordered, and amid heartwarming comradeship the prospect is encouraged to eat, drink, and be merry. And then the money player comes up with a wonderful idea.

"Aw hell," he says, "let's not pay for the lunch now. Let's settle the bill by adding it to what we play for this afternoon — just to make the game more interesting."

And so the "lamb" leaves the locker room full of good food, drink, and a commitment to play for an expensive luncheon tab. He has lost any conception of the value of a dollar, and he is willing to accept almost any further propositions these wonderful fellows have to offer. In fact, he may be so completely carried away that he will begin offering instead of asking for a few strokes handicap. Occasionally this preparation of the lamb for slaughter has a reverse twist. The confidence and relaxation acquired amid good fellowship are sometimes the underlying reasons for a neophyte's playing over his head and hitting balls 210 yards when a 180-yard slice is normal. In this case, the lamb becomes a lion, an unhappy turn of events for his opponent.

The path to the pro shop is another favorite location for the money player to ply his trade. From experience he may know that his opponent's game is erratic, and so he reasons that he must approach today's betting problem scientifically. He recognizes the fact that it is impossible to forecast his rival's score. Like many golfers, on some days his opponent is good and on others he is terrible. Therefore, the money player concentrates on making certain that his opponent's game will be as poor as possible on this particular day.

One imaginative money player relies on the hot-water theory of rejuvenation. Before leaving the locker room he holds his hands in a washbowl of piping-hot water until his opponent asks what he is doing. That is his cue to explain that the blood circulation in a middle-aged athlete (he always uses the terms "athlete" or "outdoorsman" while selling this idea) is a triffle sluggish and should be stimulated prior to a round of golf. He insists that the normal lack of stimulation reduces sensitivity in the fingertips and is one of the major causes of poor golf.

As he stands there with his hands in hot water, he says, "This type of therapy is the very latest wrinkle. I hear it is the secret of Ben Hogan's success, and Ben is scared silly that other big-name pros may find out about it."

The victim may not insist on steeping his own hands in scalding water, but often he does while his "friend" says, "Boy, this will make our hands sensitive. I promise you we will feel every shot."

Even if he is successful in keeping his hands out of hot water, as a result of all this propaganda the victim is so conscious of his hands that sooner or later he is more aware of his grip than he should be. This, in turn, causes him to

219

make unconscious alterations in his playing form.

The pro shop may also be used as a laboratory in which to practice the pseudo-science of golf psychology. And the professional himself can easily become the unwitting tool of an expert bet-maker. For example, every pro is anxious to explain the merits of his stock of clubs, because that is how he sells them. Therefore, if a bet-maker introduces his victim to the club's expert and suggests that the pro explain the advantages of a new club design, the latter will need no further encouragement. If the pro is the aggressive type, he will assure the victim that the clubs the latter now owns are largely responsible for his mediocre game.

Taking a club from the prospect's bag, he may say, "With that sand iron you have, you'll never get out of a trap consistently. You will have a tendency to dig too deep into the sand, and if you try a chip shot you'll fall short." Then he will describe the merits of a new sand wedge and go into detail about design and construction.

When a victim leaves a pro shop convinced that the clubs he is using are an assortment of antique bats, his confidence will naturally be affected a bit. Later on, when he tries a sand-trap shot, automatically he will think of the pro's warnings about his poorly designed club, and he will try to steer his swing, a poor maneuver at any time.

The pro is also eager and willing to talk about other equipment. A smooth bet-maker knows this and may suggest "helpfully" that his partner get some tips about the importance of a golf glove. This will lead to a discussion about the golf grip and make the victim conscious of his hand action. Even a conversation about the merits of long and short wooden tees can confuse a neophyte.

The first objective of a gambler is to upset his rival sufficiently to insure poor play on the first hole. A man who has bet more than he can afford is handicapped by a fear of losing. Finding it difficult enough to tee off before an audience under normal circumstances, a golfer may go to pieces noticeably in the face of added money worries. He may become so anxious to excel that he will swing his club as if the ball were a cork about to pop from a champagne bottle.

Before teeing off, the money player often uses other upsetting tricks to throw his victim's game out of whack. He may suggest trick exercises to ruin co-ordination, or fancy putting contests to destroy touch, and, if his opponent is especially vain and naive, he may ask the caddies to pay strict attention to his friend when he tees off because "this man's swing is a beautiful thing to watch."

A "friendly" money player often assumes a cloak of meekness to put over a point. By so doing, he throws his opponent off guard and makes him susceptible to later, and costly, suggestions. For instance, on the first tee he may pull his most winning smile and say, "Let's play for something small. I hate to see things get out of hand."

This sportsmanlike remark is received by the victim with enthusiasm. In fact, he is so relieved by the idea of small stakes that he overlooks the fact he should get a couple of strokes handicap.

After that, the tactics of the money player follow a regular pattern. On the fifth hole, if the money player is ahead, he assumes a surprised I'm-really-astonished-I-can-be-so-lucky look and insists that his opponent accept another bet so he can at least break even. If the money golfer is down, he will insist on another bet so *he* can break even. If the match is all square, he will say, "We're havin' a helluva match, aren't we? Whadda you say we make it more interesting?"

Also, at the proper moment, the money player may suddenly become helpful, or so the victim is led to believe. With an introductory remark, such as "I really don't care how I play today because I'm just out here for the fun," he throws his opponent completely off guard and makes himself a trusted companion. If his friend is having trouble, he offers what may at first seem to be good advice but really is sudden death to anyone who accepts it and acts upon it.

For example, the money player may be able to determine just why it is his victim has a tendency to slice. He thereupon offers a suggestion designed to make the fault even worse. If the victim is cutting across the ball, he tries to encourage an even deeper cut.

Flattery and logic are two of the basic tools in the money player's standard kit.

"Sam Snead," he may say, "keeps his wrists cocked until his hands have dropped below the level of his waist. I'll bet if you tried that you could knock the ball a mile, because I have noticed that your form is quite close to that of Sam's."

By this time, the victim is up to his neck in trouble. When he attempts to make use of the helpful tip, it fails to work and he goes to pieces. He's angry because he can't hit without slicing, and his anger is compounded because he can't hit like Sam Snead, although he likes to think his golfing form is not unlike that of the great Snead.

Money players also get excellent results by the simple but insidious device of giving unsolicited tips to an opponent who dislikes receiving such advice. As the victim strives to remain outwardly calm and tries manfully to remain a gentleman in spite of the constant flow of advice, he is unaware at first of the fluttering in his stomach. The little things have a tremendous and disastrous effect on a golfer's game, particularly if he is concerned about winning. When a player is irritated sufficiently to cause his "insides" to start churning, his whole system can go out of control before he knows it.

A chummy little device for wangling golf bets is the new game with the innocent-sounding title of "Texas." Or, if the player doesn't happen to like Texas, he might call it California, Ohio, or Georgia. But the idea remains the same, and it is this: When a side goes one-down after playing any of two successive holes, it can seek a "Texas" for the next two holes. This means that the bets will be doubled for the next two holes coming up.

Just to make the game even steeper, a gambler may suggest an automatic "Texas," "just to keep things even all the way, of course."

A neophyte who doesn't understand what this can lead to

may agree and say, "Yippee, I'm an old cow hand." Truer words were never spoken, for he is about to be taken for a rough ride. The automatic "Texas" can double the bet on every two holes, and, even if the first two holes were played for a paltry twenty-five cents, the player can quite possibly wind up playing the last two holes for sixty-four dollars, plus everything he has already lost.

By persuading a man to bet more than he can afford, a gambler can make his victim successively fearful, depressed, nervous, and angry. Sometimes these reactions will lead to utter recklessness, sometimes to extreme caution. There is only one sure thing: the victim will not be any richer after the eighteenth hole.

When teeing off for a friendly game with a "friendly" rival, it is well for a player to realize there are two times in a golfer's life when he shouldn't gamble: when he can't afford it, and when he doesn't know his opponent.

The Captain and the Secretary
Patrick Smart

Sounds like a toast, save that the secretary is often roasted but never toasted.

In any study of golf you will come across references to essentials. A good grip, full turn of the shoulders, sticking out ears so that you can't hear cries of "Fore" behind you, rhythm, and so on. Those are some of the essentials; in addition there is an *essential essential.* The club captain.

It's a must. It is simply not done not to have a captain. He is essential (a) to keep the secretary in order, (b) to perform the more difficult task of keeping the committee in order, and (c) so that there can be a captain's prize for competitors to compete for.

In ancient days the post was assumed by right of conquest. If you read the minutes, or, to be more precise, the Council Records of the City of Edinburgh in the year 1744, you will find the following: "That the victor shall be called *Captain* of the *Golf,* and all disputes touching Golf amongst Golfers, shall be determined by the Captain and any two or three of the Subscribers."

But why captain? It is not a Scottish term. One would have expected a laird, or chieftain, red in beard, flaming of hair, a claymore in each hand and a dram in the other, magnificent in the full Highland dress. What do we get? The red coat of the despised Sassenach, hired from a well-known clothes hiring agency, the hunt buttons having been replaced by plain ones. There is something ironical about this, because these captains have been complaining about moss in the greens all the winter. Captain! As a military rank it is too lowly to warrant its position in golf; even Bogey on joining was granted a colonelcy . . . but that was before the days of National Service and Questions in Parliament. The group captain of the Royal Air Force was then unknown. There is temptation to attribute it to some fearsome old sea-dog of commanding aspect, but the evidence is against it.

The first captain of the Royal and Ancient was a merchant of St. Andrews. Life is full of these anti-climaxes.

It will have been observed that in the beginning the captain's sole duty was to settle disputes in golfing matters. Since those halcyon days the march of time has brought in its civilized train disputes about the food, disputes about the drinks served, disputes about or among the staff, about bridge, dogs, about ablutions and lavatory accommodation.

A further reason for having a captain is that you have to have someone to make speeches. Which brings one to the question, why have speeches? I ask you, why?

There is the speech he must make at the Annual General Meeting. I suppose you have got to have this one. A defensive oration this for: "When the tide rises and sharks are around his voice had a timid and tremulous sound." At the Open Meeting he has to tell visiting competitors what a cracking good time they have had, and what a wonderful course they have played over. And finally at the Annual Dinner where, practically floating in port, he has to uncork a couple of golf stories that everyone in the club has heard before.

Speakers can be interesting to watch for a while. More interesting than to listen to. There are those who stand up, stand still, and say what they have to say, which is not always what they would like to say. There is the one who reads his speech in a dull monotone. Then there is the chap bursting with self-confidence. He has been reading one of those brochures on public speaking. He goes in for gestures. The wagging finger of admonition, the emphasis of clenched fist on open palm. A grandiose sweep of the arm which has you tense in your seat as it misses the wine-glasses by a whisker.

Such dramatics — pity he plays off twenty-four!

Captains vary in size, quality, and golfing ability. There is the busy one who fusses round all day badgering the secretary until the latter takes refuge in the time honoured excuse that he is out on the course.

There is the one who, like Gilbert's peers, does nothing in particular and does it very well. There is the captain who is not captain at all — his wife is.

THE SECRETARY

At the beginning of this book it was suggested that golfers are a bit rocky in the crumpet, ripe for the loony bin (nut house, the younger members of my family tell me would be more in line with modern English usage), but when it comes to secretaries we are in the higher realms of lunacy. Not, I hasten to add, in the manner of carrying out their duties, whatever members may think, but in taking the job on at all.

Fashions change. Between the wars one gained the impression that golf-clubs recruited their secretaries from a corps of colonels. Since the last war there can be little doubt that the source of intake is from a blast of brigadiers. This can be accounted for by the fact that in the last war the brigadiers outnumbered the colonels. Which must have been depressing for the enemy, and more so for the colonels.

There is a sprinkling of group captains, here and there gentlemen retired from the Royal Navy, and some malaria-ridden colonial Civil Servants. All daft.

The purpose behind this urge to become a golf-club secretary is to augment a pension coupled with a pleasant life and plenty of games of golf. Foolish fellow.

Having persuaded some gullible club that years spent in the Army, the Navy, the Air Force, some outpost of the British Empire, or commuting to and from business, have equipped you with a knowledge of greenkeeping, bookkeeping, P.A.Y.E., the Catering Wages Act, the Agricultural Wages Act, the Rules of Golf, and the answer to seven-sixteenths of the combined handicaps, you start on your new way of life.

You will have to contend with a number of people, chiefly the captain, the steward, the head greenkeeper. Captains we have dealt with, they will, however, crop up again. You arrive at the club, and are wading through a letter from which you gather there is small likelihood of the mowing-machines for the greens which were sent away last November for servicing being returned to you before May, when there is an almighty thump on the door and in clumps the greenkeeper. After a gruff "Morning," he deposits on your desk, before your astonished gaze, the lower half of a very ancient set of dentures. (This actually happened.) Then glowering at you he barks out: *"Found them there on the eighteenth green."* Outraged he is; they could have damaged the green. Sometime later, after much wild speculation as to how they got there, and with the greenkeeper still unconvinced, he announces with the voice of doom that the tractor has broke down again.

Up you get and trudge out across the course with him. You have not the remotest idea what you will do with the thing when you get there; after all, you were not a brigadier in R.E.M.E., but one must show interest. You gaze at the immobile monster with what you hope is a knowing look, and after a bit say "Ah." This gives nothing away, except that you feel inclined to fire the greenkeeper, as even your untutored eye can see the machine has not been oiled for months. But, under his baleful glare, you say nothing.

Back in the clubhouse, the steward informs you that a Mrs. Doublechin would like you to telephone her immediately. When you get through, the good lady goes off like a machine-gun: "*So* stupid of me, but one day last week . . . Monday I think, no, not Monday I had my hair done then. Tuesday? Tuesday. No, that was morning coffee with Ada. Anyway, I was playing with Mrs. Pips — I don't know if you know her, such a dear. Well, as I was saying, we came up the eighteenth — there is one thing I never do and that is leave things behind in the club. Well, what with one thing and another, I did leave something behind. I wonder if you would go into the ladies' room, and see if my . . ." (a nervous titter). "Well, perhaps not. No, don't bother, I'll fetch them myself. Thank you *so* much. Goodbye."

Being a man of iron control you replace the receiver gently, reflecting at the same time that if the Chancellor was going in for another squeeze it was a pity it couldn't be Mrs. Doublechin's throat. It was a mistake not to bash the receiver down and bust the thing. This would ensure a day or two of peace till the Post Office bestirred themselves and repaired it.

You look up to find the steward still standing there. "Sir, Cook says as how you told her that the Underwear and Corset Makers Golfing Society would be sixteen to lunch, and there's thirty-two of 'em turned up." Well, yes, sixteen matches do make thirty-two bodies.

You notice, lying on top of the post, of which so far you have opened one letter, a note from the captain, put there no doubt while you were looking at the tractor. It asks you to call an urgent house meeting for 5:30 tonight. There is no mention of why, no clue as to what is to be discussed. Five of the six members work in London, and even if you get them on the telephone you know their train does not get in until 6:30.

If you want to know what a secretary's correspondence consists of then beg, borrow, or steal George Nash's classic *Letters to a Golf Club Secretary*. Any attempt to emulate it would be an impertinence.

There are three crises during the year. The Annual General Meeting. The Open Amateur Meeting. The Dinner.

It is the preparation for the A.G.M. that will give you a

headache or two. You will be told to produce all sorts of statistics. Number of members compared with previous years. Number of resignations, giving reasons and drawing plan in each case. Number of new members. Bar profits (if any). Club ties sold. The area of each green; the chairman of the green committee wants to be in on the act. Subscriptions outstanding, etc., etc. These, with the aid of an out-of-date ready reckoner, you work out quite inaccurately and put in the wrong columns. The honorary treasurer, a retired schoolmaster, then divides the figures by half, puts one lot under assets, the other under liabilities, and says he has struck a balance. Still, in general effect it looks much like any club balance sheet, is about as much use, and, as nobody at an A.G.M. ever understands accounts, is unimportant.

And that is rather frustrating after all the work you have done, but not half so frustrating as it might be if someone got up and asked some intelligent questions.

If the meeting is a rowdy one the committee say afterwards that criticism from the members is a sign of healthy interest in the conduct of the club. If it is a dull session and over in threequarters of an hour, and no questions asked, the committee pride themselves on the confidence shown in their stewardship. The best of both worlds.

Should you be one of those fellows whose evening is spoiled if the meeting finishes too early (sooner or later your wife will find out exactly what time you all adjourned to the bar), suggest that the club should have a new design of tie. It is at present a rather nice one with stripes, but that is far too old-fashioned. And an hour or more can be spent in heated argument over the particular and peculiar heraldic design, minute in size, that should be dotted over the surface. It must, someone suggests, be subdued in colouring so that it may be worn with a city suit. Why one should wish to wear a golf tie in the city is not made clear, and it is unlikely that the proposer intends to spend his lunch hour with a wedge trying to hole out in the nearest pillar-box.

The trouble with these modern ties sprinkled with tiny

shields, animals with castles growing out of their backs, golf-clubs that look like the end of that instrument a dentist prods your teeth with, is that even with a magnifying glass you still do not know which club the tie represents.

I have yet to see a tie bearing a motif of rabbits. It seems appropriate.

It is natural to suppose that running the Open Meeting is a piece of cake. It is held at the same time every year, the programme is the same, and the competitors much the same. But it is not so. For weeks before you will be tearing your hair, which gives you an opportunity to notice how thin and grey it is getting, trying to pacify the distaff side of the mixed foursomes. They all want to play at the same time for the same reason. They get quite frustrated at your idiocy in failing to understand that children have to be got off to school, or the husband to his business.

Another thing. People still demand double the number of caddies you can muster, and you end up, or the professional does, in supplying barely weaned youngsters, and toothless gaffers whose knowledge of the course has been culled from poaching forays.

The great day comes and you feel you have done all that can be done. By the way, never hold a tournament on the 1st of April. There still comes back to me the look of desperate anxiety on the members' faces when they found an "Out of Order" notice pinned to the lavatory door. Every club has its jester.

Nor, for that matter, accept the post of secretary at a high course. Hill fog descends like a blanket, and you have to whip up volunteers to stand halfway down the first fairway, their heads protected against danger by large umbrellas, to shout all clear before you can let the next couple go off the tee. Whether these helpers regard it as danger money, or whether fog is particularly thirst-inducing, they are going to cost you a lot in the bar later.

To get on with the tournament, you pay a visit to the first tee to see if all is well there, and find the starter using quite frightful language because someone has upset what he is pleased to call his glass of water all over the start sheet, which is now illegible.

A card-collector wants to know on what ground he was asked to report at a time when competitors are setting out instead of a time when they are coming in. One feels he may be right.

A player on his way to the tee trips over a shoe-lace and in putting out a hand to save himself runs the iron spike of some railings through his hand. A doctor and a substitute player are found.

It is still early, but you have a stiff one in the bar.

You had spent some time giving clear instructions to the car-park attendant about the space reserved for the captain of the club, describing his opulent car and giving its number. You come out of the bar to see the attendant brusquely waving a massive figure riding a scooter through the park to the purlieus at the back of the club. It is the captain.

A player is helped in having slipped a cartilage walking off the tee.

An infuriated female dashes up with the news that her fellow competitor has not turned up, and furthermore she has no starting time. After a long search we find a letter from the I.F. saying that as her partner could not play she wishes to scratch. She then asks what she should do!

The heavens open and it pours cats and dogs, and in the lunch interval there are about sixty people wanting to dry sopping clothes. It is midsummer, the boiler is out, and the steward has added "run off me feet" to "only one pair of 'ands."

Later — much later — we are at the prize-giving, which has been much delayed by several ties for first place and a consequent agitated reshuffling of all the sweeps.

No sooner is the presentation of prizes over than chaos reigns. Eighty per cent of the gathering indulge in a wild scramble for the bar, while the other twenty per cent seek one another out and exchange trophies until all have the correct one. It is not surprising that a few errors have crept in, what with constant interruptions all day and constant morale-boosting visits to the bar.

That evening, you, the secretary, reviewing the events of the day, are suddenly reminded of the club that held a tournament almost as soon as peace broke out. Not one of the pre-war committee was there, and so none knew where the trophies had been stored for safekeeping. The local hunt came to the rescue and lent their trophies for the occasion. When it came to the Ladies Scratch Cup a stalwart Amazon advanced to receive her cup. There was what is known as an *awkward moment* when it was discovered too late that the inscription bore the words: "The biggest Bitch in the Show."

There is always a silver lining somewhere.

It may be questioned why, in a serious work like this, the author has chosen to introduce some fiction. With the exception of the Hound Trophy I have experienced every incident. Not perhaps all in one meeting, but they did happen.

Once again you have been warned.

The Annual Dinner is a festive occasion. It starts some weeks before with a hell of a row. Two rows. The first in house committee over the menu. The second in general committee over the menu submitted by the house committee. This touching concern for members' (and their own) welfare (no pun intended, and perhaps the wrong word for over-eating) ends in the same dishes appearing year after year.

There will be plenty to drink during the dinner, so everyone arrives an hour early and crowds into the bar shoving down enough whisky to last them for a month or more.

The secretary is having his usual jolly time, for, in addition to his dinner-jacket being too tight under the arms, he is penned in a corner by infuriated characters demanding to know why their whole evening must be ruined by being placed next to that insufferable besotted bore, So and So. Even this has its moment when two of the complainants, unaware in the hubbub that they are standing next to each other, indulge themselves with libellous, scurrilous, and damaging allegations about the moral turpitude of the other.

In due course a procession of penguins troops into the dining-room, and the roar of conversation drowns the gurgle of soup consumption. It is advisable to eat and drink as much as possible. These soporific aids come in useful during the speechifying, unless you happen to be one of those fortunate people who can drop off at any time.

The speeches. Dear me! After the loyal toast there rises ponderously a dignified character, his portly (again no pun intended) figure appearing more enceinte than ever, to propose the captain's health. This is, of course, a blatant case of collusion; the two of them have been rehearsing together for some time, and I make no apology for quoting from that classic bit with Jorrocks and his Sec discussing the speeches for the hunt dinner.

"The Chair," said Mr. Jorrocks, "that's me. Cheers, in course."

"In course," replied Captain Doleful, "I shall butter you uncommon."

"With all my 'eart — I can stand a wast of praise," replied Jorrocks.

Butter him uncommon, that's what we get. And what is more we know we are going to get it. The statisticians set their watches, the pessimists nod off, and the guests have to stay awake. Our speaker starts: "It is with great pleasure, indeed it is an honour for someone so unworthy as myself, that I, ah, er, hrrum, stand up to propose the health of our excellent captain, without whose guidance . . ." Whoppers from start to finish. It is no particular pleasure for him to propose this man's health, and if there is one thing that he does not consider himself to be it is that of being unworthy. He then proceeds to paint a picture for those of you who are not asleep, or exchanging blue stories in whispers, that leads you to suppose that without the captain the club, "this beautiful old clubhouse set as it is in heart of the country, surrounded by the course we love so much" (only yesterday he penned a searing criticism on what he called the disgusting condition of the tees and fairways), the club would have crumbled and closed down. More whoppers. The captain appears on Sunday mornings only, dressed to convey the impression he has been to church, drinks too many gins too quickly, and leaves.

Weakness, that's what it is. He hasn't got the courage of his opinions. How much more entertaining it would be if he rose unsteadily to his feet, hiccupped, and after peering squiffy-eyed upon the scene, which with wine-encrimsoned faces seen dimly through a cloud of smoke looks like a winter's evening with an unusual number of crimson suns setting, spoke his mind.

"Gentlemen, I am proposing this toast only because I have been promised an extra double Scotch if I take no more than five minutes. I require no more time than that to describe the lecherous, bottle-nosed old sinner, whom with typical lack of intelligence you saw fit to have as your captain. I happen to know the election was rigged. Only yesterday I saw him kick his ball out of the rough. Why do you think the father of that pretty waitress in the dining-room was up here demanding to see him? Why do you think he was unavoidably absent from the last meeting? Down at Brighton with her. They say a club deserves the captain it gets. You've got it."

No one would sleep through that lot.

As we have suggested before, there is always a leavening moment, and it comes when a speaker not on the toast list wobbles to his feet and with a beatific smile on his face says he wants to have the date of the dinner altered for future years, and why are the competitions held off the back tees. This startling *non sequitur* draws everyone's attention, and they listen in evident delight to a masterly display of confused reasoning, ending, in ringing tones, with the assertion that in future the dinner should be held on the back tees. Whereupon to prolonged applause he sits down where his chair was before he pushed it back to rise and speak.

This, my dear secretary, will lead you to feel that the evening has been a success. Wait till they have recovered and start in on the quality of the wines and the dilatory service. As if they could remember! Nor can you.

Excerpt from
A New Way to Better Golf
Rex Beach

I am a golfer. I have played for twenty years but I have recently made a discovery. I *hate it!*

Golf is a game only to the dub: he alone gets any fun, any satisfaction and any considerable benefit out of it. To the man who takes his game seriously, it is a torment. Annoyance, impatience, disappointment, rage — the confirmed addict suffers all of these. If he likes golf enough to try and play it well its pleasure vanishes: if he sets out to shoot a low score he dooms himself to anxiety, anguish and chagrin. For him all pleasure in the sport evaporates and the residue upon his tongue is wormwood.

The duffer, on the other hand, tastes nothing but pure satisfaction. He speeds to the links with joy in his heart, he dresses with the inflammatory eagerness of a bridegroom and he capers to the caddy house. He plays an explosion shot from the first tee, removing a great chunk therefrom with his driver. It is a shot which Kirkwood couldn't duplicate and it gains him nearly thirty yards. But is he disturbed? By no means. He goes blithely ahead lacerating the ball as he kicks it along, drinking in the sunshine, enjoying the exercise and caring little whether he does a hole in four or in multiples thereof. If by some accident he occasionally hits the ball squarely on the button he drops ten years from his age: if not, it doesn't matter. There's another hole coming.

That, without doubt, is the spirit in which golf should be played by the average man — carelessly, gladly, terribly. The advantage, mental, physical, and spiritual, which the cluck player enjoys over the low-handicap man is that he gets a great kick out of one or two good shots during a round, whereas the other, if he muffs a couple, decides to drink iodine and jump off a bridge.

But let the dub beware. He is toying with razor blades, he is juggling hand grenades. If he ever makes a decent score, ten to one he will be lost. He will begin to take lessons. He will study the science of the thing. He will sneak off and practice. He will buy a set of matched clubs. There isn't much hope for him after that. Gone are the days when he could top a ball and say something funny. As he explores the mysteries, parts the veil and gradually improves his game, a complete change in his mental and physical metabolism occurs. He grows pessimistic and apprehensive. He develops temperament and gets so jumpy that he can't putt if an ant stirs. He may, and probably will, remain a duffer — few graduate from that class — but his peace of mind is gone forever. The worst has happened. Thereafter he will be no stranger to torment of soul and bitterness of spirit.

Not long ago, in the locker room of a club, I noticed a globular little man, pink-faced and beaming. He was surrounded by half a dozen members who were clinking glasses and patting him on the bare back. I learned that they were congratulating him on having broken a hundred for the first time and he radiated happiness like a base-burner. He glowed, he expanded until he had fewer wrinkles than a grape: he was a boy again.

Presently the club champion slouched in dragging his heels. His pallid face was seamed, his shoulders drooped and in his eyes was that expression of hope abandoned which one saw in the eyes of people bent over the ticker tape in that ghastly month of October, 1929. With a deep sigh, half moan, he sank onto a bench and sat gazing at the floor, his cupped hands supporting his face.

"Hello, Jim!" somebody called. "Will you join us in a snifter?"

The champion's shoulders heaved, he shook his head without looking up.

"How'd it go today?" the other asked.

"Oh, my god!" Jim ran a trembling hand through his wet hair: in a voice that seemed to issue from the tomb, he answered: "I hooked one out of bounds and three-putted two greens!" . . . A lousy seventy-seven! I guess I'll quit the game. There's no hope for me."

235

Hope! It is all the serious-minded golfer has to cling to. And how he clings! To him the game is a dull chore, a battle in which he invariably meets defeat. Day after day it beats him and he only licks his wounds and comes back for more. But it breaks his spirit finally.

Women have the right idea. Never hurry, enjoy a cosy chat on every green, take four or five practice swings to each shot and never let anybody go through — the brutes! And don't be fussy about rules, either — they're only technicalities; improve your lie; if there's any doubt about a putt, concede it to yourself.

Other People's Golf
Bernard Darwin

It is undeniable that most of us can bear the misfortunes of others stoically and, indeed, cheerfully. Sometimes we have difficulty in realising that they are misfortunes at all. We may even think their circumstances rather enviable than otherwise.

That this is no less true of golf than of life in general I rediscovered — for I knew it tolerably well already — when I went out to play a short evening round with a friend of mine. Before we began he told me that he was suffering from a hook and consulted the professional as to various remedies. "Suffering!" thought I to myself, "I wish I had half his complaint." He proceeded to the tee and hit, as I thought, a magnificent shot. The ball started a little out to the right and then, performing what Tony Lumpkin would have called a "circumbendibus," finished in the dim distance on the left hand side of the fairway.

"Look at it!" he exclaimed, in a tone of deep disgust. "There it goes again." "My good sir," I replied, not without peevishness, "it is a very fine shot. When, before the war, I thought I could drive, I used to hit them like that and I want a share of the German indemnity about it. You will get no sympathy out of me." "Oh, if you think that, you're hopeless," was his answer. "Why, I took you out to cure me of the infernal thing."

After this little argument, I hit my tee shot. My ball also finished on the fairway and went a respectable distance, but it turned in the air so palpably to the right that I with difficulty refrained from throwing the club after it. My friend, in his turn, no doubt justifiably irritated, remarked that I had nothing whatever to complain of and that a slice was much less disastrous than a hook. We then walked on in silence, an imperfect sympathy between us, for neither could appreciate the other's point of view, namely, that the slight hook or the touch of a slice was not a solitary and negligible incident but a sorrow's crown of sorrow. The culmination of misunderstanding arrived at the sixth hole, where I, the slicer, with a fine, full-blooded hook, carried the humps and hollows on the left-hand side of the course. My opponent was generous with his pity, whereas I was radiant, infinitely more pleased with myself than if I had hit as straight as Robin Hood's arrow.

So much for the driving, but it was not only a question of driving. When we came to the green my adversary was holing out his short putts with a nonchalant grace that was hard to bear. He looked as if he could scarcely be bothered to play them, and every time the ball rattled against the back of the tin. My short ones did go in — so much I must admit — but they crept and crawled and twisted in, and I am very sure that I looked neither nonchalant nor graceful in the striking, or rather the pushing and poking of them. "I wish to Heaven," said I, in a churlish, grudging way, "that I could hole a putt like that." "It's quite simple," said he. "You've only got to hit them," and proceeded to make matters worse by explaining that he had been "off it" for some time, but had now got his confidence back. I must do him the justice to say that he added something about doing it all with the thumb and forefinger of the right hand, but he did not say it very helpfully. Besides, I had tried that several months before.

Finally, there was the pitching. Mine was comparatively

blameless. He, once or twice, when faced with a straight forward shot, "grumphed" it feebly, so that the ball spouted into the air and fell far short of the mark. "Eye off again," said he, with bitter self-contempt, and I thought of saying, "It's quite simple; you've only got to keep your head down." I refrained, but I am conscious of not having felt for him as deeply as I ought. It is altogether rather a mean and sordid story, but it has at least a happy ending. We are still, I hope I may say, friends. My tee shots towards the end of our eleven holes began to have quite an engaging little turn to the left; his hook remained under reasonable control, and his final mashie shot was wholly above suspicion. Neither of us made any attempt to go out for "just a few shots" of solitary practice, and that is always, as far as it goes, a good sign.

All properly conducted stories should have a moral. The moral of this one is that when we want sympathy and valuable "tips" for our reformation we should not play with one who is in a similar plight. Rather we should seek out that one of our acquaintance who is playing well with all his clubs. He may be in the state of mind which sees nothing difficult about the game, and that is a disadvantage. On the other hand, his mind will be void of any worries of his own, and, if flattered with judgment, he really will try to see what we are doing wrong. He will not, while perfunctorily reprobating our left elbow, be thinking chiefly about his own right knee. Scratch ninety-nine golfers out of a hundred and you will find the pedagogue underneath, but you must scratch them at the right time.

The Rivercliff Golf Killings
Don Marquis

The district attorney has given me the following certified copy of my sworn testimony, and I am telling the story of this golf game to the public just as I told it in the grand jury room.

QUESTION: Professor Waddems, will you tell the jury just when it was that you first noted evidences of the criminal tendencies, amounting to total depravity, in the late Silas W. Amherst?

ANSWER: It was on the 30th of September, 1936, at 4:17 p.m.

QUESTION: Where were you when you first began to suspect that the man had such an evil nature?

ANSWER: On the Rivercliff golf course, sir, at the second hole.

QUESTION: A par-four hole, Professor?

ANSWER: It is called that, yes, sir; but it is unfairly trapped.

QUESTION: What is your usual score on this hole, Professor Waddems? Remember, you are on oath, and you have waived immunity in this inquiry.

ANSWER: I have never yet received fair treatment with regard to this hole. My normal score on this hole is five, with an occasional par four and sometimes a birdie three. But disgraceful tactics have always been employed against me on this hole to prevent me from playing my normal game.

QUESTION: Is it a water hole?

ANSWER: Yes, sir.

QUESTION: Is it the same water hole from which the body of Silas W. Amherst was removed on October 3, 1936, a few days after he was last seen alone with you?

ANSWER: No, sir. That was the fifteenth hole. The water at the fifteenth hole is much deeper than the water at the second hole or the seventh hole. In the water at the fifteenth hole there are now several other bod ——

QUESTION: Be careful, Professor! This inquiry is devoted entirely to Silas W. Amherst, and you are not compelled to incriminate or degrade yourself. Professor, are you a nervous, irritable, testy, violent person?

ANSWER: No, sir! No, sir! No, sir! And the man that dares to call me that is . . . *(A portion of Prof. Waddems' reply is stricken from the record.)*

QUESTION: Quietly, Professor, quietly! Tell these gentlemen how you gained the unruffled patience and philosophic calm that have made you the great golfer that you are.

ANSWER: For twenty-five years I lectured on philosophy and psychology at various universities. And I apply these principles to my golf game.

QUESTION: In spite of your thorough scientific knowledge of the game, have you ever broken a hundred?

ANSWER: Yes, sir, many times.

QUESTION: Think, Professor!

ANSWER: Yes, sir; yes, sir; yes, sir!

QUESTION: Mildly, please, Professor! Quietly! I will put the question in a different way. Professor, has any opponent with whom you played ever *admitted* that you broke a hundred, or has any card that you turned in after playing a round alone been credited, if it showed you *had* broken a hundred?

ANSWER: I don't remember, sir. My game has been misrepresented and persecuted for years at Rivercliff.

QUESTION: To return to Mr. Amherst. Tell the jury exactly what happened at the second hole which revealed the man's irreclaimable blackness of character.

ANSWER: Well, sir, I teed up for my drive and addressed the ball. And just as I brought my club back, and it was poised for the down stroke, he said to me:

"Professor, you're driving with a brassie, aren't you?"

I gave him a look of mild expostulation, checked the drive, and stood in front of the ball again.

"I don't think your stance is right, Professor," he said. "Let me show you the proper stance — you don't mind my showing you, do you, Professor?"

Then he proceeded to show me — and I may say in passing that his theories were entirely faulty.

"I noticed on the first tee," he went on, "that you didn't understand how to pivot. You want to get your body into it, Professor. Like this," and he made a swing in demonstration.

240

"Your instruction, Mr. Amherst," I said politely, "is entirely gratuitous and all wrong."

"I thought you'd be glad to have me show you, Professor," he said. "And if I were you, I wouldn't play that new ball on this water hole. Here, I'll lend you a floater."

And the man actually took from his bag a floater, removed my ball, and teed up the one he had lent me.

"Now, Professor," he said, "a little more freedom in your swing. Keep your eye on the ball and don't let your hands come through ahead of the club. I noticed you had a tendency that way. I think your grip is wrong. Professor. Oh yes, certainly wrong! Here, let me show you the correct grip. And keep your head down, keep your head down!"

QUESTION: Was it then, Professor that the tragedy occurred?

ANSWER: No, sir! No, sir! No, sir!

QUESTION: Quietly, Professor, quietly! You remained calm?

ANSWER: I am always calm! I never lose my temper! I am always patient! Self-contained! Restrained! Philosophical! Unperturbed! Nothing excites me! Nothing, I say, nothing! Nothing! Nothing! Nothing!

QUESTION: There, there, Professor, easily, easily now! What happened next?

ANSWER: I took a driving-iron from my bag and addressed the ball again. I —

QUESTION: Just a moment, Professor. Why did you not continue with the brassie?

ANSWER: It was broken, sir.

QUESTION: Broken? How? I do not understand. How did it become broken?

ANSWER: I do not remember.

QUESTION: Between Mr. Amherst's instruction with the brassie and your taking the driving iron from the bag, as I understand it, the brassie was somehow broken. Please fill up this interval for the jury. What happened?

ANSWER: I can't recall, sir.

QUESTION: Come, come, Professor! How was the brassie broken?

ANSWER: It hit the sandbox, sir.

QUESTION: How could it hit the sandbox?

ANSWER: Well, it was an old brassie, and after I had made a few practice swings with it, I decided that it was poorly balanced and that I had better get rid of it once and for all. I did not wish to give it to a caddie, for I do not think it is fair to give poor clubs to these boys who are earnestly striving to educate themselves to be professionals; they are poor boys, for the most part, and we who are in better circumstances should see that they have a fair start in life. So I broke the brassie against the sandbox and took my driving iron, and —

QUESTION: Just a minute, Professor! These practice strokes that you made with the brassie, were there five or six of them?

ANSWER: I don't recollect, sir.

QUESTION: Did any one of them hit the ball?

ANSWER: No, sir! No, sir! No, sir! The brassie never touched the ball! The ball moved because there was a bent twig under it — this man Amherst had teed up his floater for me with a pat of sand upon a bent twig — and the twig straightened up and moved the sand, and the ball rolled off it.

QUESTION *(by the foreman of the jury)*: Professor Waddems, how far did the ball roll when the twig straightened up?

ANSWER: Well, sir, it had been teed up at the very edge of the driving green, and the ground is pretty high there, and the ball rolled down the slope, and it gained a great deal of momentum as it rolled down the slope, like an avalanche as it comes rolling down a mountainside, and at the bottom of the slope it struck a rut in the road the work-and-upkeep wagons use on the course, and that rut connects with the asphalt drive that leads in to the clubhouse, and when the ball struck the asphalt road it had already gained so much momentum that it rolled for some distance along the asphalt road, and then it crashed into the underbrush near the road and hit a sapling and bounded over onto the first fairway, all on

242

account of the slope of the ground, for it had never been touched with the brassie at all.

QUESTION: Professor, did this happen to the ball five or six times before you discarded the brassie and took the driving iron?

ANSWER: No, sir. I only recall three times.

QUESTION: Go on, Professor. After your breaking of the brassie, you took the driving iron. What happened then?

ANSWER: Then Mr. Amherst stepped up and said to me, "Professor, let me give you a few tips about iron play. And you must keep your head down, keep your head down!"

QUESTION: Did you lose your temper then?

ANSWER: I never lose my temper! Never! Never! Never!

QUESTION: Quietly, now, Professor. Quietly! Go on.

ANSWER: I made a magnificent drive, which cleared the water jump, and my second shot was on the green. I holed out with two putts. "A par four," I said, marking it on my card.

"You mean nine," said this man Amherst. Gentlemen, he had the effrontery to claim that the five practice swings I had made with the brassie, just simply to humor him in his demonstrations, were actual golf strokes!

(Sensation in the grand jury room. Cries of "Outrageous!" "Impossible!" "The Dastard!" from various grand jurymen. The outburst quelled with difficulty by the district attorney.)

QUESTION *(by the foreman of the jury)*: Professor Waddems, did you end it all then?

ANSWER: No, sir. I kept my self-control. Gentlemen, I am always for peace! I am a meek person. I am mild. I will endure persecution to a point beyond anything that is possible to a man who has not had my years of training in philosophy and applied psychology. I merely got another caddie and proceeded with the game, yielding the point to Mr. Amherst for the sake of peace.

QUESTION: Got another caddie?

ANSWER: Yes, sir. The one I started out with was injured.

QUESTION: How, Professor?

ANSWER: I don't remember.

243

QUESTION: Think Professor! Was it by a fall?

ANSWER: Oh yes, now I recollect! It *was* by a fall. The caddie fell from a tree just beyond the second green and broke his shoulder.

QUESTION: What was he doing in the tree?

ANSWER: He had retired to the top of the tree under a peculiar misapprehension, sir. He had agreed with Mr. Amherst with regard to the question as to whether I should take nine strokes or a par four; and I think he misinterpreted some sudden motion of mine as a threat.

QUESTION: A motion with a golf club?

ANSWER: It may have been, sir. I had a club in my hand, and I remember that my mind at the moment was engrossed with a problem connected with the underlying psychology of the full swing with wooden clubs.

QUESTION: Well, Professor, the caddie is now at the top of the tree, laboring under a misapprehension. What caused his fall?

ANSWER: I think the wooden club must have slipped somehow from my hands, sir. It flew to the top of the tree and disturbed his balance, causing him to fall.

QUESTION: Was he a good caddie?

ANSWER: There are no good caddies, sir.

(Ripple of acquiescent laughter round the grand jury room.)

QUESTION: Then, Professor, you went on to the next driving green. Tell what happened from this point on to the fifteenth hole, where the body of Silas W. Amherst was found four days later.

ANSWER: Advice, sir, advice! That's what happened! Advice! One long, intolerable gehenna of gratuitous advice! Gentlemen, I don't know whether any of you ever have had the misfortune to play golf with the late Silas W. Amherst, but if you have —

(Cries from various grand jurors: "Yes, yes, I played with him!" "Attaboy, Professor!" "I knew him, Prof!" etc., etc. District attorney begs for order; witness continues.)

ANSWER: Advice! Advice! Advice! And always from fiendish malignity of the man concealed under a cloak of helpful friendliness! Advice! Advice! Advice! And to me! I, who have studied the basic principles of the game more thoroughly than any other man in America today! Gentlemen, if I were not the most patient man in the world, Silas W. Amherst would have bit the dust twenty times between the second and the fifteenth holes that day! His explanations — to me! His continual babble and chatter! His demonstrations! Every club I took from my bag, he *explained* to me! Gentlemen, some of them were clubs that I had designed myself and had had manufactured to fit my own original theories with regard to golf! But I kept my temper! I never lose my temper! Never! Never! Never!

QUESTION: Does any particularly insulting phrase of advice stand out in your memory, Professor?

ANSWER: Yes, sir! A dozen times on every hole he would cry to me as I addressed the ball, "Keep your head down, Professor, keep your head down!"

THE DISTRICT ATTORNEY: Please sit down, Professor; and do not bang on the chairs with your walking stick as you talk. We cannot hear your testimony.

THE PROFESSOR: Yes, sir. Well, at the fifteenth hole, while he was standing on the edge of the water, looking for a ball —

QUESTION: Professor, is it true that the fifteenth hole at Rivercliff is really a pool, fed by subterranean springs, and so deep that no plummet has ever sounded its bottom?

ANSWER: Exactly, sir. As Silas W. Amherst stood on the edge of it, it occurred to me that perhaps the man's conscience had awakened and that he was going to commit suicide for the good of the human race, gentlemen. And so I gave him a little pat of approval — on the back; and he fell in. Gentlemen, he judged himself and executed himself, and I still approve.

QUESTION: Would you mind telling the jurors, Professor, just what Mr. Amherst said immediately before you patted him approvingly on the back?

ANSWER: He said, "You just stick to me, Professor, and do as I show you, and I'll make some kind of golfer out of you yet."

QUESTION: Did he try to struggle to land, and did you hold his head under water?

ANSWER: Yes, sir, I generously assisted him in his purpose to that extent.

QUESTION: What did you say while you were assisting him?

ANSWER: I said, "Keep your head down, Mr. Amherst, keep your head down!"

THE FOREMAN OF THE JURY: Mr. District Attorney, speaking for the other members of this jury as well as for myself, it is ridiculous to consider the matter of finding any true bill or indictment of any sort against Professor Waddems in the case of the late Mr. Amherst. The pat of approval was more than justified, and we consider Professor Waddems a public benefactor.

THE DISTRICT ATTORNEY: Tomorrow we will take up the case of Willie, alias "Freckled," Briggs, the caddie who met his death on October 4, 1936, at the Rivercliff Country Club. I suggest that the slight rain we have had today, which is happily over with, should contribute greatly to what is known as a good brassie lie on the fairways. You are dismissed for the day.

The 7th Hole . . .
Fred Beck and O.K. Barnes

You can always tell a home-practice addict. But what's the use? They never listen.

There is a rule about practicing pitch shots off a green. The book says nothing, however, about practicing pitch shots off a two-thousand-dollar Sarouk, and hence, unrestricted, this kind of thing is reaching evil proportions.

Replacing a divot in a rug is a pretty serious matter.

Even in its early stages, a golfer's addiction to home practice may be recognized by certain symptoms. The victim begins by bringing home little tin flapdiddles which he thinks are cups. Actually, they are just metal flangels, or flapschnangs, which trap a golf ball properly directed toward the center of one.

Home-practice addicts are bemused by these, and will play with them for hours at a time. Hotchkiss, an authority to whom the authors attribute statements which they lack the guts to make themselves, holds the opinion that the home-practice addicts cannot properly be considered golfers so much as simply fellows who never got an electric train for Christmas.

The home-practice addict labors under the illusion that he is improving his game. It could be, but the procedure certainly does not improve that living-room rug. For sheer wear and tear, the home-practice addict is rivaled only by a cocker spaniel pup with weak kidneys and no inhibitions.

As a result of these factors, the home-practice addict frequently is banned from the house. In the backyard, well, his addiction becomes obvious to the whole public, and the suffering of his family is increased in proportion to the number of neighbors who get a peek at the goings on and shake their heads significantly.

Typical of all home-practice addicts is a fellow we will call Dewey Pringle. When he took up putting with live balls and driving those knitted practice balls around his backyard, the neighbors were sure he had dropped a cotter pin. One evening, Mrs. P. came out to watch her zany mate. For no reason at all, she picked up a putter.

"Is this how you do it?" she inquired. Holding the club the wrong way, she tapped one of her husband's ninety-five-cent golf balls, which danced along and clunked into the bean can he was using for a cup.

"Hm!" he said. "Not bad if you'd been *trying* to sink it."

"But I did!" said the Mrs. "I *aimed* at that hole."

"The hell you did!" exclaimed the husband. "Bet you can't do it again." He was getting interested.

"Now hold your feet together like this, see? And be sure to line up the shot first by . . ."

"Let me do it my own way," said Mrs. P., a strong-willed

girl. She then tapped five balls toward the cup and three of them went into the can. Mrs. Pringle's performance had the same effect on Mr. Pringle that a pouchful of lighted firecrackers would have on a kangaroo. That is to say, he was impressed.

"Say!" he said. "You maybe would make a very good woman golfer."

Mr. Pringle placed one of his knitted practice balls on the greensward and proceeded to whak it some twenty or thirty feet into a hedge. "That," he explained, "is the equivalent of a 275-yard drive, maybe 285." Then he invited his Pearl of Great Price to try a drive.

Mrs. Pringle, whose shoulders are as stout as her willpower, planted her size-nine feet, brought the club back, and then swung downward with a powerful sweep. There was the sharp clack of clubhead meeting ball. Being a novice, Mrs. Pringle had not whopped a knitted practice ball. She had poked a ninety-five-cent Air Cruiser — the real McCoy.

The ball sailed over the hedge and soon there sounded the merry tickle of shattered glass. The pellet had gone through a rear bedroom window of the home of Melvin A. Faget of the South Palm Drive Fagets. Mr. Faget came back with the ball, and there was the dickens to pay. But a more serious thing than that happened, too. When Mrs. Pringle hit that ball a solid swipe, the golf bug bit her. Today, she is in her third year as champion at her club, or maybe it's the fourth year, but anyhow the Pringles can't afford golf for two members of the family and — well, you see how it is.

Furthermore, Mr. Pringle is getting very tired of cold deviled ham and crackers when Mrs. P. plays late.

That's why we view home practice with suspicion.

The Colonel and the Hunt
George Houghton

It beats me what the Colonel sees in golf. I mean his kind. Take yesterday. There has never been such rain. It was coming down in long silver pencils yet there's the Colonel and me leaning against it and trudging up the long sixteenth as if this was the only road to heaven.

Our opponent had called it a day and gone four holes earlier. Not us. The Colonel said he'd found out what was wrong with his swing (that's a laugh!) and he wanted to consolidate.

Matter of fact he actually was hitting the ball better and although this didn't mean much it didn't make sense either. Imagine. We're sodden through with cold rain. The grips of his clubs are so wet he can't hold on. Howling wind makes him cling on to the course with his toes. His specs are blurred so's he can't see. Yet the old buzzard cracks the ball as sweet as a nut.

Take last Monday. Soft sun, no breeze. Perfect golf conditions yet the Colonel couldn't hit the ball for toffee apples.

My old dad used to say that the only thing you can count on is human stupidity. You can win a bob on that any day he'd say.

Well here's the Colonel bashing on in the rain and getting us both lined up for oak boxes with brass handles when suddenly pandemonium is let loose. First of all a blinkin fox crosses the sixteenth fairway in front of us. He was a bedraggled old josser. Hungry looking. Panting and whacked. Soon we see why. A bunch of yelpin hounds comes charging through the hedge and just behind them there's the usual bloke in red coat blowing his sawn-off trumpet.

The Colonel's face was a picture. He knew danged well that if this circus of dogs and horses and that was to come crashing over our wet fairways and greens they'd damage the course more than somewhat.

He yells his head off. Pass me a club quick he says.

I did just that and the Colonel rushes into the mob of dogs swinging his club and bashing at them when they was in range. You've never seen such a sight. You've got to take your hat off to the old boy. Within three minutes and a dozen or so full iron shots he broke up the party. The dogs didn't go much for it I tell you. Some got through the Colonel's line of course and went after the fox but by then the poor brute had picked up a useful lead and was well into the woods on the right.

We never did hear if that old Raynard got clear away but just then we wasn't thinking on those lines. Our attention had been took by one helluva rumpus.

The huntsman with the sawn-off trumpet had two of his mounted pals with him and coming up behind was the gaffer of the hunt and others blowing out more steam than their flippen horses.

The first hunter got off his horse and came through the hedge doing no good to his bright red coat.

He had the right sort of Billingsgate voice for hunting. If you've injured any of those hounds you're for it he shouts at the Colonel.

But my man is right back at him. If you and your damn dogs are not off this private property in two minutes I'll throw you off shouts the Colonel.

As I said before despite the weather the Colonel had been hitting the ball well. His timing was right and that applied to the swing he took at the bitch what was leading the pack. The bow-wow was properly if not permanently out of business on account of having stopped a beaut from the Colonel's number three iron.

His nibs must have brought his right hand in just at impact because after the first yelp of defiance the bitch realised there was probably another well-timed crack due to arrive any moment. Working it out on those lines she slunk off into the hedge to take stock and comfort her bleeding snout.

The Master of the hunt was a dashing bloke in a top hat

and anyone could see that it would be good matchmaking to put him and the Colonel in the same ring.

They both shake hands like long lost brothers.

No contest. You've never seen such a flop.

Colonel gasps the hunter. How wonderful he says.

This nonsense goes on and the spectators get more restless. Finally the bloke in the hat climbs on his blinkin horse and rides off after the bloke with the sawn-off trumpet. The rest of the cavalry do the same.

Rain's coming down hard again and it seems a good idea to cut out the last two holes. Did we hell. The Colonel bashes on.

That chap was once my adjutant he says.

That so says I but couldn't care less.

Yes, says the Colonel. Pity he wastes time hunting when he could be enjoying gowf he says.

Sodden to the skin we battles on.

Are You Making Enough Fun?
Joe James

If you are thinking about giving up golf, you may not be doing enough to inject fun into the game. Golf is called a "game" but it really isn't a game at all. It is no more a "game" than an obstacle course. Golf is frustration, with rules. And you may as well face the fact that "play" is the wrong verb to use when discussing a round of golf. It would be far more truthful and accurate to say "Let's go out and *suffer* eighteen holes of golf."

To enjoy the organized frustration that is golf you must inject your own "fun" into the action. Do this and golf really becomes a "game" and you will actually be *playing* it.

You may know about the various gadgets that are available to liven up golf. Some are pretty good. A few are dismal flops. The effective ones require some imagination on your part and a little acting flair. They also require precise timing. But the results you get are worth it.

Balls with off-center gravity are readily available. When putted, these take off at weird angles. Just slipping one of these balls into the game may get a chuckle, but properly timed it can be devastating.

We had a lively match going and Wally B. had an especially hot round in the works. The next hole was a par three, across a sizeable water hazard. Wally hit first and placed his tee shot some twenty feet from the pit. He was carrying a light bag and, as we reached the green, he walked over to the green's edge to put down his clubs. I switched balls for him, replacing his ball with one of the trick balls.

The rest of us putted up and it was time for Wally to try for his twenty-foot birdie. He walked beyond the pin to survey the putt from that side. Then he took a stance below the cup to gauge the slope. Finally he took some practice swings with his putter and then moved carefully over the ball. Intense silence settled over the green. Slowly, carefully, Wally's putter moved back with pendulum-like grace and then smacked the ball. The ball came straight off the putter, then veered sharply to the right, swerving crazily like a drunken crab, and rolled off the green.

"I *shanked* it!" Wally gasped, staring at the ball lying serenely in the frog hair. "I shanked it with my *putter!*"

After we got him calmed down, we explained that the ball was really a "fun" ball designed to be injected into a match to add a little good cheer and frivolity. We did not explain this all at once, of course, but spread out the explanation during the period when we were good-naturedly scuffling with Wally and trying to keep him from splitting our skulls with his putter. When he finally became coherent, and had wiped the foam from his lips, we explained that we had carefully marked the place his ball had been and that, being good sports, we would let him putt it again from there with no penalty. Even with this second opportunity to get his birdie, Wally missed the putt.

The off-center ball is just one "fun" device. There are many more. If your golfing companions take tee shots too seriously, you might inject a plaster ball. This ball shatters when struck, disappearing with a "pow" into a cloud of white dust. Or you may switch a long-knocking buddy's ball on the tee, subbing one of those "pyrotechnic" balls from the Orient. This is really a small skyrocket that looks like a golf ball. It has to be placed on the tee with the proper side toward the golfer. When struck, the ball streaks off the tee trailing smoke. It will probably still be sizzling and smoking when your friend reaches it. These "sizzling" balls come under the classification of "fireworks" and must be handled with care. We're not recommending them, but just pointing out that they can really add "fireworks" to a round of golf.

You can also startle and delight your companions with a parachute ball. It looks like a golf ball but consists of two plastic halves that fit neatly together. A small parachute, with a tiny American flag attached to the shroud line, is first packed inside and then the halves are fitted together. You wait until a par three, where you'll use an iron, and then tee up this trick ball. When you smack it high into the air, the ball separates and the parachute comes floating down with the flag flying gaily. The fellow who hits after you is a cinch to knock his ball into the water.

If you don't want to spend good money to liven up the game, depend on your imagination to put some laughs into the action. If you have an opponent who is a "club nut" he is most vulnerable. A club nut is a guy who relies heavily on his own set of clubs, using a precise swing weight and shaft. Switch an often-used iron or wood from his bag to yours and put your club in his bag. Then how you go from there depends on the closeness of the match. You can wait until he is addressing the ball with your wood and, just before he swings, exclaim, "Hey, isn't that my club you have there?" Or you can let him use it a few times. If he does well with it, wait a few holes to call this mix-up to his attention. Say, "Hey, you've been using my four wood. I don't mind, but it is a D-1 and your clubs are all D-4's." Then add, "But you've been hitting real good with my club. I bet you oughta be using D-1's instead of D-4's!" His swing will suddenly lose that precise confidence. And what is especially nice, the confusion will be something he thinks he brought on himself.

Many golfers pursue the game with intense concentration. They are all business from tee to green and, while heading for the next tee, they are lost in a deep study about their grip, swing, or the next hole. With these guys around, there is always an opportunity to add a little fun to the round.

My cart partner was quite talkative, until he birdied two consecutive holes. He was driving the cart, and this sudden spurt of superb golf transfixed him. He headed for the next tee deep in concentration. Someone had left a cart with a flat tire next to the tee. My partner parked alongside, apparently not even noticing the abandoned cart, pulled his driver from the bag and hurried to the tee. I quickly shifted our bags to the cart with the flat tire, strapped them on, and then hurriedly moved the few other knick knacks over — my partner's cigarettes, score card, and soft drink cup.

He hit a beautiful drive. I followed with one not so good and then we walked to the cart. He dropped his driver in the bag and, as he headed for the driver's seat I exclaimed, "Oh no! We have a flat!"

He stared at the tire, but his mind was apparently still on that drive and the ball waiting in the middle of the fairway. "A flat, eh?" he muttered. "Lessee, this is the fourteenth tee. It's a long way in . . ." Then he noticed the other cart (our cart). "Wonder why somebody left that one?" he exclaimed. "Probably had a dead battery. Maybe it's up now enough to run." He climbed in, stepped on the accelerator, and the cart jumped forward. "Hey, we're in luck!" he shouted. "It runs!"

So we unstrapped the bags from the cart with the flat tire and put them back on the other cart, where they had been for thirteen holes. I brought the score card, cigarettes, and soft drink cup over and we charged off down the fairway. Meanwhile the other two in our foursome were weaving along behind us, doubled over with laughter. We never did tell our buddy the truth about his amazing bit of good fortune on the fourteenth tee.

Some foursomes play a taut, business-like game. These are the ones that usually break up and refuse to speak to each other any more. Or three will ostracize the fourth, casting him out like an ugly duckling. If you are one of those cast out, do not give up the game. Somewhere there is a happy, frivolous threesome looking for a non-conforming guy like you.

Joining one of these "loose" threesomes can be as unnerving as being the proverbial illegitimate child at a family reunion. I wandered into such a group at Lubbock recently. At the first tee, there was the usual coin-flipping to see who got to hit first. Then as the lucky guy started his back swing, one of the two golf carts leaped ahead, then screeched to a halt. The fellow on the tee finished his swing smoothly, sending the ball streaking down the fairway. Out on the fairway another player started to hit a four-iron shot. A bag of clubs, with help, fell off the nearby cart. When we reached the green, a golfer with a long birdie putt asked for someone to pull the flag. His opponent stood behind the flag; his feet formed a big "V" just beyond the hole and the flag rattled in the cup. The putt was up for a gimmie. And so the game went on, with putters being dropped "accidentally," much loud talking at all points, and every type of distraction used that you can imagine. None of it seemed to bother these golfers.

We teed off on eighteen with the usual presses working. Again, as the players stroked putts, putters dropped with dull thuds. No one was bothered. Then one of our opponents lined up his crucial ten-foot putt. Perhaps the first whiff of hay fever season rolled in at the precise moment. For just as he started to stroke his putt, I sneezed a hellacious sneeze. He banged the ball fifteen feet past the cup.

"I'm sorry," I gasped, but my partner was hopping about in delight. "That closed 'em out!" he chuckled. "We won the press on the press!"

"Well, I'm sorry," I repeated to our crestfallen opponents. "I never dreamed a sneeze would bother you guys, not after the routines with the carts, the dropped clubs, and all that other noisy stuff you've been doing to each other."

"That was different," our opponent growled as he paid off his bet. "We expect that sort of thing from each other. But we never expected it from you, our *guest!*"

U.S. *versus* U.K.
Stephen Potter

Something must be said in this book of the gamesmanship of Anglo-American golf play, U.S. *v.* U.K.* with particular reference to the U.K. man in the U.S. and occasional reflections on the American in Britain.

How stands all this today? So far as top golf is concerned, America has established a massive one-upness. We, of London, bring congratulations to American top golfers, but it does not stop us from being deeply fed up.

Here, surely, is the prime problem of International Gamesmanship. How to make the invincible vincible. How to reduce the great American one-up to parity.

Hints for the Salt of the Earth

Before we put forward our first pioneering proposals for international golf, let us discuss a few basic principles, with special reference to the ordinary average or salt-of-the-earth golfer, so-called because salt is typical handicap 10.

Lifemanship's attitude to America is well-known but it should be cleared up. Where new things are concerned, America is more-so, England less, and *vice versa* with the old, it may be said, even if there are more exceptions than there is rule.

Since the publication of *Gamesmanship* America has excelled in going one further in gamesmanship as well. Let us take one instance — the original Ploy of the Straight Left Arm (recalled here above). On the New Canaan course, in play with R. Massey, I found the technique already in use *and improved*, by this version of the essential dialogue or "parlette":

* My own view is, at present, definitely a minority one. But I hold increasingly to the belief that Britain and the U.S. should play on the same side, so far as golf is concerned. I envisage matches against France for instance. We and the States are brothers.

U.S. GAMESMAN: I was going to say do you mind if I watch your drive rather close, from here? I think I know *why* you're shooting them so straight.

OPPONENT: Oh yes?

U.S. GAMESMAN: It's that spiral movement starting *from the left instep.*

What one must ask oneself, when v. America, is "Have they any weaknesses?" Is your U.S. friend inclined to health fads, for instance? Are some Americans allergy-minded herbalistical hypochondriacs? No harm in asking your man, anyhow, whether there is bone in his shirt buttons, or telling him that the ring you are wearing has an iodine core and you don't know what you'd do without it.

Another method, when the Americans are being more so in golf, is to try to be more more so than their more so. English golfers who reach the heart of the American golf belt sometimes write exaggerated accounts of the "Ordeal by American Four Ball," in which "believe it or not, every shot is played out, including the tiddliest putt."

"What, not if it's eighteen inches?" says admiring stay-at-home.

"Yes, even if it's two inches," says traveller, calmly. "We started at 9.30 and came in a 4," he goes on, laying it on slightly. "Two rounds, you may well think . . . . Not a bit of it. One."

"What about lunch?" says novice.

"Lunch at 4.30," says Traveller.

"Any tea?" said Wiffley, whose Furthest West was Barnstaple.

"No."

During my first year of playing four balls in America I made the mistake of referring nostalgically to my Wednesday morning meetings for golf with Edgar Lansbury, when we always got through two rounds by lunch time. I at once noticed that the look of admiration I had expected simply was not there, and nobody made any comment whatever. Indeed a strong article of mine, friendly but firm, which I titled "American Golf — Speed Up!" was sent back by the *New*

Yorker and the *Saturday Evening Post.*

"If prejudice against a view exists, change sides." This has always been my rule. And this is my present policy. *Be more so than the more so.*

In other words I decided, in the four ball, to be the slowest. I held it up. A touch here, a device there. I cleaned my ball on the green — but first I unscrewed a tin and sprinkled a little shampoo powder on the wet sponge. A small "Speedi" portable drier useful for hurrying up moisture evaporation on the ball yet took up time because the leads needed fixing to a battery inserted in the golf bag. I specialized in flattening out pitchmarks, not only on the line of my ball to the hole but beyond it.

"Why do you do that?" said one of my American opponents, with friendly curiosity, smiling.

"So often the ball deviates from the straight after passing hole," I said. "We want to minimize this risk."

"It takes time," he said, thoughtfully.

"Half an hour a hole, Cyril reckoned, on the Downs Course (Eastbourne)," I said. "Why rush?" I was inventing at random of course, but I wanted to bring in C.J. Tolley, whose hand I shook in 1923.

Of course a lot can be done on both sides with national habits of hospitality, difference in changing room standards, agreements by small golf ball nations to use large ball, and *vice versa.* Talk about golf ball diameters must leave a trace of confusion, particularly if a decimal point is involved, and when expert opinion seems to state that the small ball is easier *and* that it is impossible to win if you play with it.

Americans must pride themselves on their hospitality which is kind, imaginative and refreshing, thereby putting an unfair burden on guest golf opponent, who is likely, if he tries to get the better of his noble opponent, to feel remorse — something which in its most exaggerated form can mean the loss of three straight holes.*

---

* Cf. losing behaviour of Valjean, potentially a 7 handicap man, in the first episode of *Les Misérables,* after stealing the bishop's candlesticks.

Odoreida, invited through some error or misprint, found himself staying in a gracious and leisurely home, near Charleston, W. Va. At breakfast, he did not want the beautiful bacon, crisp yet mild, and the simple perfection of egg. He wagged his foot.

"Have you any brown bread with sultanas in it?" he said. There was always a suspicion of wheeze in his voice.

"And if you've got it, Keiller's marmalade. No chance of the *Yorkshire Post?*" he added.

So far as the comforts and hospitality of American club changing-rooms are concerned, what is the English visitor to do?

A Canadian gamesman goes round taking photographs as if he were a professional — "the Brussels edition of *Paris Match* . . . interested in your *moeurs* — it means your life, the sort of people you are . . . yellow filter . . ." He then takes a low angle shot of some woman asleep on a balcony who, he says, "is" this place (ugliest woman present).

The Rigor Cup

But we must not shirk the prime problem: the one-upness of American golf. Year after year either the professional contests, the Rigor Cup, or the Amateur, the Walkover, (to say nothing of the ever charming Courtesy Cup) turn up to remind us of the old sequence. The British captain is "full of confidence."* Our fine English professionals, at home and among themselves the dashing destroyers of par, the Herculean drivers, gymnasts of the iron and wizards of the green, are most (but not all of them) transformed, when they get to the States or play against them here, into the kind of player who, one up and one to play, is destined, inevitably, cowed by some grim gods of the Americas, biting the hand which bit them, to take three putts.

Superstition aside, by what forces are they controlled? I

_____
* Always bad gamesmanship, this non-ploy is borrowed from the world of boxing.

259

will enumerate them.

(1) By the atmosphere and suggestion, artificially produced by Britain, that for Britain everything is about as serious as a major operation. This is something to do with the English Press, implacably leaden hearted on these occasions and the traditional ENGLAND FACED WITH DISASTER type of headline, which in June means that three England wickets have fallen at Lord's before lunch time.

(2) By the sense that to the American players, inevitably, it is all a gentle interlude. Where in October 1967 was Julius Boros on the day before the Ryder Cup started? Practising on the difficult Champions course? He was fishing on the bank of the water hazard.

(3) By the sense that though, for him, the British Professional, the pay is worth earning, the American players know they are probably losing money. Here we are faced with the one-upness of the preternaturally prosperous.

(4) By a sense of the inevitability of history, and the feeling that we were once so they must be now.

Here is a problem worthy of the highest gamesmanship. If I were to leave to my heirs a plan of attack, I am sure now of the general trend. Be more, or be the opposite, should be my guiding principle. As for seriousness, why not go the whole hog, spend the night before the match in meditation, and light a little fire, as a sacrifice, at break of day? Be on the practice tee at first light. Associate yourself with a peculiar religion. "A dedicated man," they will say.

But I would prefer places in the team to be given to the happy-go-lucky, the dashing, the debonair, and the handsome. We have not yet discussed the importance of looks in international golf. Many British players are handsome but they are not produced properly. Besides being handsome he has to look handsome. As for money let them be financially independent or perhaps real estate men with oil interests, to whom a million dollars, plus or minus, is rather small feed to men who could and would buy the golf course if they wanted to.

As for the inevitability of history, keep repeating that

progress is not a series of slices piled up like a club sandwich, that regress is just as common, and that according to Spengler, and possibly Toynbee, the beacon of American golf eminence may be showing already the dubious and phosphorescent light of incipient decay. I intend, when I meet Arnold Palmer, to tell him this, in almost exactly these words.

To Each Course Its Own Daemon

Daemon in Latin: δαίμων in Greek. The different spelling is a reminder that the original meaning of "demon" was different. There was nothing horrid about it. On the contrary. The classical word could be translated as "spirit" — the protective or determining spirit which gives and controls character.

The fact that each good and memorable golf course in Britain and America has its own essential eccentricity can be an important factor in gamesmanship. Possibly the most startling *daemon* courses occur in the United States, at any rate the proportion is high in those I know. A few of these examples may seem far fetched but I have the feeling that I was myself directly subjected to able gamesmanship in a way which some may find surprising.

The course which put me on the alert was in Kansas. I was lecturing at Kansas State University. All Englishmen who find themselves 1500 miles from the nearest sea water feel particularly high and dry; but the hospitality was perfection, and I felt I had made some good new friends — until golf was arranged for me next morning. Talking about my game the night before, I had told the Lecturer in Italian Renaissance Architecture that I would like to play, although I was suffering at the moment from a serious tendency to hook.

"Good," he said at once. "I should be lecturing tomorrow morning but my student is sick. Let's play."

No discussion as to which course — and in fact the one chosen for me was built round the sides of a conical hill which was played clockwise. With my hook, every ball I drove went bouncing down the slope into what seemed to be almost a different geological formation.

Chance, the reader may think: but what of this example of what I can only call DCmanship?

My hosts were distinguished members respectively of the C.I.A. and the *Washington Post*. I was longing, as always in America, for exercise. Burning Tree was suggested — which attracted me because I knew that the then President, Eisenhower, sometimes played there. I was putting well for some reason; and one thing about America is that one can take one's time on the greens. On the 8th green I looked up. My opponents were talking. They sounded fidgety.

"Sorry," they said. "Only —"

"Anything up?" I said.

"Only that we think the President's here."

"Oh yes?"

"Did you hear that plane 20 minutes ago. It's best to *keep going*, you know? On we get."

He made a sweeping forward motion with his hand.

"He likes to do the course at some speed, you know?"

"Naturally."

"Those two fellows ahead — probably got guns."

In spite of all my experience, my game showed a hairline fracture, and I had to admit I was outgambited when I read next morning that the President was in Palm Springs. It put me on my guard for the future. "Don't slice here, my friend," said my opponent at Paradise Valley. This was one of those oasis courses, a sudden green place in the middle of the Arizona desert.

"Why, particularly?" I said, non-commitally.

"You might find your ball in a nest of side-winders."

I smiled, but there *were* snakes and I *had* seen a caddy with his arm in a sling. How can one be sure? Even when I first tasted the beauties of Cypress Point, the oldest member of our four-ball — actually he had a white goatee beard — told me at an important hole, made still more beautiful by the sparkling of the Western sun on the Pacific, that "this was where we could see the seals — and hear them too, at this time of year."

"Rather sweet," I said, thinking of my shot.

"Listen. At this time of year it's their sexual roar."

Old World Equivalents

English and Scottish courses have their own *daemon*, but it is more of an elf, very often, or sprite. Both countries excel in settings of fabulous beauty — ideal conditions for missing the ball completely on the first tee, courses like Pine Valley, emperor of the American East, Pine Valley the majestic, almost compelling the newcomer either to attempt ridiculously enormous shots, or pokey little prodding shots, from nervousness and a feeling of inferiority.* In Scotland there are famous hostile courses, like Carnoustie — Irish Portmarnock could be included here — which have this effect: or dramatically handsome courses like Newcastle, County Down, bristling with quotes about the Mountains of Mourne. There is a new-boy-at-school feeling when we first play such courses. And has the Old Course, St. Andrews, itself got a total gambit? For the new player there is a specialized form of hallowed turfmanship, world famous bunkers, sanctified burn, the immortal anxieties of the 17th, and a general feeling that one is playing not only the course but history, behind the backs, turned indifferently towards us, of the ghosts of the most celebrated names in the game.

An interesting variation is the Killarney course, where the almost overpowering beauty of the rock and water type is

---

* When I played Pine Valley I was at my worst and shortest, taking the "Newcomer's Nine," standard for the first hole. But I had little chance. The famous captain of the Club, John Arthur Brown, then 70 and handicap four, received me. It is said that he was under the impression that I was Stephen Spender whose name of course stands high in literary circles in the U.S. He then entertained us, lunched us, and played with me: and it is the custom, at Pine Valley, for other players to stand aside and allow the Captain and his guest to play through. Many couples had to stand aside for quite a time.

softened by the acceptance of fishing as an O.K. alternative. It might be added here that the acceptance of fishing as a sideline grows daily, particularly in our Municipal Club, where the first tee is half under a gasometer and any visible stream is not quite perfect in content.

Muirfield has its own variation on the same theme. Here history is infrequently mentioned. Famous finishes over the last few holes in the Open are taken for granted. But one is faced with the nobility of pure golf in a Club where the ban on business talk is so complete that there is no professional's shop, and where the players are so single minded in the play that none of them have handicaps.*

Finally let us look at a few typical gambits peculiar to individual clubs. Many of these are haunted by an out-of-bounds reputation. "Mind you don't slice at Lytham, pull at Hoylake, and above all in spite of that bunker on the left, don't slice on to the railway alongside the 4th at Woking." This is a standard way of stiffening up the newcomer and being careful lest, because he doesn't know the dangers, he is going to be carefree. "So flat," they said of Royal Mid-Surrey. And who was J.H. Taylor to contradict them? Just the local pro., who covered the course with such a variety of traps and hummocks, slopes and pimples, that the stranger off line finds himself continually playing off some of the most discouraging angles in golf.

Then there is Rye, whose resident *daemon* presides in summer, when the course is dry, when putts which are overhit on the 1st or the 5th green for instance scamper off the green on the other side,** or where some of the holes seem to be played on the crest of a smooth ridge, the back of a long

---

* Compare the fine gambit of the Portland Club where, in the bridge room "they play no conventions." "Same with my car driving," said Gattling to me, noticing my surprise at finding him in this Club. "Let me take you home." He was, I thought, a little "on."

**"It'll be better in winter," the gamesmen of Rye say to their visitors. In the winter, for some reason which has never yet been explained, the greens are even faster.

animal — the 4th particularly, where one seems to be coaxing the ball along the backbone of an early cretaceous animal. Few can look, as they wander through the fossil reptile rooms of the Natural History Museum, at the interminable backbone of *Diplodocus Carnegii,* without thinking of the fourth hole at Rye.

Or there are "Beware" courses, like North Berwick, with those low stone walls.

"I should take a more lofted club if I were you," I was told. "If you hit that No. 5 a bit thin, it just won't carry the wall. Might do you an injury."

"Well, actually I belong to Aldeburgh," I used to reply. "Those sleepers in the bunker at the short 4th. Simpson nearly lost an eye there."

Sometimes the local put-offs can be unexpected. It is compulsory at Guadalmina, on the Costa del Sol, to have caddies, and to ask for them at their school, by the nearby hotel. On demand two are at once forthcoming. At the age of approximately nine, the ecstacy of being removed from the classroom is so great that joy and laughter and a desire to rush about cannot be confined. No need to say how putting-off this is to the player, who has to learn especial Spanish phrases to keep them in order. How different the atmosphere of Woking or Worplesdon, with their melancholy Autumn beauty. I think it was on the water hole at Worpers, last time I played there, that Darwin asked me, as I played my ball out from the trees into which my ball had unluckily rolled, not to "hack about" to much.

"Why?" I said.

"Middlewick's ashes," he said, in a for him almost poetic sort of voice. "They were scattered on this place."

Excerpt From **The Bogey Man**
George Plimpton

The round the next day, the third of the tournament, produced an odd shot. Larry Mancour was our professional, and on one hole he drove a three wood on a line into a high palm just at the edge of the fairway. After we had trudged around the tree for a while it was apparent the ball had not dropped out. Mancour climbed the smooth bole of the palm some thirty feet up and discovered that his ball was impaled on a thorn. He took a swipe at it with an iron, leaning far out from the tree trunk to do so, and brought the ball down with the thorn and a network of fronds still attached. No one knew whether Mancour was allowed a free drop, or if he was required to scrape along with the original ball, its branches flopping, until he got to the green where he could presumably "lift" it and clean it. A marshal appeared and allowed him a free drop.

The rules were not always so lenient. In *The Golfer's Handbook* I discovered that one R. Andrew, playing for the Hillhouse Cup at Troon, found his ball impaled on a hairpin. He had to play the hole with the hairpin intact. It never came out during the play of that hole, and it was Andrew's estimate that the hairpin had cost him ten strokes.

As usual, the *Handbook,* under its heading "Freak Shots," had pertinent material to enjoy that evening, some of which made Moncour's shot seem pretty small potatoes. In 1953, for example, a Scottish golfer trying to sink an approach on the 5th hole at St. Andrews duck-hooked his shot which rolled up on the adjacent green, the 13th, and dropped into the hole. On that same round, obviously inspired, this same golfer sliced his second shot on the 18th so severely that it bounced off the roof of a lorry and sailed through the front door of the clubhouse and rattled around until it ended up in the bar.

Another example, one of the best from the *Handbook,* I think, reads as follows: "A member of the Wildernesse Club,

266

Kent, drove a ball from the first tee through a window of the professional's shop, where it ended up in a cup of tea which the professional was about to pick up. The cup was undamaged, but the professional was slightly cut by broken glass from the window."

Much of the talk around the bar that evening — inspired by reports of Mancour's odd difficulty — was about freak shots. Bob Rosburg said that he had once hit a shot that went up a drainpipe into the men's locker room and rolled out on the carpet.

"I know a guy," said someone at the table, "who putted into his own hat. Guy called John Beck, an Englishman, a good golfer, and his hat blew off while he was making his putting stroke and damned if it didn't land out there where the ball went right into it."

But the golfers didn't seem at home with the subject — true duffer's shots were an indignity to their profession.

Johnny Pott leaned across and said to me: "I guess it's the 18-handicappers who are what you might call experts on such shots."

"I'll say," I said.

I began describing a shot I had seen my brother hit. We were in England on a vacation together, and on impulse had gone out to play a round at Sandhurst, one of the historic courses of England. Our caddy was an elderly, stooped man who expressed at the start his warm admiration for the United States and its golfers. He had caddied at one time for Bobby Jones, he told us. My brother and I are both tall and big, and he expected, I think, a powerful round from each of us. He handed my brother a driver, and then with a cheerful smile, standing off at right angles, just where a caddy should be while the golfer shoots, he recommended that my brother favor the right side of the fairway, not too much, just a wee mite.

My brother nodded and then hit the ball off the toe of his club just ticking it with the rush of his club so that the ball went off nearly at right angles, on a line, rather softly because it had been grazed, directly into the kneecap of the caddy. The caddy gave out the following sound:

"Awks!"

He sat down. My brother was very contrite, of course. He rushed up and did what he could. The caddy was unable to continue. He went back to the caddy house with this rather forlorn look, not of pain, but disappointment, as if my brother, as a representative of his country, had not lived up to . . . well, expectations.

"Yes," the golfers said.

"I wish I had had a tape measure there at Sandhurst," I said suddenly.

"What for?"

I told them about the statistics in *The Golfer's Handbook* — that one of the categories was the length of rebound shots hitting caddies. The record, I told them, was a 75-yard rebound off the forehead of a caddy on the Premier Mine Course, South Africa. The caddy's name was not recorded, but the ball was. It was a Colonel.

"The ball that my brother hit wasn't truly a rebound," I said. "It went a long way, but it was more a grazing shot. I guess it wouldn't have counted."

"No," said the golfers.

"In any case, I didn't check the name of the ball."

I was very enthusiastic that evening. I went on to describe another misplay. I told the golfers about a shot hit by Alex Karras, the Detroit tackle. They'd told me about it, his Lion teammates, maybe five, maybe ten times. He hit this shot on the first tee at Red Run Golf Club in Royal Oak, Michigan. He's a terrible golfer, Karras — almost all big football tackles and guards seem to be, I suppose because of the lack of suppleness in their upper limbs — and what happened was that he stepped up and smacked his drive off the end of his club, very much as my brother had, and it went right through the big plate-glass window of the clubhouse. The entire glass front disappeared — the glass simply dropped out of its supports with a roar, and Karras, with his club over his shoulder in the follow-through, and the rest of his foursome could look into the interior of the clubhouse front room.

There wasn't anyone in there. Karras went up and looked in over the sill. Of course, the glass collapsing had made this terrific crash, and after a while down at the end of the room a waiter appeared in a doorway, balancing a tray with someone's lunch on it under covered plates, staring up the length of the room.

Alex couldn't see his ball on the carpet, but he yelled down to the waiter: "Hey, is this room out of bounds?"

The golfers laughed, or murmured, rather. They did not warm to the subject. One of them ordered a round of drinks. The talk drifted on to something else. I had a few more shots I could have described. I'd seen a Random House editor, Joe Fox, hit a drive off the heel of his club *between his legs* into a large shrub off the tee. I could have described that. Or a shot I had seen Peter Duchin, the orchestra leader, make from the flat roof of the Shinnecock Hills Golf Club at Southampton where he had skyed his approach. He climbed up a painter's ladder to get there, outlined against the sky with his putter, and he skillfully punched the ball from the roof over the drain gutter down onto the green where he got his putt down for an interesting double-bogey.

Then it occurred to me, sitting with half an ear to the golfers' conversation, that the ultimate in bad shots had been described somewhat tartly by Abe, my caddy. One day during the Crosby, I had asked him if he would describe what he considered the worst shot he had ever seen in the Crosby.

He thought I was speaking generally about bad shots, and after thinking a while, he said: "Well, the worst shot I seen, if you want it straight, are them that go nowhere. Them that sit on the tee."

I must have looked puzzled.

"The golfer swings and *misses*. That's the shot I'm talking about," Abe said.

"Oh, yes," I said. "You know what the *easiest* shot in golf is, Abe?" I had asked.

"What?"

"The fourth putt. Ring Lardner wrote that."

"Yah?"

269

That night, just by chance, I looked into the book bag and found a story of Vardons about the worst shot *he* ever saw. He had once seen a beginner at a place called Totteridge miss the ball completely and yet lose it. This fellow had lashed at the ball, his eyes apparently almost shut tight, with a lofted iron, and hitting far behind the ball he had lifted up a divot, a piece of turf, as large as a soup plate which had dropped on the ball. "Where is it? Where'd it go?" he asked, peering down the fairway, shading his eyes, and then someone said "ahem" and it was pointed out to him that the ball was directly under his divot.

Watching My Wife
John L. Hulteng

My wife was playing in a golf match the other day in the National Women's Championship, and I was in the gallery.

Fortunately, I'm never nervous on such occasions.

They teed off, and my wife's opponent dropped a magnificent putt for a birdie and won the first hole. There was a man in a yellow jacket who kept following along beside me and he turned to me:

"What are you doing?"

"I'm writing down the score," I told him.

"Hadn't you better turn the pencil around? The lead is on the other end."

"Thank you," I said, with dignity.

My wife lost the second hole, and was two down. A woman in a long peaked cap came up to me.

"Things aren't looking too bright, are they?" she said sympathetically.

"Oh," I said airily, "it's nothing to be upset about. After all, it's only a molf gatch."

She stared at me a moment. "Yes," she said. "Yes, of course."

Neither my wife nor her opponent won either of the next

two holes. Then they came to a short, par three hole. My wife was about to hit her drive. The man in the yellow jacket was beside me again.

"She's about to drive," he said. "Aren't you going to watch?"

"I have to tie my shoelace," I told him.

"You've been tying that shoelace during every shot for the last three holes."

"It's an old lace," I told him. "Very slippery."

Finally the match stood all even after six holes. Then my wife hit a shot into a bad piece of rough.

"Don't be jittery now," said the man in the yellow jacket. "She can still get out of it all right."

"I'm not the slightest bit jittery and I wish you wouldn't keep talking about it," I told him, edging away.

"Hey," he said. "Watch where you're —"

Two gallery marshals helped me up out of the sand trap and brushed the sand off the back of my shirt.

"I ought to penalize your wife two strokes," one of them said darkly; "it's against the rules for a competitor to use any implement to test the consistency of a sand trap."

Around the middle of the match my wife took a one-hole lead. The tension grew. It was blazing hot on the course. I reached down for my handkerchief and mopped the perspiration off my brow.

"Do you always," said the man in the yellow jacket, "use your tie to wipe your face?"

"There are so many other matches to watch," I told him. "Why don't you go find one of them?"

My wife won another hole, and was two up with only a few holes left.

I was standing at one side of the fairway, in the shade of some trees. The woman in the peaked cap came up behind me.

"Well," she said, slapping me on the shoulder. "How do you feel now?"

"Fine," I told her from ten feet up in the tree. "Just fine."

"That's good," she said. "Don't try to get down. I'll go find a ladder."

The sun grew hotter and the tension tighter. But as it turned out my wife won the match on the sixteenth hole. Someone went up to congratulate her and asked her how she felt.

"I'm hungry," she said.

And I'm proud to say that I maintained my own icy calm right up to the final moment of the match.

In fact, I never felt more relaxed than I did as they carried me into the clubhouse.

Muny Golf Takes Guts — Right, Mac?
Jay Cronley

I requested a tee off time at 10 a.m. on a Saturday that was promised lovely — temperature between 70 and 80 and a fast track. Wind: none. Moisture: in Coors cans.

"No."

Well, yes, I see, Let's make it 9 a.m. Should be able to shake it up by then.

"No. Full."

Eight? No. Seven? No. Noon? No way. One? Ha-ha. Two? You a comedian. Three, four, five p.m.? Three no's. Six a.m.? Out of the question. When then? Which is where 5:30 a.m. comes in.

It comes in quickly. It is not completely light at 5:30 a.m. It is not anything, except mighty still — still dark, still before the newspaper, still stiff. Any false hopes you had about feeling heavenly vanishes between squints. If you are not the son or daughter of the pro, chef, parking lot guy, mayor, or keeper of the greens, you are out of luck, Mac. Municipal players are best characterized as Macs.

We drink beer, clonk around in any number of stripes and dots, stand in line and get wicked sunburns.

Don't feel all that sorry for us. We get to play golf without shirts. The men. We can find from one to 20 golf balls per 18-hole round. The country club player pays for the right to shoot a quick, comfortable, fashionable 90. We do it furiously, for maybe $10 total, if we get the bounce.

There are those who have never played a municipal golf course, the Esquires and III's and Van-Somethings, and it is to them that I dedicate this material. While you are scratching your toes on rich carpet in the men's lounge, we are trying to hit an 8-iron off bare dirt that is nourished only by spilled pop.

No, I have played some splendid municipal golf courses, one in Albuquerque with fairway grass thick as welcome rugs, and one in Ireland that played through castle ruins. The difference then is psychological. You must summon inner courage to tee it up with a man dressed in sneakers, an ascot, and a glove on the wrong hand, who says, "Mind if I play through?" on the No. 1 tee.

I find a particular thrill in standing on the putting green and being watered down by an attendant in a plantation hat who "speek no Eenglish, Meester."

It is my contention that anybody, with proper money, can play a country club golf course. It requires I'll-lead-us-to-Omaha-Beach-boys, why-don't-we-step-out-back, race-you-around-the-block guts to play a municipal golf course.

Down the No. 1 fairway at shortly after 6 a.m., as the sun pulls away from the horizon, displaying the hole in pink glow, there is still some fog, but you can see 14 guys trying to tee off. There is an official "starter," a retired gentleman with a microphone who says, mostly during backswings, "Mr. Snodgrass next on the tee." If you venture forth alone you are paired with other jokers who generally range in handicap from four to 30. I got a used truck salesman and his buddy who sold books, a 17 and an 18, and one of the oldest men I have ever seen upright. During a splendid round last year he shot 134, his age.

Hello, glad to meetcha. Me, oh I'm an eight handicap or so. The old guy and I will play them for two bucks a side, lowball. The old guy can't hear for beans, YOU AND ME. PARTNERS. TWO BUCKS. DOLLARS.

The tee area is roped off, like a bullfight. Behind, the thumps of practice swings echo off the asphalt. My partner had four clubs. Can he use my putter? Sure. SURE.

Mulligans — hitting drives, machine-gun style, until one finds the fairway — are as common as elm trees. The theory of mulligans at a municipal course is that 11 mulligans are no worse than one. If you are going to violate the Rules of Golf you might as well go ahead and violate the heck out of them. Golf balls are flying from the tee. I promise you that for the briefest of moments, both our opponents were teeing off at the same time.

The law of averages once again prevailed and they are down the middle.

My partner nudges it dead left into the driving range, and he plays one with a stripe around it.

Once on the course you must adjust your game and your behavior. It is not uncommon to be "hit into," which can result in serious injury, not to mention bogey. On one municipal course I saw a man hit into a group, the drive coming within inches of a skull. The player owning the skull walked back to the tree and hit a perfect 9-iron across the forehead of the man owning the driver. The latter passed out, cold. Somebody called an ambulance. No big deal. Par for the course.

It is not unusual to find strange objects in municipal sand traps, even bones. Some players think the rake by the side of the trap is a hazard itself, and that it is a two-stroke penalty if you touch it. Putting out of a trap was invented on a municipal course. Also, throwing it out of a trap. Also, leaving it in a trap.

There are many reasons why play tends to be slow on a municipal golf course. A main one is that a golf ball, however wounded, is a sacred object, and when one is hit into wood, over road or into water it is searched for. Other people's balls also are searched for. A view of the public course from above must look like the biggest Easter egg hunt of all time.

Another reason for slow play is inferior play. When you seven-putt a green, it takes time. When you forget where the green is, it takes time to find it. When you stop to climb a fence and get a Coke from an adjoining supermarket, it takes time.

You are always hearing, "Excuse my buddy here, he is just learning."

Another reason is that nobody lets you play through, as if it were a sin. You ask to play through, then put 'em up and get ready to fight. Hit into them, they will hit back, and pretty soon it will be just like volleyball. It is as if letting somebody play through means you are a sissy.

As we completed No. 9 at 10 a.m. there was much teaching activity on the practice tee. It takes a real man to give lessons at a municipal course. You must spot improvement in a series of flailing arms, you must iron out slices, fade hooks and keep a straight face because no, Mr. Whomple, it isn't like croquet.

A municipal golf course is two parts, the front nine and the back nine. It is not a whole. There were six groups on the ninth tee, one of which should have been there, five of which had sneaked on when the back nine attendant, age 16, ran off after a girl from the pool.

We waited a six-pack worth, 35 minutes. My partner napped. I read half of a 200-page novel, and our opponents went to practice putts on the 18th green, which was near. When I looked up there were nine golf balls on the green, and the group coming up the 18th fairway was only a sixsome. Illegal, but fun.

The 18th is appropriately uphill, and, as the most logical placement of all, the bar and grill is just behind. You could fly one there and remain. The grill is what it is all about, the place where competitors fret over the scorecard as if it were Form 1040, shoes off, bag lumped in a corner, beer frothing, body still rippling like you just drove Kansas City-Las Vegas, non stop.

This is where you add the eights and nines and discover where the $4 is headed. The money is handled gently, like a Master's jacket. Losers crumple the proof, scorecard, as if it had been a poorly selected ticket at the $2 window. The sandwiches are the greatest, the beer the coldest, the companionship the best.

Remember No. 17? Flew an 8-iron. Flew it over the green, over the water fountain, over the fence, over the road. Should have choked a wedge.

Sometimes you have to go as far back as No. 2 to find that one crisp shot that will bring you back. My partner is exhausted, pale. I get some beer in him and he wants to go nine more. We make a game for next week and we are good friends.

To hundreds of thousands who go to drive-in movies, shop sales, buy golf balls at the drug store and putt from 10 yards off the green this is the only game in town.

It is the same great game they play on television for all that bread. When you check to see who is watching the next big tournament it will be the same person who is out Saturday morning, elbowing his way onto the first tee, wearing a baseball cap and a dedicated look.

Golf is great because you can give it to the people. If you want to watch some of us play, I'll give you a ring some morning about 5, but if you want to come later and start on 13, well who's to know. Right, Mac?

Just bring your lunch.

Golf is a Funny Game
Ronald Heager

"GOLF IS A funny game, caddie."

"Aye, sir, but it's no' meant to be."

The old time Scot was showing the true regard of his race for the royal and ancient pastime. But truth is the game has been contradicting him ever since it began. Golf *is* funny. It just cannot help itself.

Take Arnold Palmer, most regal golfer of his age. The first time I met him was on his visit to Portmarnock for the 1960 Canada Cup. He was U.S. Masters and Open Champion, on the crest of a wave. It was his first taste of British conditions. The golf writers swarmed round him at the end of his first practice round. Deftly, good-humouredly, Arnie answered all the questions.

Inevitably he was asked: "What about the small ball, how did you get on with it?" Palmer added a regiment of friends to his "Army" with the reply:

"I like the small ball. It makes the hole look bigger."

I have found Arnie's off-the-cuff quips and repartee rolling forth ever since. Even in his blackest moments.

After the Open Championship triumphs of Royal Birkdale and Troon, Palmer had to strike his colours at Royal Lytham in 1963. He never got his game going and finished joint twenty-sixth.

On the final day the outgoing champion endured the indignity of an early starting time at the back of the field while Bob Charles, Phil Rodgers, Jack Nicklaus and Peter Thomson fought it out for the title. I was among a band of loyalists on hand to greet Palmer as he finished his fourth round in 76.

The path from the eighteenth green ran between the ivy-clad, red-brick clubhouse and a temporary television tower. Arnie strode in with his card, tight-lipped and grim. But as he drew abreast of the tower he saw a few familiar faces and with an upward glance at the tubular scaffolding he remarked laconically:

"Is this where you hang yourself?"

The Palmer stories are legion. My favourite is related by former Walker Cup player Guy Wolstenholme.

Guy, in his second year as a professional, began a tour of the American winter circuit in January 1962. It lasted three weeks, tragically cut short by an accident in which Guy broke his left arm.

It happened at Cypress Point, one of the three famous Pacific Coast courses on which the annual Bing Crosby tournament is played. Guy, in his last practice round, jumped on to what appeared to be the stump of a tree. It turned out to be a loose log which gave way and sent Guy crashing to the ground.

The scene was the tee of the sixth hole, one of the toughest and most renowned par three's in golf. It is 222 yards, a full drive across the yawning blue waters of the Pacific to a peninsula green. If you miss the green, it's down the cliff into the foaming seas below.

After the accident a woebegone Wolstenholme, with arm strapped up, encountered Arnold Palmer. Arnie consoled Guy and said: "I always knew it was one helluva hole, but I did not realise it was so tough it could break your arm!"

Palmer's great American rival, Jack Nicklaus, looks just as stern and serious as Arnold while taking a golf course apart. Yet Jack, too, has a sharp and spontaneous wit.

The second round of the 1964 Open championship was a disaster for him. He was blown out of it with a round of 74, containing 40 putts, the most he had ever had in a tournament. Next morning he made his move in what proved to be the vain chase of Tony Lema with a scorching third round of 66.

Before Jack begun the final round, an American journalist, Tom Reedy, encountered him in the Royal and Ancient clubhouse and said:

"Well, Jack, I see you've discovered the secret of the Old Course."

Replied Nicklaus, with a grin: "Yes. Fewer putts."

Nicklaus visited England for the Piccadilly tournament at Southport in his first year as a professional in 1962. We were old acquaintances from the Walker Cup matches at Muirfield and Seattle. We talked of this and that and I said: "Where was your last tournament, Jack?"

"At Burneyville, Oklahoma. Just a place with two houses," he replied.

"Good course?" I asked.

"Just like you'd get at a place with two houses," was Jack's all-embracing reply.

All the fun of the fairways is no monopoly of the Americans, even though the flamboyant Walter Hagen contributed more than his share in another era. It is not the monopoly of the moderns, either.

Like the best of golf and golfers, some of the loveliest stories come from Scotland. The hero of every other one of them is the legendary Andra' Kirkaldy, a rugged native of St. Andrews with a salty turn of phrase. Frank Moran, doyen of golf writers and fifty years the *Scotsman's* correspondent, has a treasure house of Scots stories. I retell three of them.

The craggy, powerful Kirkaldy formed a colourful partnership with "Wee Ben" Sayers, for more than forty years the golfing monarch of that other famous citadel of the game, North Berwick.

They played many important matches together around the turn of the century. One of them was at St. Andrews at a time the railway line bordering the right of the fifteenth and sixteenth holes was not out of bounds as it is now. Sayers cut his shot on to the lines, giving Kirkaldy a horrible lie among the sleepers and flints.

Andra' was far from pleased. He climbed the railings, saying: "This is a time for sweerin'. Staund back, you wimmen."

The dimunitive Sayers came over to the railings as Kirkaldy fumed over the lie, in time to hear Andra' say: "Lend us that wee mashie of yours."

"Na, na," replied Ben. "Brek yer ain bluidy club."

Kirkaldy's challenge matches with Sayers took them all over the country. Once Andra' was one of a quartet seeking a restaurant in the West End of London. They eventually settled for what the itinerant professionals would have classified as a "posh" place. The meal was excellent. But the bill was a stunner. As the party left an obsequious and slightly anxious waiter helped Andra' on with his coat and murmured:

"You won't forget the waiter, sir?"

"Naw," Kirkaldy answered huffily. "Ah'll never forget ye. And what's more, ah'll never forgie ye!"

St. Andrews is as inseparable from the fun of the game as it is from golf itself. The Old Course has a short hole which few would challenge as being the greatest par three in the world, the 170-yard eleventh, with its Shell and Cockle bunkers, the estuary of the Eden at the back, and the fiendish slope of the green towards the tee.

One of the pillars of golf as a pastime early in the century was the Rt. Hon. A.J. Balfour, a leading politician who probably did as much for the game in Britain as President Eisenhower was to do later in the United States.

Mr. Balfour was a regular visitor to North Berwick and St. Andrews. At the time he was Secretary of State for Ireland, his golfing excursions demanded the attendance of a couple of armed detectives. It all helped to publicise golf and make people think there must be something in the game. It also left the locals of St. Andrews in no doubt about the importance of Mr. Balfour.

One day Balfour was playing the Old Course and duly reached the short eleventh. His tee shot found the green but he was left with a long, long, difficult putt. He consulted his caddie about the line and was told:

"Hit it a yaird to the left."

The ball finished a good yard to the right of the flag. Whereon the caddie snorted to a companion:

"And these are the b.....s that are running the country."

There is no end to the classic caddie comments. Among my favourites is that during the club consultation routine between hacker and caddie at a hole where the tee shot has to traverse a lake.

"What shall I take here?" queries the player, gravely.

"An old ball," is the brutal reply.

Then there is the pun to end all puns from the Scots caddie wearied at too frequent replacing of divots:

"It's no' replacing the tur-r-f I am. It's retur-r-fing the bluidy place."

The companion one to this is:

Player: "I'll move heaven and earth to play this game properly."

Caddie (a few holes later): "Well, 'e's only got 'eaven ter move now."

Bad-tempered golfers and bland caddies are a prolific source of golfing fun. Few match this gem:

"You must be the worst caddie in the world."

"Gawd, no, sir. That would be too much of a coincidence."

It is said the Scots themselves invent tales like that in which the Scots golfer asked his boy caddie: "Are you guid at finding balls?"

"Aye, sir."

"Away then and find one and we'll start the game."

Thirty years ago Henry Longhurst, who has a most perceptive ear and joyous pen for the lighter side of golf, collaborated with Robert Graves on an anthology of caddie stories, *Candid Caddies*.

The one I cherish most from their researches concerns the Colonel given to explosive language on the course. His efforts to curb the violent expression of his wrath reached the stage of giving his straitlaced, chapel-going caddie a sixpenny fine for every oath.

The old man was said to flinch with horror at his master's outbursts. But he made sure of collecting the sixpences.

At the end of one round the Colonel made his calculation and handed over 4s. 6d. for his cuss words.

The old man counted it and said: "Beg pardon, Colonel, but ain't ye forgotten the b..... on the fourth green?"

The caddies are vanishing. But the fun goes on.

Mention of Henry Longhurst brings back memory of a gorgeous aside he made at the 1959 Ryder Cup match in America. The opulent background of the Eldorado Country Club — members, President Eisenhower, Bing Crosby, Bob Hope — gave the Americans the perfect setting for putting on the show they love at golf's international occasions.

Among the amenities was the band of an American Air Force unit. They confined their efforts, of course, to the morning flag-raising ceremony and the luncheon interval.

During lunch one of the tunes they played was what the airmen no doubt knew as the theme music from that splendid war film, "Bridge on the River Kwai." The British party thought of it as the rousing, ribald "Colonel Bogey" march.

As Longhurst and I walked past the band, Henry remarked tartly: "I wonder if they know the words?"

The late Bernard Darwin, Longhurst's predecessor as a golfing laureate, contrived his mellifluous essays and reports with a gentle, chiding humour which mirrored his life-long love affair with the game of golf.

Darwin was an accomplished player — Walker Cup, England, Cambridge University — but if things went wrong on the course he had a reputation for exploding into a raging fury. His imprecations had to be heard to be believed, say those who knew him.

Beset with bunker trouble one day, he was heard to invoke the Lord to damn and blast the bunker to everlasting hell-fire. And as a rider to his oaths he raged:

". . . And don't send your Son down. This is a man's job."

An event specially cherished by Darwin was the President's Putter, which he won in 1924. This hardy annual winter frolic of the Oxford and Cambridge Golfing Society ranks second to none in the standard of its gaiety, humour and wit.

The participants, men honoured and respected in the highest walks of life, enjoy the nicknames of their youth. Each year the entry will contain: "The Emperor," "The Poet," "The Monk," "The Camel," "The Italian," and the like.

In a recent "Putter" Donald Steel was playing another past winner, Michael Anderson, a doctor from Liverpool, in a third round tie so desperately fought that it went to the sixth extra hole, the twenty-fourth.

As the large gallery surged onward from the twenty-fourth tee the talk turned to the possibility of calling a halt because of failing light. This brought up the question of the longest match in the history of the event, that in which Tony Duncan defeated John Beck at the twenty-sixth hole in 1948. This duel was halted by darkness, Duncan winning on the resumption in the morning and going on to win the final.

I was reporting the Steel-Anderson match and was able to check all the facts of the 1948 marathon with John Beck himself, who was walking in the crowd beside me. I shall always remember his concluding remark: "We had to stop not so much because we could not see the flags, but because we could not see each other."

This was in the highest tradition of the event, which January's rawest weather has only once prevented finishing on schedule.

Gerald Micklem, staunchest of Oxford and Cambridge golf supporters, has done everything and met everybody who is anybody in the game. From his term as Walker Cup captain he reveals a delicious anecdote which displays how in some ways Britain and America live in two worlds of golf.

A prelude to the Walker Cup matches is always a joint conference of the teams to make clear the conditions and form of the match and any small differences existing between R. & A. and U.S.G.A. rules.

In 1957 when the match was at Minikahda the teams duly assembled. Some of the Americans had to be carefully briefed about the foursomes, a form of golf rare in the United States.

As the explanation regarding playing alternate strokes drew to an end one of the newcomers to the American side put the ultimate question: "Does it mean if my partner holes the putt, I drive off at the next tee?"

In the ghastly hush that followed this boner, the abashed player asked his captain, Charlie Coe: "Do I still play in the foursomes tomorrow, captain?"

He did. His name — Arnold Blum.

In the 1955 Walker Cup match at St. Andrews I recollect watching the morning singles beside the thirteenth green in the company of a group including the American captain, the charming "Big Bill" Campbell, who as recently as 1964 won the American Amateur title at the age of forty-one.

Campbell had crossed over from the outgoing matches and was waiting to pick up the top single between Britain's Ronnie White and Harvie Ward, winner of both U.S. and

British titles and one of the greatest amateur golfers since World War II.

"Having a good game, Junior?" said Campbell, addressing handsome little Harvie.

"Heck, no," Ward replied, "It is all even."

Ward proved the killer with a smile; he pulled away to crush White six and five and end Ronnie's eight-year record of not losing a Walker Cup single.

Amateur golf has few personalities more droll than cosmopolite Harry Bentley, Lancashire born but equally at home at St. Andrews, Sunningdale, Royal St. George's, Paris or Monte Carlo, and appropriately once captain of the International Golfers' Club.

Harry's presence was felt in British and Continental golf from the early nineteen thirties until the mid-fifties. He won the French Open Amateur championship in both 1931 and 1932. After his second successive victory Harry was asked: "What are your immediate plans?"

Harry still has a Mancunian accent. Thirty years ago it may have been even more pronounced. This did nothing to stop the twice French champion stating: "I am going to Paris to address my people."

After Henry Cotton's first Open Championship victory in 1934 he was favourite almost everytime he started. Hoylake in 1936 — Alfred Padgham's year — was no exception. Cotton played superbly but could not set his putter alight.

On the final day that regal golfing figure Raymond Oppenheimer, Henry's friend and contemporary, was acting as chief gallery steward to the very much in contention Cotton, then the magnet of the crowds.

A newcomer to the vast throng was overheard by Raymond to enquire: "Is Cotton driving well?"

Spontaneously from Oppenheimer came the words: "Sir, it is impossible to tell whether his drives are finishing on the right half or the left half of the fairway."

It is impossible to tell whether this story more typifies the wit of Oppenheimer or the majesty of Cotton at that time.

The 1963 Ryder Cup match at Atlanta was the first time I heard an amazing sidelight to the great American Bobby Jones's first victory in the British Open championship in 1926.

It came from Jones's own lips at a dinner to the British and American teams.

He revealed that he and his chief challenger, Al Watrous, decided during the interval between the third and fourth rounds to seek rest and quiet at the peace of their hotel instead of at the clubhouse.

They laid on a taxi to do so and returned by the same means. They had walked straight from the last green to the waiting cab in their golfing clothes.

When they got back to the Royal Lytham and St. Annes clubhouse they found that neither had a badge or documents of any kind identifying them as players.

The gatekeeper was adamant. No badge, no entry. How did he know it was Mr. Jones and Mr. Watrous?

Time was running short. Jones made up his mind on a course of action. He took Watrous by the arm and led him to the public paying entrance where he handed over two half-crowns. And that is how the men who finished first and second in the championship got on to the course to play their dramatic final round together.

Jones's legendary 175-yard shot from sand at the seventeenth clinched the issue for him.

Amid the sandy wastes of the seventeenth fairway today lies a plaque purporting to mark the spot from which Jones played his ball.

A woman golfer was taken to this spot one day. She said in tones of due solemnity: "Oh, is this were poor Mr. Jones is buried?"

It could be said that the professionals of the modern age are taking over from the candid caddies of yesteryear when it comes to golf humour.

Perhaps it all began with Andrew Kirkaldy. Among the immortal pro's ripostes is that of pipe-smoking Ted Ray, contemporary of Vardon and 1912 Open champion.

Ray was once asked by an aspiring golfer: "How can I get more length?"

"Hit it a bloody sight harder, mate," was Ray's unequivocal answer.

How is this for wit? A gushing female admirer charges up to the very bronzed and healthy looking Dai Rees — incidentally Harry Vardon's long serving successor at the South Herts Club near London — and burst forth: "Dai, what a simply marvellous tan you have. South of France?" "No. Just South Herts," was Rees's succinct reply.

Or this? Scot John Stirling, one of the liveliest-minded professionals, who serves at Meyrick Park, Bournemouth, was telling me once that he came under the spell of the drowsy rhythmical swing of America's Julius Boros, twice U.S. Open Champion, after watching a film of the great man.

"I tried to mould my swing on Julius Boros," said Stirling. "I ended up swinging more like Julius Caesar."

A professional on the receiving end of a classical remark was Peter Thomson while practising one year at St. Andrews with his well-known local caddie, Wallace Gillespie.

Gillespie gave Thomson the line at a certain hole. Thomson hit the shot perfectly.

They walked on and came to the ball and it lay between two little pot bunkers with only five yards dividing them.

"You didn't give me much margin," said Thomson. "Well, you are the Open Champion, aren't you?" replied Gillespie.

Much of the humour in tournament golf comes from gallery reaction as they faithfully follow the masters.

The spectacular Harry Weetman always brings forth the best of comments.

At the Sonning Club in Berkshire I overheard in the clubhouse one day: "You know that bush beside the ninth green?"

"Yes."

"Well, Weetman put his ball in there today. The bush isn't there any more."

The Americans have a salty turn of golfing language. I once heard one say of Weetman: "Did you see the size divots

Harry Weetman takes? They are as big as beaver pelts."

I reserve my favourite story about a star professional for the close. It concerns Irishman Fred Daly, the 1947 Open Champion.

Some years later he was playing in a professional tournament near Edinburgh. It was shortly after the victory of Ed Furgol in the American Open. Furgol had become a legend because of this wonderful achievement despite the handicap of having his left arm shorter than his right.

Daly was staying at a hotel near the course where a huge but friendly Great Dane had the run of the house. The knowing dog would stroll into the dining room and encourage guests to give it titbits. Daly was among those unable to resist the dog's pleas.

The hotel manager saw Fred throwing a biscuit on to the floor near the dog. He said: "He is quite harmless, Mr. Daly. You can give it to him in your hand."

Daly hesitated — then still continued throwing the biscuit.

"No fear. Do you think I want to become the Irish Ed Furgol," said the cautious Fred.

I have gone all this way relating stories concerning famous people and things that actually happened or were said. I have taken no account of the humours of club golf or the mountains of fiction which deal with the lighter side of the game.

Golf is rich in its humorists. Patrick Campbell, George Houghton, Keith Marshall, Rex Lardner, Ring Lardner, Stephen Potter and George Nash have all delighted us with their amusing invention and who is there to equal the heyday of P.G. Wodehouse, who once wrote: "The least thing upsets him on the links. He misses short putts because of the uproar of the butterflies in the adjoining meadows."

I am convinced golf is a funny game — in every sense of the word. For every humour I have dredged my memory to recall, I know there are a dozen others which I have forgotten.